Manor Lessons
Commons Revisited

PARK BOOKS

> Comment veut-on que des idées nouvelles puissent se développer? A peine peuvent-elles se faire jour sur le papier; comment pourraient-elles se traduire en pierre? C'est à développer l'indépendance de l'artiste et à lui assurer cette indépendance qu'il faut tendre si l'on veut avoir un art de notre temps.[1]
> — Eugène Viollet-Le-Duc

Teaching and Research in Architecture

From classical antiquity to the 15th century, architects were both planners and builders. As "master builders," architects were responsible for both the design and overseeing of construction. The master builder was a highly skilled and highly experienced leader of the construction team. He was apprenticed in all of the main construction crafts, such as masonry, carpentry, plumbing, and roofing. He possessed a range of skills that were immediately related to the design, the engineering, the materials, and the overall concept for construction.

From the 15th century onward, the unity of art and technology, of designer and craftsman, began to disintegrate. This was due primarily to the emergence of a less regulated, expanded concept of art. In the quest for a new complexity in art, the loss of the unity of the conceptual and the practical was less of a preoccupation. In consequence the concept of the master builder disappeared, and the process of designing and constructing a building became fragmented. This division was further underlined by the foundation of the École National des Ponts et Chaussées in 1747, when training in engineering became independent of architecture.

The architect's influence on the shape of our built environment has declined ever since. There has been a dramatic reduction in both the variety and range of the architect's activities. Whereas architects once designed a building by themselves, they now share the task with many consultants. In addition, the range of the architect's involvement in the process of planning and construction has diminished over time. As such, the architect's traditional role of integrating and coordinating the entire planning and building process is undermined.

Today, architecture finds itself in the paradoxical situation of being more popular than ever before, but at the same time being exposed to total decline. Never before has architecture had such a high profile. Yet never before have architects had so little influence on the actual construction of buildings. What does this mean for teaching and research in architecture?

laba's primary goal is to ensure the architect's continued role in the planning and building process and to reinforce the architect's position as a central, integrating, and coordinating force. Architecture is understood as a technical and scientific yet artistic and creative discipline. Architecture is an instrument of perception and as such a tool for understanding the world and society.

The working methodology proposed by laba merges analytical research methodologies with creative design, developing investigative processes for urban design and architecture. This procedural approach promotes the interdisciplinary process of planning production. The teaching objective is to show that the role of the architect is not limited to the planning and design of the individual building but that it encompasses the construction and operation of the built and natural environment in its integrity. Students are asked to develop a frame of mind that engages in critical dialogue, and they come to the realization that design is not a mathematical process of solving problems, but a creative process of consciously confronting them.

Each academic year laba chooses a specific territory as the focus of its teaching and research project. Sites are selected based on their relevance for the investigation of the manifold phenomenon of urbanization with the mission to question the age-old opposition between architecture and nature—the object-sculpture and the landscape-background—in light of today's ecological crisis. At present the idea of Nature (as something nurturing, autonomous, and in continuous renewal) is put into question by both the natural and the social sciences.

How can architecture contribute to this larger ontological debate? The Anthropocene has proven and doubled down on William Morris's eminent statement that "everything except the desert is architecture."[2] It demands that architecture no longer stops at the threshold of the window sill or the edge of the building plot. It asks us to question the fundamental opposition between architecture and nature and to disrupt the relation of privilege between the meaningful object-sculpture in the foreground and the unconscious landscape background. Amid wider struggles for environmental justice and rights of nature, we need ways of integrating ecology into architecture as more than just a collection of techno-engineering fixes (green roofs, solar appliances, energy efficiency plans) but as a collection of aesthetic principles and values that promote an environmental architecture.

Each research and teaching project brings together specialists and project partners to expand the field of research in order to ensure the inclusion of contextual factors and relevant issues that affect the overall methodological approach and the design results. The approach to teaching in architecture at laba is informed by the procedures and project experience of international practice and the desire to establish a comprehensive and transdisciplinary culture of analysis and design in architecture.

— *Harry Gugger*

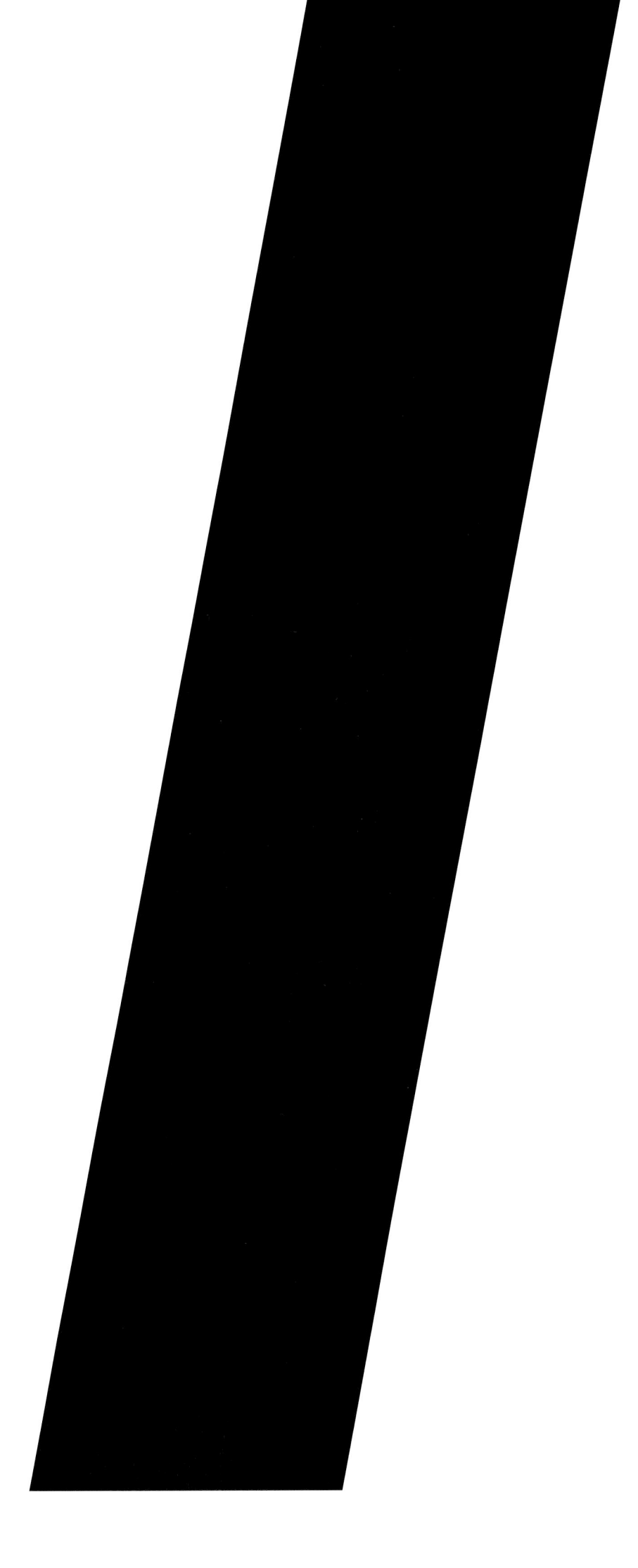

Introduction

The Commons Revisited
   1. Enclosed Ground   9
   2. Country Is a Modern Invention   10
   3. The Lie of the Land   10
   4. Landscape and Nationalism   11
   5. Heritage Landscapes   11
   6. Good Fences Make Good Neighbors   12
   7. The Fate of the Manor House   13
   8. Lessons from the Manor   14

The Commons Revisited

> You paint with memory, even when you are there, there is no such thing as objectivity really. We always see with memory.
> — David Hockney[1]

David Hockney returned to Yorkshire at nearly 70 years old to "compete with the camera."[2] After spending over 40 years in Los Angeles, his attempts to capture the landscape of the Yorkshire countryside led to a new period of landscape painting, eschewing the camera and attempting to recreate almost cinematically immersive images. These paintings from the 1990s depict journeys through North Yorkshire. Completed mainly in the studio, they draw strongly on memory and childhood associations with the landscape. [Fig. 1] In contrast to the later Yorkshire landscapes in the 2000s, which are deeply embedded in their scenes, these take a slightly removed perspective. With Hockney still flying in regularly from America, they hint at the airplane window perspective of the British landscape, and also to a deep-rooted idea of a quintessentially English scenography, a patchwork of fields stitched together with hedges, thickets, fences, roads, paths, ways, and trees.

Hedges, seemingly inconspicuous, are however codes sewn into the landscape, and like codes can be deciphered; these barriers each tell a story. The shape, density, thickness, and composition of the field divisions help to identify how and why they were formed. The most telling sign of age is the density and variety of plant species, as a rule of thumb, counting the number of species in a 30-yard length and multiplying by 110 should give a rough idea as to how long ago it was planted.[3] Apart from some Iron Age and Roman exceptions, most boundaries dating from before the Middle Ages are irregular and unsymmetrical, adapting to the climate, methods of cultivation, and specific needs of the smallholding. Those which are subtly S-shaped and roughly 200 meters long are normally the traces of the open-field system, the shape and size determined by the oxen-drawn Anglo-Saxon plow. The Celtic plow was simpler and required fields to be plowed twice, once horizontally and once vertically, leading to smaller, squarer fields which were typically fenced or walled in pre-Anglo-Saxon rule, meaning that their forms remain in place to date.

The roughly square, larger fields painted by Hockney are most likely to be late 18th or early 19th century, formed during a period of Parliament sanctioned enclosures of common grounds across England when over 2000 Enclosure Acts were passed.[4] Peter Linebaugh describes these "hundreds of miles of quick set hedge" as symbols of a post-enclosure landscape, as "barriers between people and land."[5]

Much has been written about the long process of enclosures in England, particularly in response to Garret Hardin's now infamous 1968 address, "The Tragedy of the Commons" advocating for authoritarian control and structured management of common shared resources at all scales.[6] The commons, as well as the process of enclosure, have been scaled and used as the basis for contemporary theories applied to models from grazing rights on grasslands to global greenhouse gas emissions. As a brief overview, Elinor Ostrom has examined historical and contemporary examples of working common resources, Peter Linebaugh has explored enclosures' relationship to colonization, John E. Martin has looked at their use in the transition from feudalism to capitalism, Silvia Federici at their instrumentalization in the suppression of women and knowledge, and David Harvey in relation to cultural capital and ownership rights.[7] The simple act of fencing in a piece of land inevitably touches upon both sociopolitical and geopolitical histories.

If we are to learn lessons from the manor, then we must revisit "commons" and "enclosures," and what better lens through which to frame them than the instances of boundary markers: the ditches, fences, hedges, and ha-has embedded in the British landscape and embodied with its histories.

1. Enclosed Ground

The history of English enclosures, although dating back to the 13th century, witnessed peaks in the 15th and 16th centuries, and then again in the late 18th and early 19th centuries. It has been estimated that in 1688 around a quarter of England and Wales was common land. Parliamentary enclosures from 1775 to 1825 allowed a politically dominant land-owning class to pass nearly 4 thousand acts, enclosing more than 6 million acres of land.[8] The late 18th-century enclosures are worth examining in more depth as they coincide with the period of industrialization and rapid expansion of urban areas, but also with a particularly aggressive period of the British Empire's activities. "When the English took possession of lands overseas, they did so by building fences and hedges, the markers of enclosure and private property."[9] The map and the survey profoundly changed the way the state imagined its territories and allowed for the transfer of lines on paper to physical dissections of the land.

For as long as the practice of enclosure has been in place, theories have been written extolling, justifying, and disparaging the practice. The same justifications based on John Locke's theories were used to condone both English enclosures and the claiming and fencing of land overseas. As Locke argues in his treatise "Of Property," labor, when mixed with land, is the means by which ownership is created. Locke makes associations between the English commoner living off shared lands and the Native American living off of the unenclosed bounty of the American landscape. However, because of his lack of understanding of the cultural practice already in place between people and land in the pre-colonized Americas, he wrongly assumed that, contrary to true English commons, where collective ownership is evident in their collective use and government, the American landscape was wide open and available to all. Without the visible presence of fences to indicate a management of livestock, Locke wrongly assumed that the lands were entirely "wild." There was of course agriculture in the pre-Columbian Americas, yet because this consisted mostly of crops rather than livestock there was less need for physical systems of enclosure and therefore less evidence of what the colonialists could recognize as ordered systems of land use.

The cash crops returning from overseas colonies required processing at greater speeds and efficiencies than cottage industry could accommodate. Mills, warehouses, and factories—the foundations of industrialized towns—arose from the need to process the cotton, sugar, tobacco, and tea arriving by the boatload. The coinciding of the growth of industrial urban centers and the spike in enclosures across the country is of course no coincidence, although it would be a mistake to draw a causal conclusion between the two. The drive toward efficiency and scales of production, although often touted as "progress" toward a general societal modernization, was mostly completed with the aim of capital accumulation, inevitably resulting in the misery and poverty suffered by those carrying out the work in factories and towns.[10]

2. Country Is a Modern Invention

> "Nations are modern, as is nationalism, even when their members think they are very old and even when they are in part created out of pre-modern cultures and memories."
> — Anthony D. Smith [11]

The 17th century drastically and permanently shifted the common perspective toward an image-based culture with the invention of the concept of "landscape," a painterly term used to describe a particularly aesthetic, usually rural scene. Partly as a reaction to the exponential growth of industrialized urban centers, and the terrible living conditions witnessed within them, an ideal rural aesthetic was formed, and more importantly, framed. Creating a window onto this pastoral world positioned the viewer outside of it, rather than within it.

Prior to print capitalism making the reproduction of text and images available to mass markets, prior to the railway and penny post fostering mobility and communication across the length and breadth of the country, the common imaginary would have been held orally. Storytelling traditions passed down through spoken, performed, and sung histories were replaced by imagery. A visual tradition was born through the reproduction and mass distribution of descriptions and images of Britain, at the same time boosting the sense of belonging due to the sense of a shared language across a vast territory.

Although it can be argued that the sense of belonging to a nation could be traced back to the Middle Ages, those who would have had a true concept of this belonging, and to what exactly they belonged, would have been limited to those scholars and monks who had the resources and education to formulate these ideas, and the time and freedom to conceptualize them. Nations are undeniably modern. Described by Benedict Anderson as an "imagined political community," nationality is assigned to every modern person, and yet it must be imagined, as knowing all of this "community" to which one belongs is clearly impossible. The origins of national consciousness are located in the requirements and the technologies of modernity. We cannot therefore imagine that pre-Enlightenment inhabitants of Britain would have had the need nor the desire to conceptualize the notion of a "Nation," contested as that idea is upon the British Isles.

3. The Lie of the Land

It is no coincidence that the terms used in this book to describe the group of 6,000 islands to the northwest of mainland Europe seem to differ in relation to the time and place under discussion. The lands, borders, and names are still disputed. The group of islands commonly known as the British Isles, for example, is a term not officially recognized by the Government of Ireland, containing, as it does the term Britain and including within it the Republic of Ireland. In general, the term Britain has been used in relation to the countries of England, Scotland, and Wales, during those historical periods when they have been united under the same government. Despite the three countries' unification, Wales formally in 1535 and Scotland formally in 1707, each has retained their individual culture and language and retained their status as separate countries, while also united under the British flag. The United Kingdom of Great Britain and Northern Ireland, shortened to the UK includes the country of Northern Ireland and unites all four countries under the British Monarchy.

The term England really only refers to the country itself and not the island as a whole which is, since 1707 the Kingdom of Great Britain.

> Before I built a wall I'd ask to know
> What I was walling in or walling out
> — Robert Frost [12]

The complexity of the terminologies lay claim to a contested territory which has left its marks on the landscape. The Roman remains of Hadrian's Wall still roughly divide England and Scotland, while the peace walls of Northern Ireland still cast a huge shadow over Belfast in particular, their 34 kilometers a much more recent reminder of bloody conflict.

This mixed and disputed history does not allow for a shared cultural identity within language, religion, culture, or history. What the Britons truly share, however, is a deep-rooted association with the land itself. Projecting a common culture into the cultivated ground allows for a shared lineage to be traced, for the ground to become "storied" and shared between countries as a common cultural asset.[13]

4. Landscape and Nationalism

The term "cultivated" is important here, as the ethnic self-consciousness of the British is linked to a particular type of worked ground. Thomas Gainsborough arguably pioneered landscape painting in Britain, and his earliest landscapes—rather than depicting mythical, historical, or biblical scenes—tended to show inhabited lands, in the process of cultivation. The figures are collecting wood from commons, fishing in streams, spinning wool, driving cattle. Gainsborough sets up a romantic mythology of an aestheticized working rural country. The national idea of "country" is "countryside" and that countryside is cultivated.

The distinctive value placed upon the British landscape is not that of authenticity or wilderness; it cannot hide from the many hands which have shaped the ground and can therefore never be imagined as in any way "untamed." Rural is the prized and quintessentially English ideal, a landscape suggestive of prolonged human occupation.[14] National identity, history, and landscape tightly bound together.

> Behind much of the feeling of the landless, however, the idea of an earlier and uncorrupted age persisted.
> — Raymond Williams [15]

What Gainsborough perhaps unwittingly began and many artists, poets, and writers have followed was a trend toward the romanticization of a simple rural past, a "golden age of labor," competing versions of which can be put to use simultaneously. These versions of the past share "an idealization of feudal and immediately post feudal values: of an order based on settled and reciprocal social and economic relations of an avowedly total kind."[16] Although painting and literature spoke to those who had lost land through enclosures, or to those who were sympathetic to the cause, the application of a moral order from a feudal society to the contemporary post-industrial conditions was both impossible and unhelpful. And yet the British psyche cannot help but go in search of picturesque scenes of the countryside where the genuine labor and hardship of life has been reduced to a scene of rural simplicity. [Fig. 2]

5. Heritage Landscapes

As the proprietorial common ownership of the land was eroded by the enclosures, the collective public ownership of the view onto them inversely increased. Preservationists began to place value on landscapes due to their association with the past, and to stake out these places as an inheritance to which the nation had a claim—an ownership based on access for leisure rather than sustenance. The institutional expressions of the preservationist movement—the National Trust and the Campaign for the Protection of Rural England—formalized the idea that landscapes, like historic houses, were a part of national cultural heritage, amenities to be enjoyed and appreciated, but not used.[17]

Currently boasting over 500 historic houses and 5.6 million members, the National Trust's beginnings were, however, more concerned with land than with property. Prior to World War I, approximately two-thirds of the Trust's acquisitions were open spaces.[18] The early days of this super-major charity, which has now become synonymous with the English country house, were foundational in cementing the idea that the English countryside landscape was a national cultural asset. Indeed 13 years after its foundation, the Trust acquired its first country house, taking a further 13 years to restore it.

High maintenance costs as well as taxation in the form of death duties eroded the succession of wealth through generations of families. Large numbers of country houses were sold, demolished, or abandoned before the treasury began accepting donations of these properties as settlements of tax bills. Turning over these houses to the stewardship of the National Trust transformed the charity into a landlord of epic proportions.

The fascination with the built heritage of the countryside lies not purely in the objects; visitors to these former seats of great wealth and power come to imagine the lives once lived there. Tourists to an unfamiliar class and status, they come to marvel at these symbols of dominance and the territories they commanded.

Political action was not confined to the societies and to the charities pressuring government to safeguard access to the country's cultural assets; cultural propaganda also played a part in cementing the British cultural identity into a romanticized and historicized pastoral ideal. Three quarters of a century after Gainsborough painted scenes of rural simplicity, John Constable's *Hay Wein* (1821) would have us believe that the English countryside had not been affected by industrialization, depopulation, and enclosures. An idyllic scene of Suffolk, it could be seen as a reaction to the massive expansion of the industrialized cities of the time, and to the mechanization of the agricultural industry. Thomas Cook, the popular British travel agency, was already organizing tours to "Constable Country" as early as 1890. The National Trust has subsequently bought not only the cottage, but several of the landscape features which constitute the scene.

Literature has shaped the national relationship with other British landscapes. If Wordsworth's poetry laid the groundwork for the preservation of the Lake District, the realism of Thomas Hardy's descriptions of the South West have also entered into the national psyche. [Fig. 3] Although "A Taste of Hardy's Wessex" can now be bought at travel agencies, the books which form part of the Wessex series are a radical description of the everyday hardships and economic struggles of the rural working class of the late nineteenth century. The novels, often bleak in their narratives, are always accompanied by sublime and evocative descriptions of the physical conditions of the landscape. Rather than offering an escapism as a counter to the conditions of the time, Hardy forces his Victorian readership to encounter their own ideas, values, and dealings with class.

6. Good Fences Make Good Neighbors

A seminal moment in the picturesque tradition of landscape design was the separation, and counterintuitively, inclusion, of the wider landscape into the domain of the country house. Using the device of the hidden wall within a ditch, a ha-ha, the landscape designer was able to provide a physical boundary between garden and landscape, while giving the appearance of continuity between the both.

The Wessex countryside is marked with the scars of palimpsest boundary markers, the oldest of these are the Bronze Age reves—a system of parallel walls defining large areas of moorland for grazing and smaller enclosures around round dwellings. Archaeologists and historians have speculated that these large-scale landscape structures point to an ancient practice of commoning on this land.

Tracing the walls and boundaries of our study area back through the 4,000 or so years between the reve and the ha-ha would allow us to witness the rise and fall of feudalism, and the manorial system's impact on the landscape. [Fig. 4–5]

True and widespread feudalism arrived in England only after the establishment of Norman rule in the latter part of the 11th century. Within a generation after the conquest of Anglo-Saxon England in 1066, the Norman court had implemented a structured society based on the division of the land, regulated through survey.[19] A form of the manorial system was present in South West England before this time—essentially a village community working off the land which was kept in Royal Service by a "Lord," who would act as a local magistrate and as the collector of duties in the form of produce. The size and distribution of these manorial systems differed widely across the English Kingdoms, as well as their management and taxation; only after the great survey of 1089–1090 were roles and rights to tenure and inheritance defined, and a standardized taxation of payment or of military service implemented based upon these roles.[20]

Whether dating from Norman rule or residual within post-Roman Britain, the structuring of the landscape in South West England by the time of the great survey was heavily influenced by the open-field system. Each situation being different according to its specific relationship to the geography and topography of the territory, there are many physical features common to all. Arable land was divided, usually by roadways or waterways into large open fields which were in turn subdivided into rows of long thin strips of around 200 meters long and 20 meters wide.[21] This most distinctive cartographic feature of the manorial territory represents a working method rather than tenure with individual holdings made up of many different whole or partial acres spread across the territory of the manor. The two or three open fields would be cultivated on a rotating system utilizing fallow years to graze livestock and to simultaneously regenerate the soil. Under a manorial lordship, the arable land of the open fields could therefore be seen as common to all of those within the village community.[22] Any forest or non-arable land, as well as the arable fields after the crop had been gathered, was designated as common land, upon which the villagers had rights to graze livestock and to collect firewood. Tools and the infrastructure of production were also common property although the use of the mill was strictly regulated by the manor as a way of documenting, controlling, and taxing the productivity.

The system of two or three large open fields, commons, roadways, and waterways hold together the domain of the manor like a net cast over the territory. Caught within this web would also be the communally used infrastructures such as fishing ponds, mills, and presses as well as the collection of dwellings forming the village, often arranged either along a roadway, or gathered around a green. This is of course an idealized description and in reality, the land was not so neatly divided, many parishes having multiple manor houses with peasants under the tenure of multiple landlords. [Fig. 6] The manor house itself was nonetheless a distinct presence within the villages of medieval England as the administrative and juridical center of the community.[23]

These houses were not the grand chimneyed and crenelated postcard villas we see across the British countryside today. The ennoblement of these houses mainly occurred in the 15th centuries onwards as a way to garner royal favor and prepare for state visits, or to demonstrate personal wealth and power accumulated through petty capitalism and investment in trade and the cloth industries.

> In the eighteenth century the network of great houses or neoclassical mansions was formed establishing strong points of the rural ruling class. This, along with colonial expansion, constituted the architecture of enclosure.
> — Peter Linebaugh [24]

It is far from easy to identify all of the factors leading to the current system of individual land ownership and commercial large-scale farming, but a gradual shift in the economic, political, and social systems influenced by war, famine, and peasant revolt as well as the Black Death's devastating effect on the population, all had their interwoven influences on the progressive shift away from the village as commons. The growth of the wool trade led to enclosures of many common pastures, and woodland commons were also eroded by clearances for ship building and to make space for more livestock. The rough model which emerges from feudalistic beginnings is one of a landlord as capitalist owner, collecting rent from the farmers who are businessmen, and who in turn employ the landless poor as wage laborers.[25]

Little trace of the open-field system remains in the South West of England, most of the land farmed within this structure having been consolidated into larger fields and farms and privatized through enclosure. Essentially privatizing the country, parliamentary enclosure acts passed the rights to ownership of arable land across Britain to individuals, and succeeded, along with the agricultural revolution, in feeding a rapidly expanding population and at the same time creating a rigid class structure of wealthy land owners and laboring poor. The mass enclosure of around 4.5 million acres of common land though parliamentary acts took place chiefly between the years of 1760 and 1820 and created a new upper class of landed gentry who by virtue of land ownership saw gains in both their private wealth and political power. It also created the pauperized laborer whose common rights to the land were lost and who became economically dependent on the tenant farmer, landlord, or church.[26]

What remains of the feudal structure is partial, yet certain villages will at their core have kept the faint traces, perhaps in the gentle S-shape pattern of the field boundaries or the 914,307 acres of common land which remain. Otherwise the most striking feature from these now ancient landscapes is the relationship of a great manor house and the territory over which it presides. Raymond Williams describes these houses as the "visible centers of the new social system. A more settled and centralized order—a system of social and economic rather than directly military and physical control."[27]

> Following the fortunes, through these centuries, of the dominant interests, it is a story of growth and achievement, but for the majority of men it was the substitution of one form of domination for another: the mystified feudal order replaced by a mystified agrarian capitalist order.
> — Raymond Williams [28]

Walls once built around fortified farm complexes to protect their inhabitants fall out of necessity after the end of the civil war, and the manor houses built after this period tend to omit defensive features. The protective circumscription of the estates of the 19th and early 20th centuries with stone walls and grand gatehouses come to signify a different kind of separation, that of social and political separation between land owners and the landless; a physical demarcation of private property.

> There where it is we do not need the wall:
> He is all pine and I am apple orchard.
> My apple trees will never get across
> And eat the cones under his pines, I tell him.
> He only says, "Good fences make good neighbors."
> — Robert Frost, "Mending Wall"

7. The Fate of the Manor House

William Cobbett's shock at the number of derelict country houses he discovers on his journey down the Avon Valley in 1826 [Fig. 7] points to a decline predating the agricultural depression in the late 19th century, the two world wars, and the inheritance taxes, which were to lead to the permanent loss of many of these estates. Over the following century it is estimated that 24 percent of all country houses were demolished.[29]

The fate of many of those houses which remain is bound up either with tourism or to the individual outcomes of a handful of old families. But what of the fate of those whose future lies neither in dwelling nor tourism? Can these houses and their environments, considered as a whole, become a form of activated heritage?

8. Lessons from the Manor

This book presents the results of the studio course offered in the 2019–2020 academic year by laba (Laboratoire Bâle), the architecture and urban design studio of the Ecole polytechnique fédérale de Lausanne (EPFL). *Manor Lessons: Commons Revisited* is the third in a series of studio courses dedicated to researching an approach to environmental aesthetics in architecture that focuses on modes of ecological contextualism. The book's three-part structure reflects the academic method employed in the studio. Part 1, "Territory" presents a regional reading based on cartography. Part 2, "Field" shows photographs of a trip to the South West of England that took place in February 2020. Part 3, "Architecture" presents architectural designs produced by laba's students as critical syntheses and proof of concept of the constitutions generated in the territorial research.

By expanding the field of architecture onto the territorial scale, laba aims to claim the urban-environmental system as part of the architectural object, and foster an engagement with the "big picture" that is reflected in both design practice and critical thinking. Operating under the orientation "Urban Nature", laba wishes to question the age-old opposition between architecture and the environment in light of today's ecological crisis. Our research on the idea of "environmental objects" is both a mirror and a subversion of this opposition—the environment is a space that surrounds, encloses, and encircles; the object is a thing that limits a place and a point of view. In questioning this dynamic of separation, we want to imagine a discipline that amplifies its context, attunes to it, and renders it conscious.

With this in mind the studio turned its attention to the South West of England. Relatively distinct from the country's main urban centers, it provides an opportunity to question what the "countryside" in Britain stands for today and how the pervasiveness of planetary urbanization has decisively eroded the classic opposition between "city" and "countryside."

By revisiting the manor, the studio addresses the idea of dwelling as a testing ground to investigate the confrontation between object and environment, stretching its understanding to utopian approaches which venture into radical readings of the territory and go decisively beyond standard strategies and typologies.

— *Amy Faith Perkins*
— *Harry Gugger*

[Fig. 1] David Hockney, *Garrowby Hill*, 1998. Oil on canvas.

[Fig. 2] Thomas Gainsborough, *Landscape in Suffolk*, 1748, oil on canvas. Gainsborough, early pioneer of Landscape painting in Britain, tended to depict romanticized scenes of an idyllic working countryside.

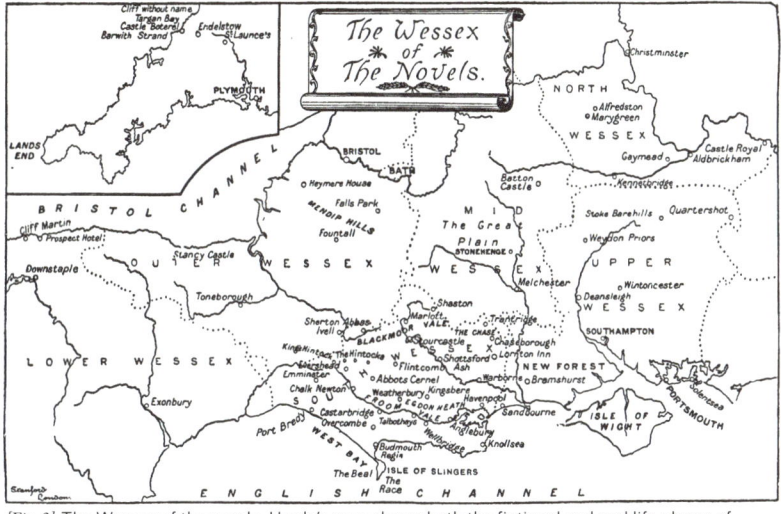

[Fig. 3] The Wessex of the novels. Hardy's map shows both the fictional and real life places of his Victorian graphical realism depicted in the poems and novels.

[Fig. 4] Reave below White Tor, Dartmoor, Devon, England.

[Fig. 5] An aerial view of the Bronze Age Cholwichtown Main enclosure built onto the long line of a reave on Dartmoor.

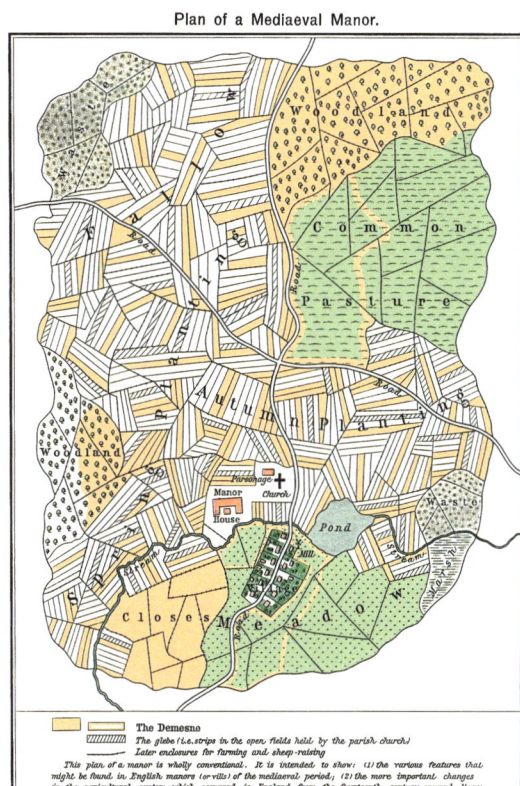

[Fig. 6] Plan of a fictional mediaeval manor. The mustard-colored areas are part of the demesne, the hatched areas part of the glebe.

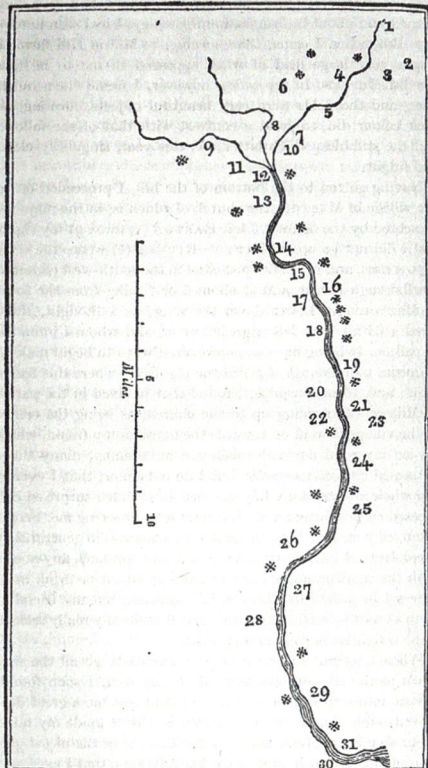

[Fig. 7] "The stars in my map, mark the spots where manor-houses, or gentlemen's mansions, formerly stood, and stood, too, only about sixty years ago. Every parish had its manor house in the first place; and then there were, down this Valley, twenty-one others; so that in this distance of about thirty miles, there stood FIFTY MANSION HOUSES. Where are they now? I believe there are but eight, that are at all worthy of the name mansion houses; and even they are poorly kept up." William Cobbett, *Rural Rides*.

Introduction 15

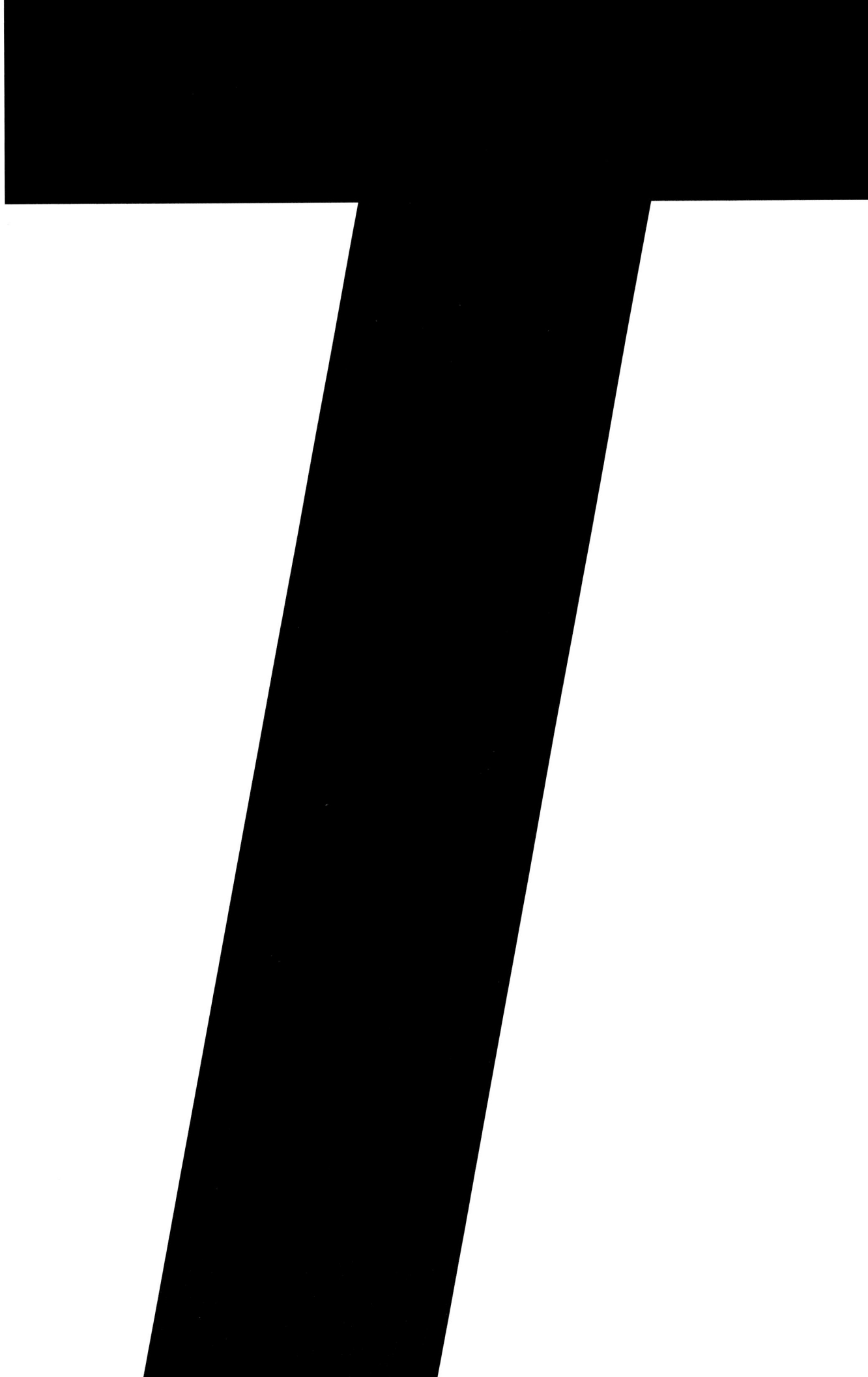

Territory

Wessex: General Facts — 19

Avon Green Belt: Distributed Urbanities — 24
1. The Place by the Bridge
2. A Girdle of Land
3. Constitution: A Resilient Network of Towns

Dorset Coast: Area of Outstanding Natural Beauty — 42
1. A Protected Territory
2. The Politics of Regional Development
3. Constitution: From Manors to Community Land Trusts

South Hams: Town-Country-Magnet — 56
1. Moorland Maritime
2. A Contested Agricultural Territory
3. Constitution: Manors Maintaining the Town-Country-Magnet

Taw & Exe Valley: Remote Communities — 70
1. A Remote Valley Territory
2. Higher Education
3. Constitution: New Commons

Wessex: General Facts

The study area of this publication is most easily described cartographically, with an imaginary line drawn between the mouths of the River Severn and the River Stour to define its eastern boundary, and another along the Cornwall-Devon county border to define its western limit. The Bristol and English Channels enclose the territory to the north and the south respectively, forming not only physical but national borders where this strip of England is sandwiched between Wales and France. The term 'Wessex', referring both to an ancient English Kingdom and to the semi fictional setting of a series of Thomas Hardy's novels and poems, has been used throughout this chapter to describe this central portion of the West Country. [Fig. 1]

The proximity of the ocean on both sides of the South West of England leads to milder winters and cooler summers than the UK average, although the south coast does benefit from the presence of the Azores's high pressure zone leading to a higher than average number of sunny days and warm summer temperatures. Coastal areas experience a relatively high rainfall of around 1,000 millimeters annually, although this varies greatly from month to month, with much less rainfall between May and September and higher rainfall between October and March. Due to their high altitude, the rocky high lands of Dartmoor and Exmoor, formed of carboniferous granite basement rock and Devonian sedimentary rock respectively, experience double the amount of annual precipitation.[1] [Fig. 2–6]

According to the UKCIP02 climate modeling study, the South West of England is due, over the coming 60 years, to experience hotter, drier summers and milder, wetter winters, with an expected increase of between 1.5 and 4.5 degrees Celsius. Along with the potential adverse effects of a rise in surface sea temperature leading to coastal erosion and flooding, the increase in temperature and duration of milder weather will have other effects on agriculture. Growing seasons are likely to be longer and the upwards trend of summer and winter mean temperatures are likely to result in a favorable growing environment for new crop types such as citrus fruits. The effects of global warming on the agricultural sector are now fairly well understood, although measures to adapt within the region's farming communities have not been widely developed or implemented due to many other pressing concerns such as the exit from the European Union and the aftermath of the BSE and Foot and Mouth disease crises as well as changes to the Common Agricultural Policy.[2]

The territory contains a large number of designated protected landscapes, National Parks and Areas of Outstanding Natural Beauty, including the north and south Devon coasts and the two National Park moorlands of Dartmoor and Exmoor, [Fig. 7] making tourism a significant contributor to the economy. South West England receives more domestic visitors than any other English region. Tourists are welcomed in the largest hotel and restaurant sector in the country, with service industries employing four out of every five workers in the region.[3]

Facts and Figures [i]
Population (2020)   3,241,397
Area   14,100 sq. km
Density   230 p./sq. km (UK 275)
Rural population (2011)   54%
Age Structure (2020)   <16: 18.2 %
   16–64: 58.4 %
   >64: 23.5 %

Coast at Golden Cap [ii]

Moorlands at Dartmoor [iii]

Rainy day in Dartmoor *iv*

Sheep in Dorset *v*

Lacock Abbey *vi*

Agriculture, though in decline, remains an important economic and territorial feature of South West England. The majority of the agricultural land is nonarable and used for livestock, dairy farming being especially significant in Devon and Dorset. *[Fig. 8]* A combined area of 9,117 square kilometers of pasture and grassland allow the 1.76 million dairy cows to graze and their milk to be transformed into some of the region's most well-known specialties: cheddar cheese and clotted cream. Other local produce, such as cider and seafood, are nationally renowned and have helped to contribute toward a new wave of food- and farming-focused tourism to the area.

Despite the growth of tourism and agriculture, statistics show a trend toward decreased employment opportunities in rural areas and a general gravitation of the younger working-age population toward urban centers. Inhabitants of rural communities have high numbers of part-time workers, those with more than one job, and those who are self-employed, compared with the national average. The prevalence of protected countryside has led to a high number of second homes, more than in any other region of England.

With a combined area of 14,100 square kilometers and a population of 3,241,397, the region sits well below the English national average density of 430 people per square kilometer, at 230 people per square kilometer, although the distribution of the population is far from even across the territory with Bristol, Plymouth, Bournemouth, Poole, and Exeter accounting for around a third of the total at 1,238,792 inhabitants. Our study area, despite Bristol's relatively young demographic, is also significant for its aging population, its percentage of over 65-year-olds being 5.5 percent higher than the national average and accounting for 32.7 percent of the population.[4] *[Fig. 9]*

Although not considered part of the same legislative metropolitan area, the conurbations centered around Bristol and Bath are, when considered together, by far the largest urban settlement of the study region.[5] The urban centers along the south coast were also founded as port cities and currently serve as regional administrative centers as well as popular centers for leisure, education, commerce, and services. *[Fig. 10]*

Formerly an agrarian society with a network of small villages based around manor houses, connected by paths and roads, a centralized system with a stark urban rural divide now spreads like a web across the landscape. *[Fig. 11]* Outside the urban centers, the majority of the region is rural, with more people living in villages, hamlets, and isolated dwellings than in any other region of England. A gradual erosion of the manorial system—due to the privatization of the land through the practice of enclosure and the monetization of the products of the land through industrialization, capitalism, and trade—and the development of the railway system has contributed to a different web structure over the land. By 1850, the railway lines connected ports, mines, and mills across the region, settlements forming where employment could be found, subsidence farming no longer viable in a post-enclosure and industrialized land. *[Fig. 12]*

[Fig. 1]
Study area

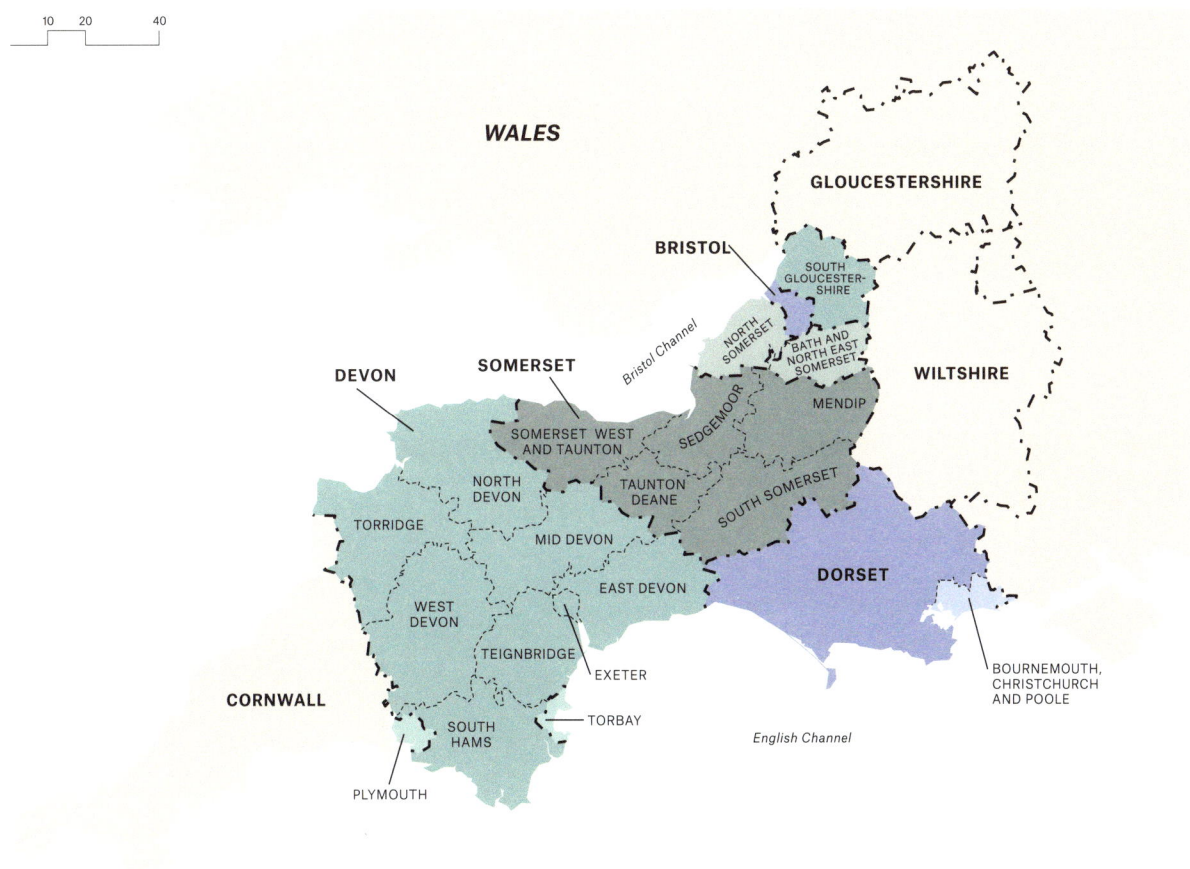

[Fig. 2]
Topography
Highlands of Dartmoor and Exmoor and the Bristol lowlands

- >300 m
- 150–300 m
- Study area
- Alluvium and lowland peat
- Major scarps
- Coastal cliffs >30 m

[Fig. 3]
Sedimentary rocks

- Oligocene
- Cretaceous
- Jurassic
- Triassic
- Permian
- Carboniferous
- Devonian
- Silurian
- Ordovician
- Proterzoic
- Early Precambrian
- Igneous rocks

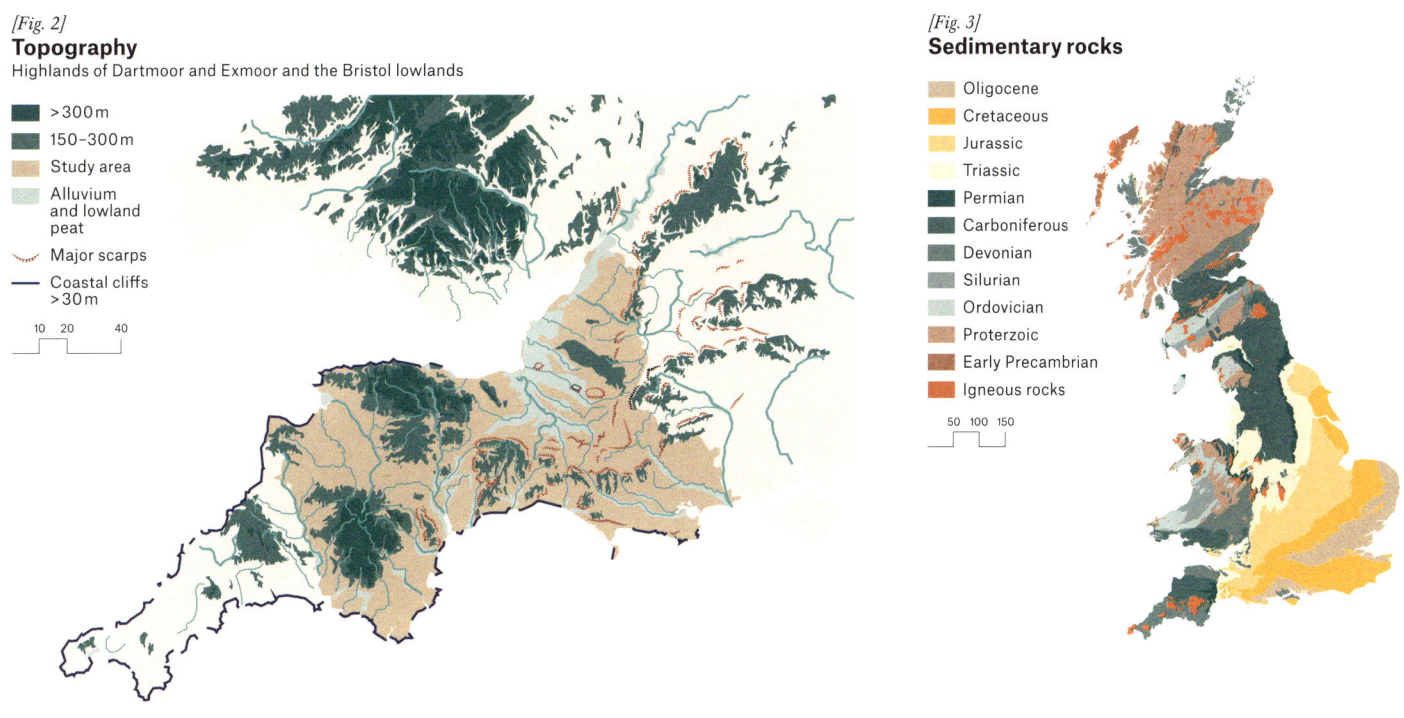

Territory: General Facts

[Fig. 4]
Sunshine
Annual average (1982–2010)

▮ >1,600 hours/a
▮ <900 hours/a

[Fig. 5]
Rainfall
Annual average

▮ 3,000 mm/a
▮ 400 mm/a

[Fig. 6]
Winter temperature
January average in °C

▮ Max 6°C
▮ Min −1°C

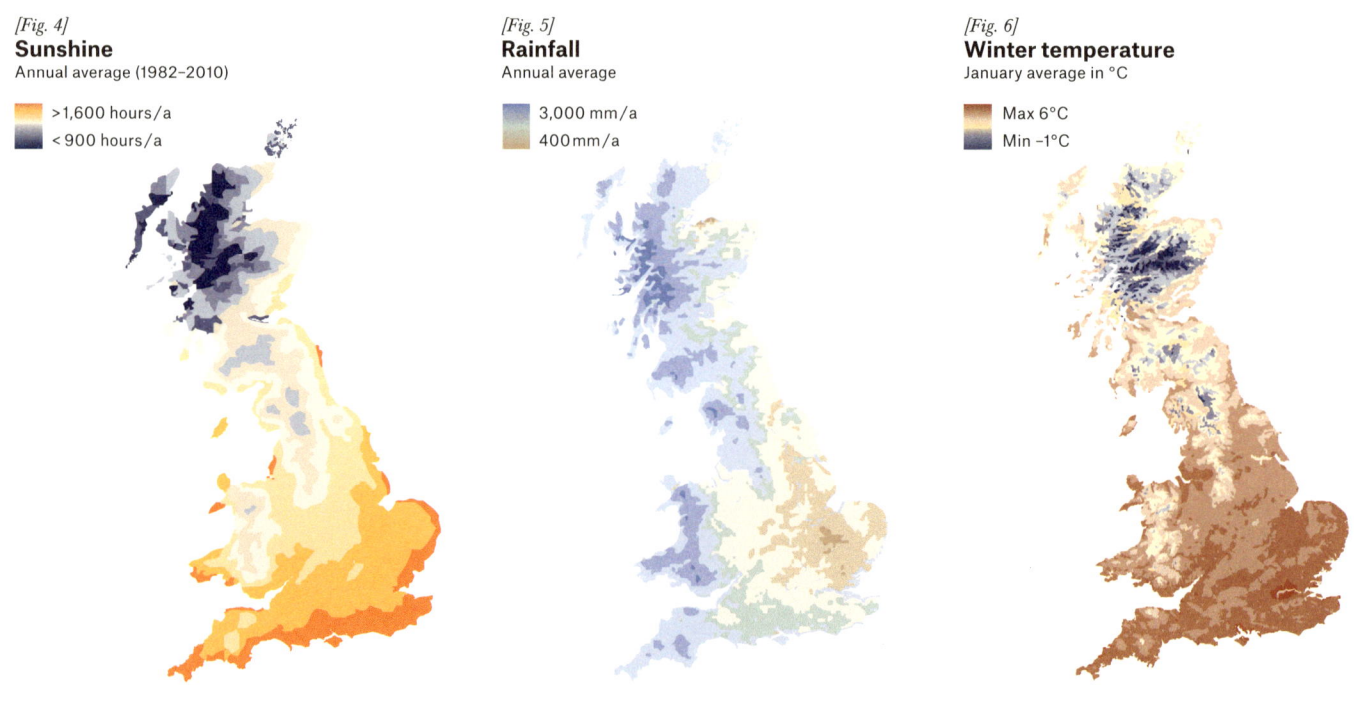

[Fig. 7]
Protected countryside

▮ National Parks
▮ Green belt
▮ Areas of Outstanding Natural Beauty (AONB)
▮ Area of Great Landscape Value (AGLV)
▮ Heritage coast
▮ Study area

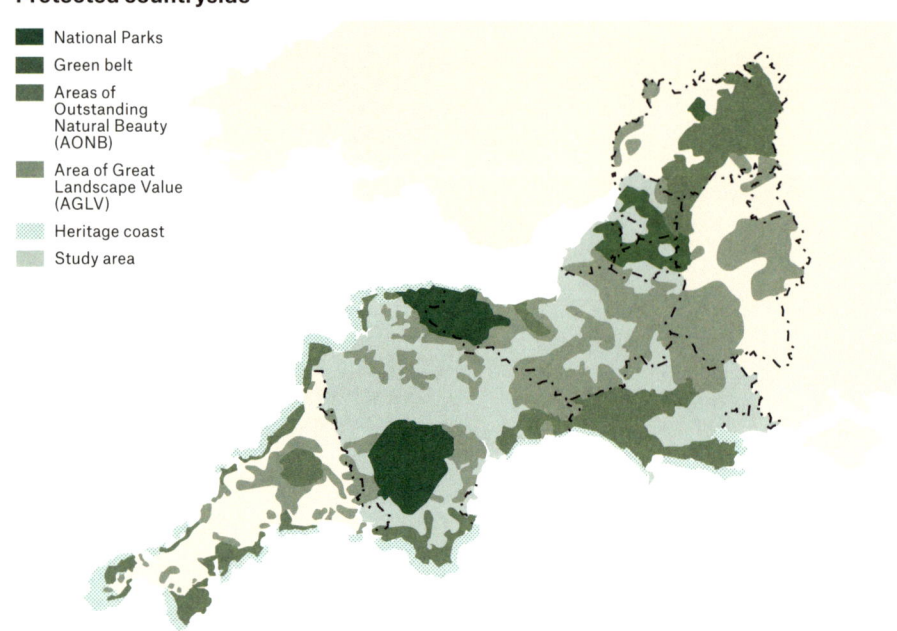

[Fig. 8]
Agricultural land classification

▮ Urban
▮ Non agricultural land
▮ Excellent
▮ Very good
▮ Good to moderate
▮ Poor
▮ Very poor
▯ Study area

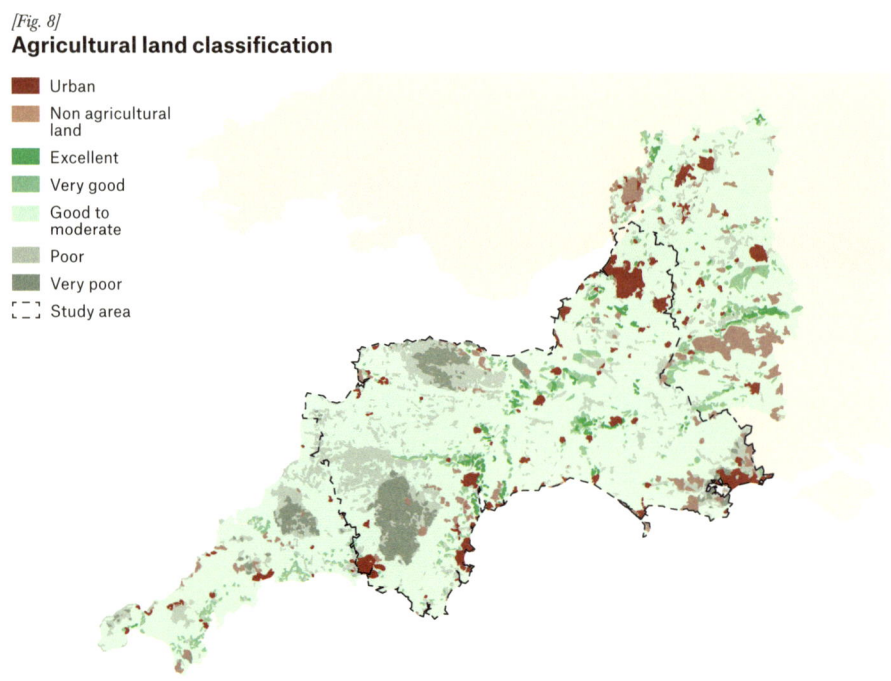

[Fig. 9]
Aging population
Percentage of population over 64 years of age

▮ >25%
▮ <12%

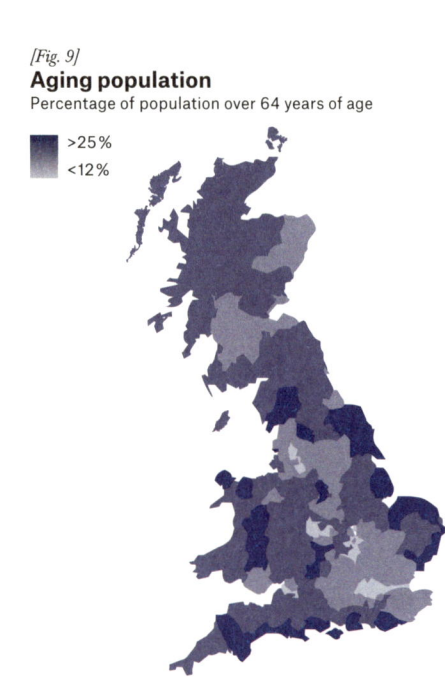

[Fig. 10]
Urban centers

- Urban center
- Study area
- South West England

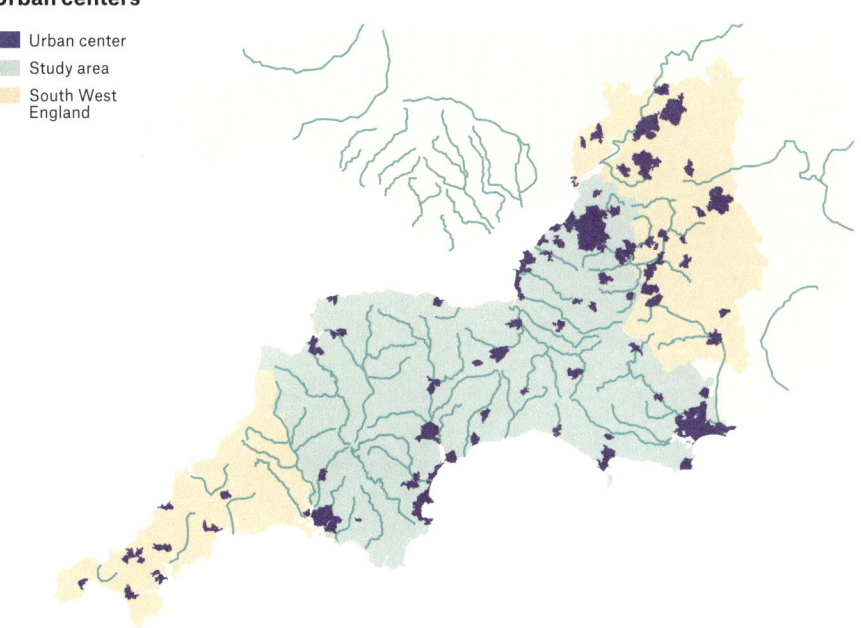

[Fig. 11]
Road network

[Fig. 12]
Railway network evolution

- Railway line
- City

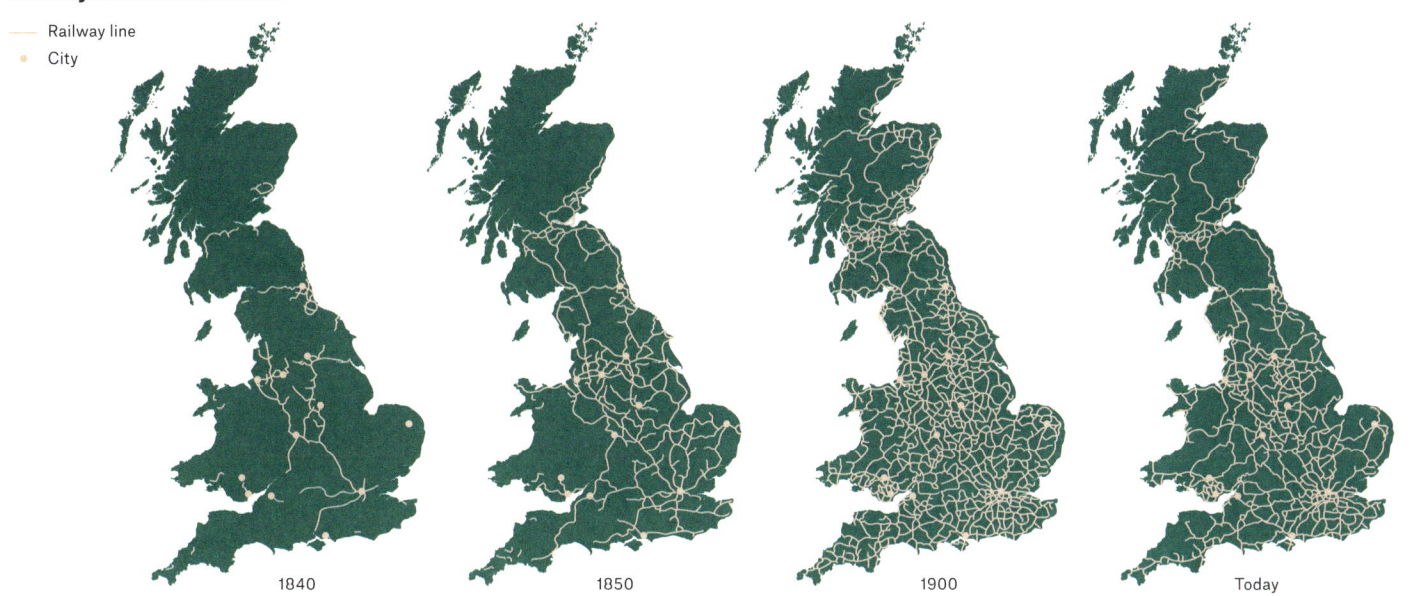

1840   1850   1900   Today

Territory: General Facts

Territory

Avon Green Belt: Distributed Urbanities
   1. The Place by the Bridge   25
   2. A Girdle of Land   32
   3. Constitution: A Resilient Network of Towns   36

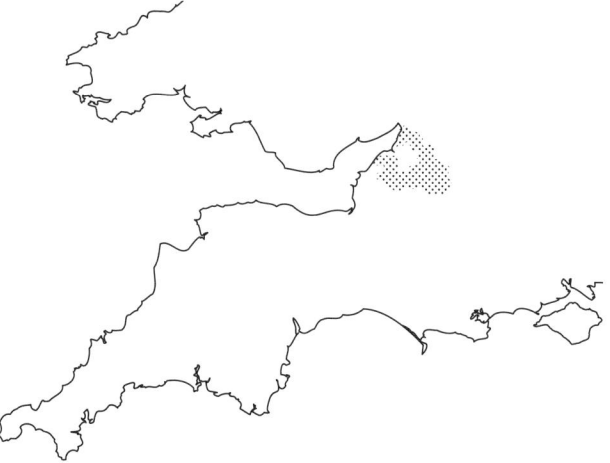

Avon Green Belt: Distributed Urbanities

Although not considered part of the same legislative metropolitan area, the conurbations centred around Bristol and Bath are, when considered together, by far the largest urban settlement of the study region. Bristol is historically a port city based on trade, yet known today for youth culture and a grass-roots arts scene.

1. The Place by the Bridge

Derived from Old English, meaning "the place by the bridge," it feels natural that Bristol's name reflects its long history with crossings. The city has an emblem in the elegant engineering of the Clifton Suspension Bridge, sailing high over the Avon Gorge, as well as being the gateway city to the two 5-kilometer-long motorway bridges across the River Severn, connecting Cardiff, Swansea, and south Wales via the M4 to London and the South East of England. Looking back further, we discover Bristol as the place of departure for some much longer crossings. Through its port, it joined the British Empire to trading posts across Europe and Africa, and bridged the Atlantic, acting as the gateway to the British colonies in the Caribbean and North America.

Clifton Suspension Bridge *i*

1.1. Crossings

Officially given city status in 1542, Bristol's gradual growth in wealth and population over the following centuries was fed by the extortion of land and the exploitation of people. At the height of the Industrial Revolution and the transatlantic slave trade during the 17th and 18th centuries, Bristol was England's second largest city, after London, and its main slaving port. Today Bristol's maritime connection, the Port of Bristol, is based further down the River Avon, at its confluence with the Bristol Channel, a neat air-gap between today's city and the memory of its foundational role in the kidnapping, sale, and shipping of African people to the Americas.

The Bristol Harbour, formerly at the heart of the city, at the meeting point of the River Avon and the River Frome, was, in the late 15th century, the point of departure for several exploratory voyages to North America, funded by the crown. The new-found land and its colonization for military and economic power remained an interest for centuries to come. Deportation of convicts and the enticement of the poor to populate the colonies did not provide enough labor to produce the newly planted cotton, sugar, and other cash crops.

In the 17th century, the triangular trade model was developed with the Port of Bristol playing an important role, eventually becoming the leading slaving port in Britain during the early 18th century. Triangular trade is the term used to describe the routes of the ships sailing to the West African coast carrying manufactured goods, which traded rum

Old Bristol Harbour *ii*

Edward Colston's controversial statue *iii*

Proposed plaque for the Colston memorial statue *iv*

Toppling of the Colston memorial statue during 2020 Black Lives Matter Protests *v*

and cloth for enslaved Africans who would be transported and sold to the plantation owners of the British Caribbean, Virginia, and South Carolina. *[Fig. 1]*

In Britain, the shipping and trade activity attracted peasants, whose livelihoods were eroded by enclosure, to the towns and cities. A class system based on wealth widened divisions and solidified a small number of very wealthy families and a vast number of extremely poor people into society.

Private wealth contributed disproportionately to Bristol's physical appearance and civic structure during the rule of the British Empire. Many streets, schools, hospitals, alms-houses, and charitable foundations in Bristol still bear the name of their wealthy philanthropist supporters such as Edward Colston. His generosity in donations to the city and inhabitants of Bristol led to the erecting of statues and naming of streets and institutions in his honor. Celebrations in his name continue to be held today despite the recent revelations that his money was partly made through the transportation of 84,000 enslaved men, women, and children, over half of whom would perish within three years.[1]

1.2. High society in the town and the country

The region's geological situation gives rise to natural thermal springs whose mineral-rich waters were exploited by the Romans as early as the 1st century, and heralded by generations of inhabitants to come, for their health-giving properties. *[Fig. 2]* From the 17th century onward, the healing properties of the waters were brought to the attention of the aristocracy and Bath's location between London and Bristol made it the city of choice for leisure, socializing, rest, and recuperation. Both historically wealthy families and those who had made their money in trade took long stays in the city.

While Bristol's docks and warehouses, the built paraphernalia of trade, stood adjacent yet juxtaposed to the grand philanthropically built gestures of those who had profited from it, Bath was imagined in a more coherent fashion. Largely designed by John Wood the Elder, the neat terraced façades of the Circus, the Crescent, North and South Parades, and Queen's Square were examples of speculative building. The land was leased from its owner, the plot divisions were fixed, and the façades were designed. Each plot was then sold to a builder who had two years of low rent to erect the building and find tenants or buyers for the house. The elegant stone façades, all designed by John Wood the Elder, acted as composed screens, hiding buildings behind them which are irregular in both their form and tenure.

As wealth and status were being bestowed on Bath, they were also returning to the country residences of the aristocracy. Manor houses in the countryside surrounding Bristol and Bath, which had once been the administrative centers for agrarian communities, became the demonstrative tool for the display of privately owned land and wealth. Enclosure of common land, and the move toward larger scales of production and trade, led to individual families amassing huge private fortunes. The manor houses of the 17th and 18th centuries required a different expression and relationship to the landscape as new emblems that represented the ownership of a territory, rather than housing the

[Fig. 1]
Transatlantic triangular slave trade

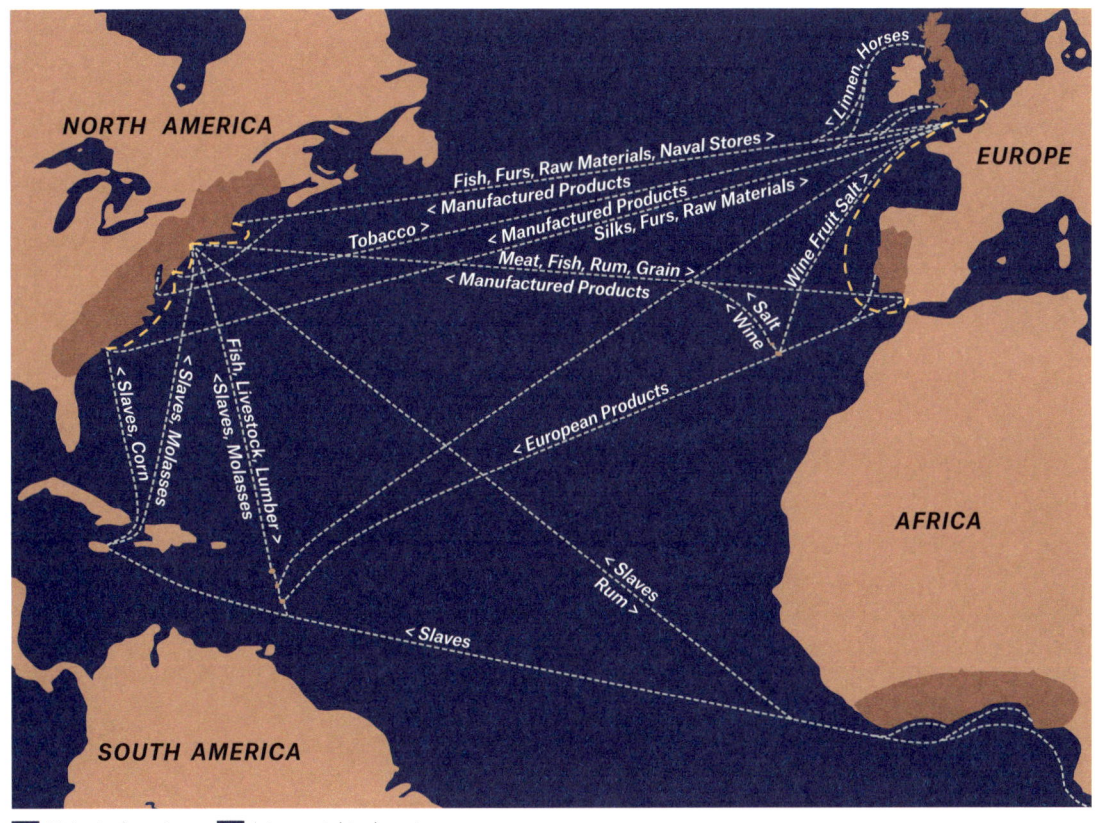

- - - Major trade route   - - - Intercoastal trade route

[Fig. 2]
Geology and thermal springs around Bath
Hotwells Springs and Bath Springs

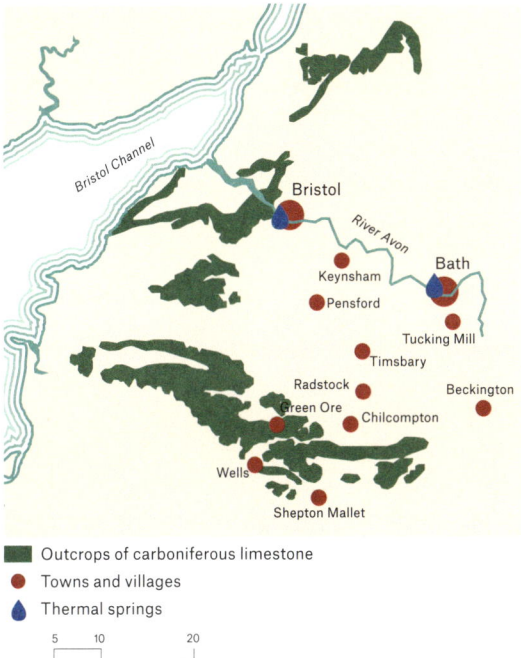

- Outcrops of carboniferous limestone
- Towns and villages
- Thermal springs

[Fig. 3]
Population density
per square kilometer

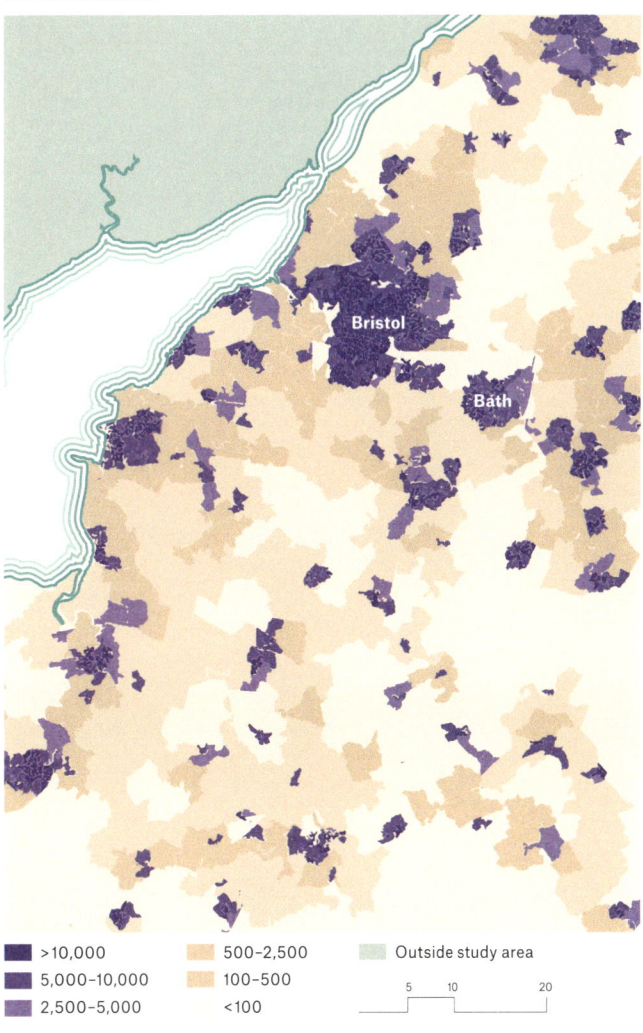

- >10,000
- 5,000–10,000
- 2,500–5,000
- 500–2,500
- 100–500
- <100
- Outside study area

Territory: Avon Green Belt   27

organizational structures for the communal use of the land. Like in Bath, many were supplemented by new stone façades and wings, which grouped and organized ad hoc additions over the previous centuries. Grand estates were created from former agricultural peasant communities, and the importance of the landscape's productivity was eclipsed by its new leisure functions. [Fig. 3]

1.3. Demographics

Despite many of the wealthy merchants opposing the abolitionist movement, British law banned the trading of slaves in 1807 and the ownership of slaves in 1833, beginning a slow process of liberation by which most former slaves became "indentured apprentices" to their former owners. Nonetheless, the politics and wealth of the British Caribbean remained largely in the hands of the white descendants of plantation owners, with little, if any, capital reinvested in the development of local economies. By 1933 wages for the descendants of freed slaves had not risen in real terms since emancipation a century earlier.[2]

Migration from former colonies

The Circus, Bath *vi*

Citizens from former British colonies were encouraged to make the crossing to the British Isles to help rebuild a country devastated by World War II. Many of the old British port cities including Bristol, Liverpool, and London became the new homes of the Windrush generation, named after the first passenger ship to arrive from the Caribbean. Spurred by the government to emigrate and fill vacancies in the public service sector, many were also drawn by educational opportunities and the prospect of better wages. Migrants from the Caribbean, however, faced a fair amount of racism and xenophobia on their arrival. Discrimination on the grounds of race, ethnicity, and gender was still legal in many circumstances until the Race Relations Act of 1976.

A lingering memory of slave uprisings, passed down through generations of rumor and hearsay, was confounded by the British press who painted a picture of all black people as dangerous and violent. A deeply engrained racist sentiment that is slowly unraveling, yet still lingers in places to this day.

Demographic divides

Architecture faculty, University of Bath *vii*

Bristol enjoys a reputation as a multicultural city, yet despite this, its population consists of 77.9 percent of people who identify as White British. [Fig. 4] As seen in many urban environments, the city center contains the most diverse districts with a much higher than average percentage of the city's Black and Minority Ethnic population. [Fig. 5] This trend continues with more recent migrants to Bristol: the 2011 census showing that new arrivals to the UK, who have settled in Bristol, have also tended to do so at the city center. [Fig. 6]

Bath, whose history lies in the leisure time of the wealthy and fashionable upper class of the early modern period, has experienced far less immigration. The 2011 census showed 94.6 percent of the population identifying as White British. [Fig. 7]

[Fig. 4]
Demographics of Bristol's population

Total of 428,234 residents

Subdivision of ethnic groups

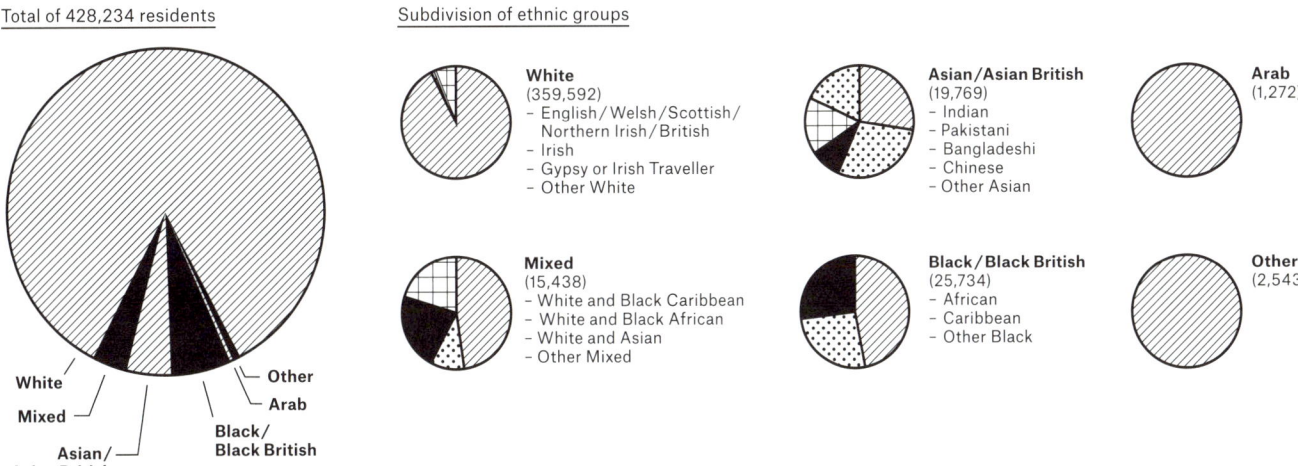

White (359,592)
- English / Welsh / Scottish / Northern Irish / British
- Irish
- Gypsy or Irish Traveller
- Other White

Mixed (15,438)
- White and Black Caribbean
- White and Black African
- White and Asian
- Other Mixed

Asian / Asian British (19,769)
- Indian
- Pakistani
- Bangladeshi
- Chinese
- Other Asian

Black / Black British (25,734)
- African
- Caribbean
- Other Black

Arab (1,272)

Other (2,543)

[Fig. 5]
Black and minority ethnic population in Bristol
as % of total population, in relation to Bristol average, 2011

[Fig. 6]
Migrants arriving in UK since 2001 in Bristol
as % of total population, in relation to Bristol average

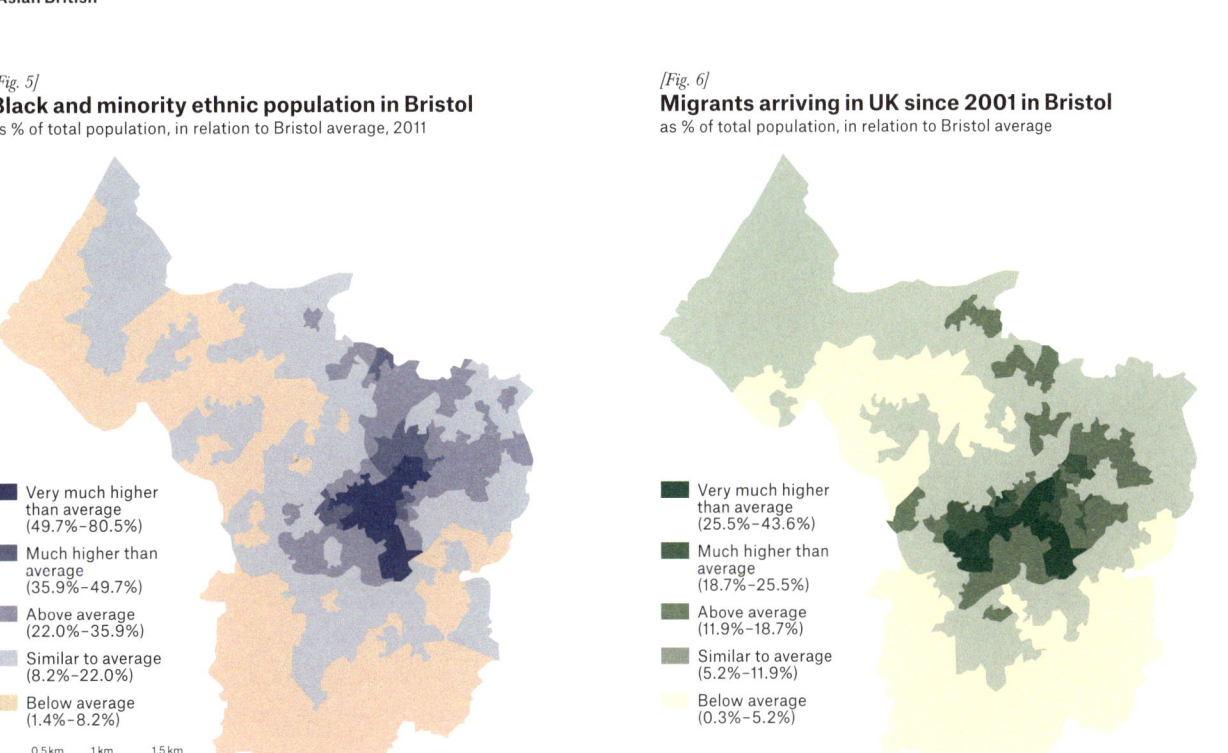

Very much higher than average (49.7%–80.5%)
Much higher than average (35.9%–49.7%)
Above average (22.0%–35.9%)
Similar to average (8.2%–22.0%)
Below average (1.4%–8.2%)

0.5 km 1 km 1.5 km

Very much higher than average (25.5%–43.6%)
Much higher than average (18.7%–25.5%)
Above average (11.9%–18.7%)
Similar to average (5.2%–11.9%)
Below average (0.3%–5.2%)

[Fig. 7]
Demographics of Bath's population

Total of 176,016 residents

Subdivision of ethnic groups

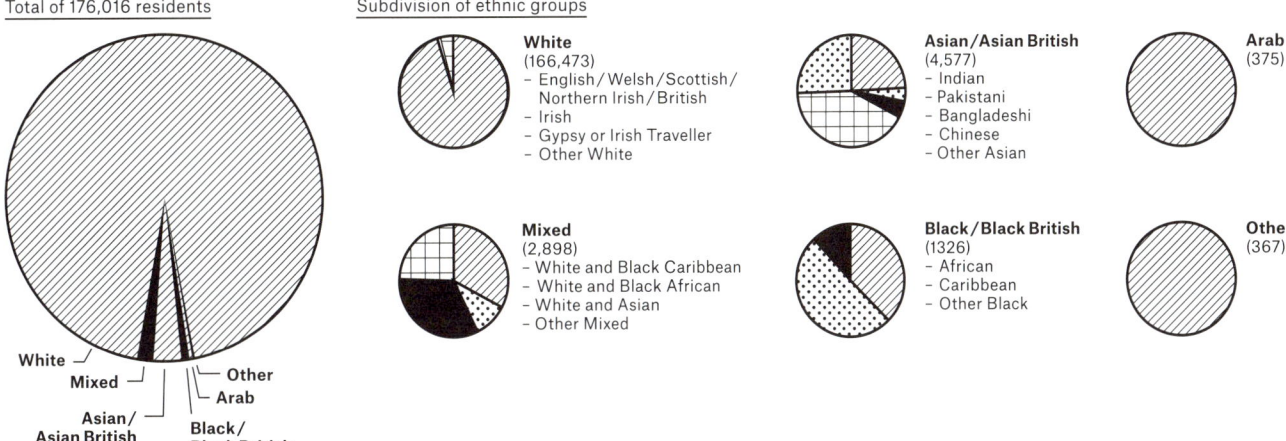

White (166,473)
- English / Welsh / Scottish / Northern Irish / British
- Irish
- Gypsy or Irish Traveller
- Other White

Mixed (2,898)
- White and Black Caribbean
- White and Black African
- White and Asian
- Other Mixed

Asian / Asian British (4,577)
- Indian
- Pakistani
- Bangladeshi
- Chinese
- Other Asian

Black / Black British (1326)
- African
- Caribbean
- Other Black

Arab (375)

Other (367)

Territory: Avon Green Belt   29

Street art in Bristol *viii*

Poster for the sell-out Banksy exhibition at the Bristol Museum *ix*

Bristol Underground

Bristol enjoys a reputation as the region's cultural capital, its alternative music and arts scenes stemming from its history as a multicultural city. In the 1980s Bristol became synonymous with grassroots youth culture. The many immigrants who made the city their home as well as the non-conformist and punk movements contributed to a vibrant alternative music and arts scene. A strong connection to the visual arts was shared among the Bristol Underground scene; graffiti, rap, and performance artist as well as protester often being interchangeable roles for members of collectives. Artwork such as Banksy's anti-war, anti-capitalist, and anti-establishment stencil graffiti pieces brought international attention to street art and to Bristol's arts scene in general.

Being the largest city in the region, Bristol is home to a number of cultural institutions, from the old and established that attract national and international artists, to those supporting the careers of young contemporary artists. In 2009 the Edwardian baroque Bristol City Museum hosted Banksy's largest international exhibition to date, where it was reported that queues lasted as long as seven hours.

A thread of activism ran through the Bristol Underground scene, many of its artists speaking out openly against the Iraq War and boycotting venues such as Colston Hall, the grand classical music and theater venue named after the 18th-century slave trader. The hall is due to reopen after renovation, rebranded with an as-yet-undecided name, as a result of sustained pressure to relinquish its links with its divisive namesake.

Bristol's reputation as a young city is reflected in its current demographic with a median age of 32.5;[3] its steadily increasing population weighted disproportionately toward those under 40 years old. The percentage of children and young people in the city is increasing as well as the transient student population. Bath presents a similar portrait, although not growing as fast as Bristol. The student population is represented by a spike in the residents aged 20–24. *[Fig. 8–10]*

1.4. Resilient economy / footloose industry

Heading out of the Welsh industrial heartland of Port Talbot toward England leads you to two incarnations of elegant bridges crossing the River Severn estuary as it widens to become the Bristol Channel. Both suspension bridges at one point carried the M4, beginning in south west Wales as the country's only stretch of motorway and drawing a near horizontal line due east, across the border to England, finally terminating in London. *[Fig. 11]* Built over a period of 32 years from 1961 to 1993, the first bridge was already obsolete by the time the whole motorway was constructed, leading to the construction of a second connection between Bristol and south Wales.

Industries such as electronics, aerospace, and computer component manufacturing do not have the same geographical ties to geology, natural resources, and shipping as heavy industry. Cheaper tracts of land, lining the M4 just beyond cities and towns, became ideal locations to base these types of "footloose" industries. High-speed railways and road links provided convenient connections to Heathrow Airport and major technology research centers in universities. The density of urban centers

[Fig. 8]
Population pyramids
Percentage of population in age band, 2016

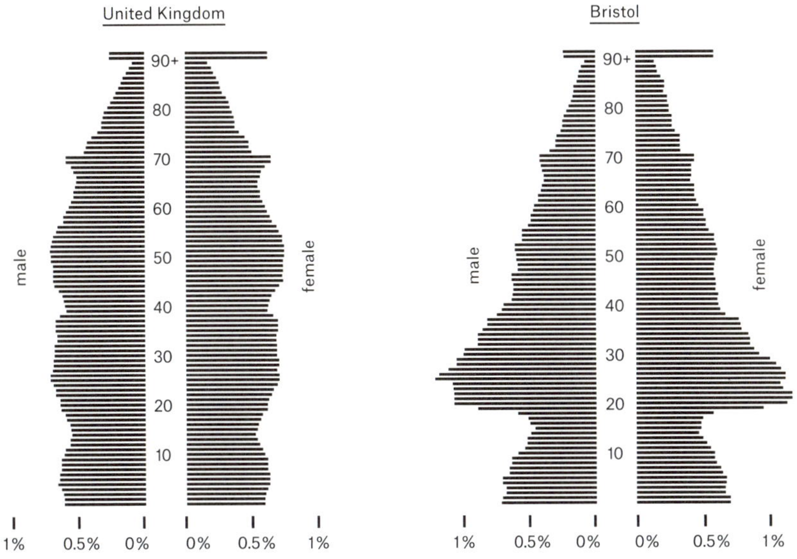

United Kingdom

Bristol

Bath

[Fig. 9]
Universities in Bristol

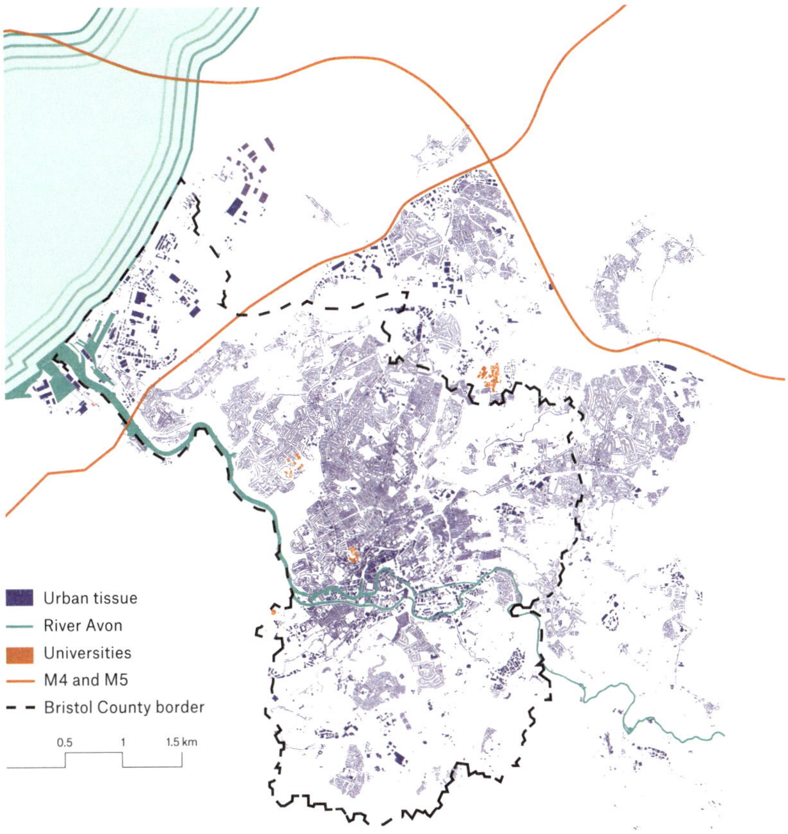

[Fig. 10]
University on the outskirts of Bath

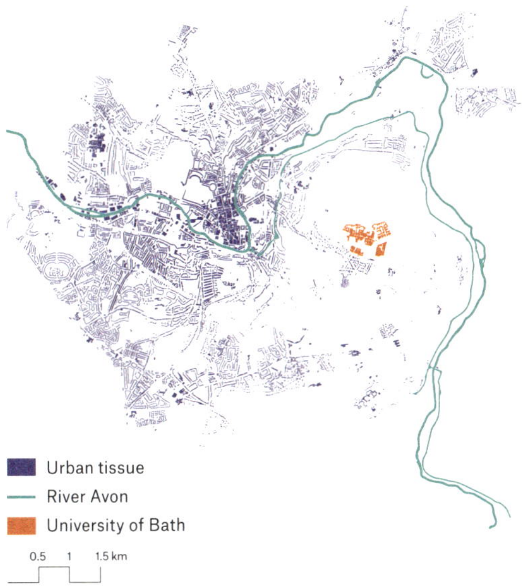

- Urban tissue
- River Avon
- Universities
- M4 and M5
- Bristol County border

- Urban tissue
- River Avon
- University of Bath

[Fig. 11]
The M4 corridor
Connecting South Wales with Bristol, London, and Heathrow Airport

Territory: Avon Green Belt

also provided a stable workforce. This phenomenon—beads of digitally focused industries dotted along the thread of the motorway—is known as the M4 corridor.

In 2018 the digital tech businesses clustered around Bristol and Bath produced an annual turnover of £7.9 billion and employed 24,754 digital workers.[4] Indeed, Bristol's economy is one of the fastest growing of any city in the UK. Employment rates are currently the highest of any of the UK's Core Cities, at 77.6 percent.[5] The city has a long history of engineering and innovation and has become, in more recent times, a haven for start-ups.

BAE Systems, formerly British Aerospace, has been based in Bristol since 1910, and manufactures commercial and military aircraft, naval vessels, defense electronics, munitions, and land warfare systems. Its research and development helped to create the Comet, the Concorde, and the Harrier Jump Jet—the first commercial airliner, the only supersonic commercial aircraft, and the subsonic attack craft respectively. South West England's aerospace cluster is now the largest in Europe and is worth more than £7 billion, with many of the big-name companies such as Airbus, Boeing, and Rolls-Royce based in the Filton area, where the M4 skims the north eastern outskirts of the city.

Start-ups are drawn to the region through multiple factors: three leading UK universities provide a stream of young, educated employees; the region boasts relatively low rents compared to the South East; and funds continue to be invested into science and technology parks. These hubs foster exchange between larger more established firms and support the development of young businesses through innovation centers and subsidized collective work spaces. The Bath and Bristol Metropolitan area is primed for substantial growth in jobs and residents as well as needing to accommodate increases in the student population. An urbanistic question arises about how to accommodate this growth in an already densely built environment.

2. A Girdle of Land

> Walking still toward the outskirts of the town, we come upon the "Grand Avenue." This avenue is fully entitled to the name it bears, for it is 420 ft wide, and, forming a belt of green upwards of three miles long, divides that part of the town which lies outside central park into two belts. It really constitutes an additional park of 115 acres—a park which is within 240 yards of the furthest inhabitant.
> — Ebenezer Howard [6]

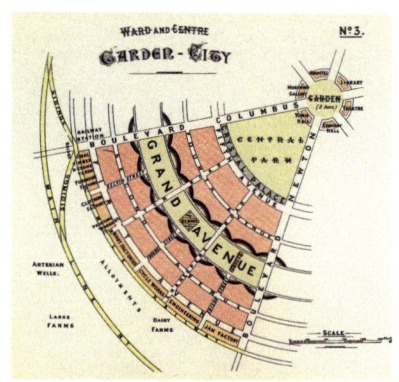

Diagram of a portion of a Garden City by Ebenezer Howard [x]

In recent years one of the mainstays of British Planning Law has been called into question, compelling us to look again at the idea of a green girdle of land constraining the development of urban conurbations. Outside the Bristol–Bath Metropolitan Area, the majority of the South West of England is rural, with more people living in villages, hamlets, and isolated dwellings than in any other region of England. Bristol itself has been surrounded by a green belt since 1958, which restricts the development of the city and prevents its physical connection with nearby towns and settlements.

2.1. Garden City Movement

Nineteenth-century Britain saw an unprecedented growth in cities. By 1850 more of the population lived in cities than in rural areas, and by 1939, two in every five people were living in one of seven great conurbations.[7] The development of this urban explosion tended to form along major transport routes such as railways and canals, and later along roadways, spreading out from the city centers in great threads. This great migration from the land to the cities resulted in overcrowding, extreme poverty, and horrendous living and working conditions. In his introduction to the *Garden Cities of Tomorrow,* Ebenezer Howard wrote:

> There is however, a question in regard to which one can scarcely find any difference of opinion. It is well nigh universally agreed by men of all parties, not only in England, but all over Europe and America and our colonies, that it is deeply to be deplored that the people should continue to stream into the already over-crowded cities, and should thus further deplete the country districts.

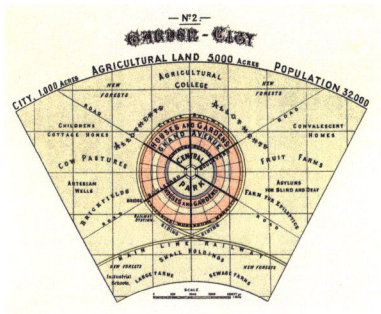

Diagram of a Garden City and the surrounding agricultural land by Ebenezer Howard [xi]

His solution was to restrict the development of larger cities and to plan a network of smaller, self-contained satellite settlements of 6,000 acres, one-sixth of this land planned as a small city of around 30,000 inhabitants. In many ways what Howard was proposing was a feudal village society, scaled up to the size of a small city, where the local government administration took on the role of feudal landlord: collecting taxes, administering the law, and managing public amenities.

The first incarnation of Howard's city planning idea at Letchworth Garden City is encircled by a "greenway" of unbuilt land reserved for leisure and sports. It is in many ways a precursor to the green belts implemented around cities later in the 20th century, although it is much smaller and more focused on the leisure activities of residents than on agriculture and open space. Letchworth's Greenway would eventually be swallowed up by the enormous ring of land designated as London's Metropolitan Green Belt.

2.2. Green gap

If Howard's ideas had a humanist foundation—the creation of cities with better working and living conditions for their residents—the policies seen later in the 20th century looked at the issue from the outside in. Political figures such as Sir Patrick Abercrombie campaigned against urbanization from the standpoint of environmentalism and the protection of a rural lifestyle and landscape. Abercrombie, through his charitable foundation Campaign to Protect Rural England (CPRE), lobbied against the unchecked urban sprawl of the early 20th century. In the CPRE's initial address at the Royal Institute of British Architects, Abercrombie described these "ribbon developments" as carving up the countryside.

The idea of a wide strip of land surrounding larger urban settlements, protected from development by planning laws, was put forward by several urban planners including Abercrombie and Raymond Unwin. Similar to Howard's description of the Garden City's limits being clearly defined by an encircling ring of parkland, the policies put for-

Traffic jam around Bristol *xii*

Aerial view showing a sharp division between town and countryside *xiii*

ward by Abercrombie in his Greater London Plan suggested something of much grander proportions. Rather than simply a park, he proposed that the city would be contained by a ring of unbuildable land between 7 and 10 miles wide. In certain places around London this is an entire county. As it was implemented, existing towns and villages were totally engulfed by London's Metropolitan Green Belt. Today it covers an area three times that of the built city itself, in many ways coming closer to Howard's 5:1 ratio of an ideal Garden City—albeit missing his radical and detailed utopian ideas about land ownership and management of common assets.

Green belts were suggested within the Town and Country Planning Act in 1947, the first attempt at implementing a national zoning plan for the whole of England and Wales, before which all rights to build lay with the land owner. Opposition came mainly from those who owned land at the outskirts of cities who suddenly saw their own development potentials vanish, and from the local councils who lacked finances and legal power. Since their first implementation in the UK, green belt policies have found themselves as part of city development plans worldwide and are generally accepted as a positive measure to manage urban growth. Indeed, the green belts are potentially the single universally popular part of the British planning system.[8] As of 2010 13 percent of land in England was designated as green belt. *[Fig. 12]*

2.3. Avon Green Belt's makeup

The Bristol and Bath Green Belt was formed in 1957, expressly to prevent the merger of the two growing cities, and the stark division between town and countryside is made clearer by the green gap surrounding the settlements. A detailed plan defining the purpose of the green belt land surrounding Bristol and Bath was first made in 1966 as part of the County of Somerset Development Plan. The Avon Green Belt had five original aims: firstly to check the unrestricted sprawl of the Bristol conurbation and Bath; secondly to assist in safeguarding the surrounding countryside from encroachment; thirdly to prevent neighboring towns merging into one another; the fourth was to preserve the setting and special character of villages, towns, and historic cities; and finally to assist in urban regeneration.[9]

The distribution of land uses in the total area of 669 square kilometers of the Avon Green Belt and the 1,804 kilometers of public rights of way reflect these different aims. *[Fig. 13–14]*

This land, however, is under a huge amount of duress from housing development; local governments are both pressured and encouraged through financial bonuses to provide new homes. The city's housing delivery plan set a target, in 2019, of 33,500 new homes by 2036 and the local council is under pressure to reevaluate the qualities offered by the land within the current green belt. *[Fig. 15–16]*

2.4. Criticism of the green belt as a planning tool

Many people criticized Abercrombie's movement of the "drawbridge effect," where wealthy middle-class individuals, who have moved to

[Fig. 12]
Green belt
13% of England is designated as green belt

- Green belt
- England
- Wales and Scotland

[Fig. 13]
The Avon Green Belt
Connecting Bristol and Bath along the river Avon

- Urban tissue
- Green belt
- Bristol Airport
- Motorway and Interchange
- Main road
- Railway
- Local authority boundary

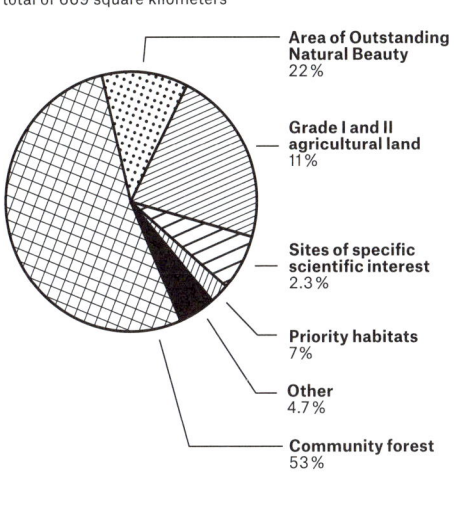

[Fig. 14]
Land use of the Avon Green Belt
total of 669 square kilometers

- Area of Outstanding Natural Beauty 22%
- Grade I and II agricultural land 11%
- Sites of specific scientific interest 2.3%
- Priority habitats 7%
- Other 4.7%
- Community forest 53%

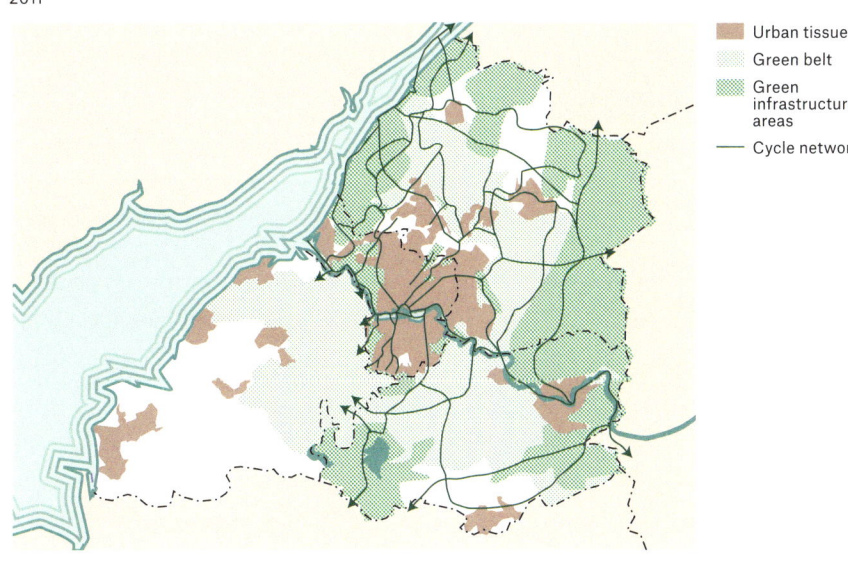

[Fig. 15]
Avon Green Belt green infrastructure and cycle network
2011

- Urban tissue
- Green belt
- Green infrastructure areas
- Cycle network

[Fig. 16]
Priority growth locations
New homes and jobs, 2006–2026

- Urban tissue
- Priority growth locations
- Greater Bristol bus network (in progress)
- Rapid transit
- Future potential airport link
- Bristol Airport
- Priority employment sites
- New Park & Ride site

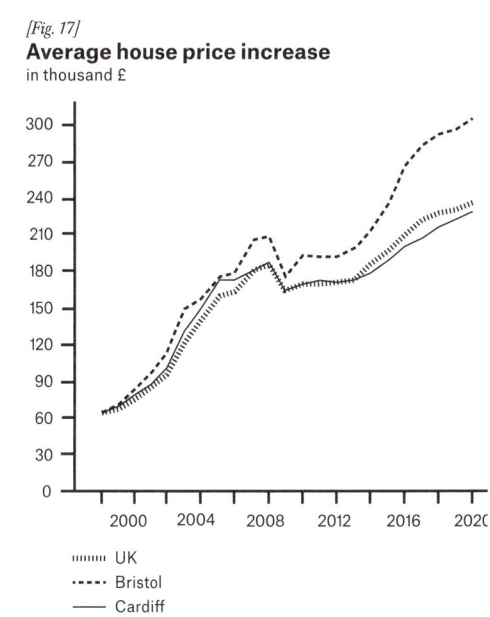

[Fig. 17]
Average house price increase
in thousand £

- UK
- Bristol
- Cardiff

Territory: Avon Green Belt   35

the countryside to improve their own quality of life "pull up the drawbridge" to others who might wish to do the same. The fear was that if all inner-city residents were to decamp to the green and leafy suburbs, the idyllic rural setting would be undermined as well as the clean air and space, proximity to nature, and property values.

Green belts have also led to the extreme densification of the cities they surround. Restricting outward expansion while maintaining population increase naturally results in taller buildings and less open space within the cities themselves. Older, less dense, yet still good housing stock is often replaced by denser high-rise new-builds, using the argument of protecting the green belt as justification.

Higher demand for land within the city, with no regulation on house prices, also results in a marked increase; few people are able to afford to rent, let alone buy, within the cities themselves. Bristol's average house price in February 2020 was £283,230 compared with £44,387 in 1995, a trend not followed by average earnings which have risen by only 50 percent.[10] Compared to a city without a green belt in force such as nearby Cardiff, a university city with a similar population as Bristol, Cardiff's house prices remain below the UK average of £230,332 at £208,329. [Fig. 17]

Those wishing to retain the cultural and employment benefits of the city itself, yet live outside of it, put extra pressure on housing in the villages and towns just beyond the green belt.

These "leapfrog developments" lead to a semi-urban "commuter belt" just beyond the green one. Those settlements with good public transport links become commuter hotspots, driving up house prices and overburdening rail connections. [Fig. 18] Those commuters lacking train services use automobiles to enter and leave the city each day, congesting the vehicular arteries leading to the heart of the city. Paradoxically the ring of unbuilt land designed to improve air quality in the city and provide a clean and healthy space for leisure is the recipient of increased exhaust fumes from commuters "leapfrogging" in and out of the city each day.

Protesters against expensive student housing [xiv]

3. Constitution: A Resilient Network of Towns

In an attempt to improve food security and provide homes and employment for the ever-increasing population of Bristol and Bath, we imagine a distributed isotropic territory of nearly self-sufficient parish communities. Shifting developments away from centralization would reduce pressure on the already highly disputed terrain of the green belt, simultaneously reducing its necessity.

3.1. Feeding Bristol

The topic of food autonomy in a society increasingly aware of the effects and causes of climate change has become critical. Studies have periodically been conducted since Kenneth Mellanby's seminal book *Can Britain Feed Itself?* in 1975, and all conclude that the current available agricultural land is sufficient for feeding the British population.

However, this statement comes with the huge caveat of dietary change; self-sufficiency is only possible with a diet based largely on grains and cereal, with a significant reduction in the amount of meat and dairy consumed. A 2018 government report, however, shows that the total cereal crop in Britain is decreasing while livestock numbers are increasing. Furthermore, 61 percent of the cereal crop produced goes toward feeding the millions of livestock and poultry being reared.[11]

3.2. Food Security

A report by the Department for Environment, Food and Rural Affairs (DEFRA, 2006) looking into Britain's food security concluded that food autonomy was both unrealistic and undesirable.[12] Globalized economies favor specialization and export in order to drive international trade. Producing an excess of that which can be grown, reared, or manufactured efficiently within the country for export, while importing those products cheaper to produce in other regions. Societal taste drives this system, rather than local manufacturing conditions or skills. Britain generates billions of pounds worth of annual revenue from the export of cereal, meat, eggs, and dairy. When we look at the issue from an ecological perspective, however, the idea of the industrial production of food for export while importing 80 percent of food starts to make much less sense in light of the costs of transport, the detriment of soil fertility, nitrate leakage, greenhouse gas emissions, and packaging.

The DEFRA report of 2006 predates the economic crash of 2008, the vote to leave the European Union in 2015, and the global pandemic of 2020. The statements regarding the security of the food market in the current context seem out of date. Instead of relying on international imports and exports for national food security, the government should now be looking at diversification within the agricultural industry, while simultaneously encouraging the populous to shift their consumption habits towards home-grown produce.

3.3. Is the Avon Green Belt serving its purpose?

Also in 2006 Bristol City Council set itself a target to deliver 26,400 new homes by 2026,[13] while Bath & North East Somerset set the target of 7750 new homes between 2019 and 2029,[14] a difficult task when 70 percent of available land is designated as green belt. The development proposals currently being formulated by the Local Authorities for the two cities risk overloading those existing settlements that fall in the strip of land between the edge of the greenbelt and the district's jurisdictional boundary.

And yet proposals for building on the green belt are met with fierce criticism, indeed political suicide for those politicians who dare to suggest that this land may be part of a solution to what was initially a housing shortage and is currently a housing crisis. Despite pressure from groups such as the Campaign to Protect Rural England, studies have been commissioned by the Local Authority questioning the use, effectiveness, and potential of the land currently designated as the Avon Green Belt.

3.4. An isotropic territory

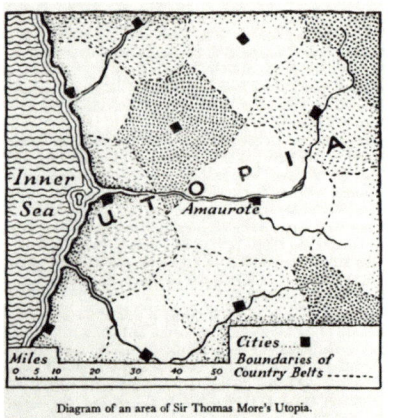

Diagram of an area of Sir Thomas Moore's Utopia [xv]

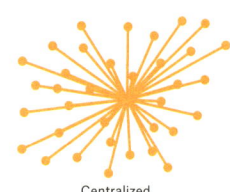

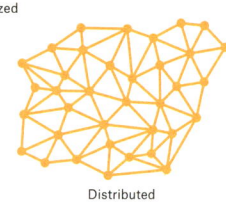

Models of development [xvi]

> Imagine an urban countryside, a highly varied but humanized landscape. It is neither urban nor rural in the old sense, since houses, workplaces, and places of assembly are set among trees, farms, and streams. Within that extensive countryside, there is a network of small, intensive urban centers. This countryside is as functionally intricate and interdependent as any contemporary city.
> — Kevin Lynch [15]

With the gradual population increase, the need for more homes is a widely accepted reality, yet footloose industry and digital employment no longer root people so firmly to a place.

Thomas Moore's *Utopia* describes a fictitious island where small, dense, self-governing, and self-sustaining settlements, each surrounded by agricultural land are distributed in a network across the territory. The trope is revisited throughout urban theory, by the likes of Ebenezer Howard and Kevin Lynch, who both describe dense and punctual nodes of inhabitation evenly spread across a territory.

With a density of 2,000 residents per square kilometers, compact settlements spaced approximately 6 kilometers from one another, based on existing transport networks, amenities, and villages, could form an isotropic territory out of the existing rural landscape.

If we take decentralization as a model for the future growth of the area, we can reimagine the wider territory surrounding Bristol and Bath into a system of these smaller and denser urban nodes, surrounded by an expanse of agricultural land sufficient for its alimental and recreational needs. Analyzing the current landscape in terms of administration and amenities, a series of overlapping layers identifying potential locations for the implementation of the dispersed system can be found.

Disregarding the areas of agricultural land surrounding the current urban settlements of cities and towns, which would be required for their own self-sufficiency, the remaining civil parishes provide an existing system of local governance from which to build larger communities. [Fig. 19]

Enticing residents to move to a new self-sufficient settlement is a problem recognized by Howard in his three magnets diagram. It has been shown that "amenities" directly affect personal decisions around housing desirability. Amenities can be thought of in terms of natural, historical, and modern—a natural amenity being an aesthetically pleasing topographical feature, a historical amenity being a well-preserved building with a connection to the history of the place, and a modern amenity as a service or provision. Analyzing the current distribution of these amenities, we see a relatively heterogeneous spread across the territory. [Fig. 20–21]

The civil parishes already provide a local system of governance and the natural, historical and modern amenities offer pleasant features to future inhabitants. By creating an inviting, denser, and more resilient network of towns, the current issues facing the Avon Green Belt begin to lose their relevance.

Avon Green Belt: Constitution Map [Fig. 22]

[Fig. 18]
Leapfrog effect of the green belt
80,907 commuters to Bristol every day

[Fig. 19]
Agricultural land around existing settlements
Required for self-sufficiency

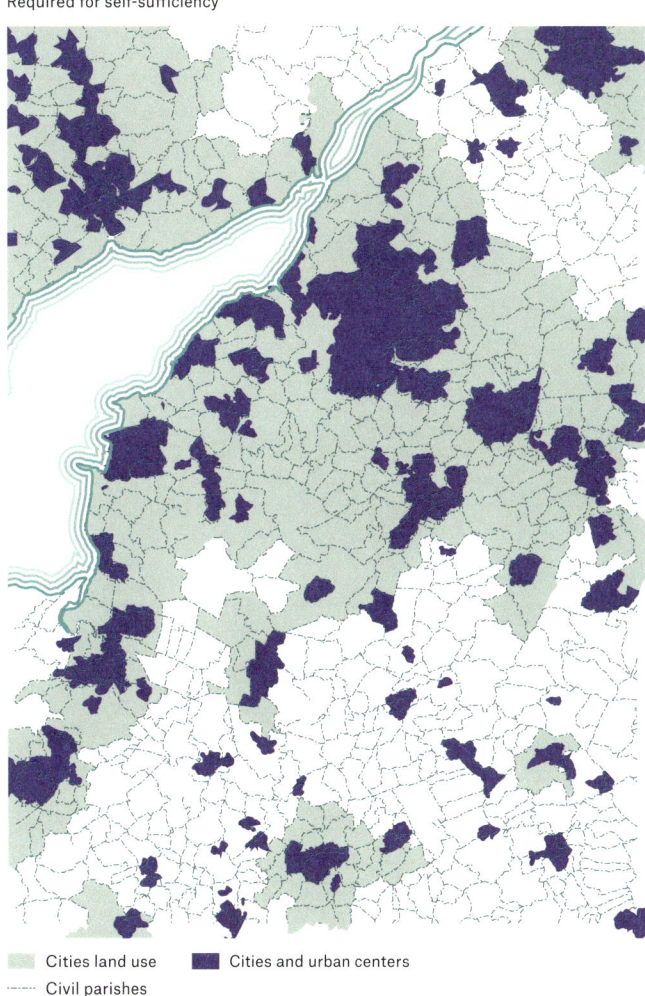

▫ Avon Green Belt
— Commuting arteries

5   10   20

▫ Cities land use   ▪ Cities and urban centers
---- Civil parishes

[Fig. 20]
Natural amenities

[Fig. 21]
Amenities around Bristol and Bath

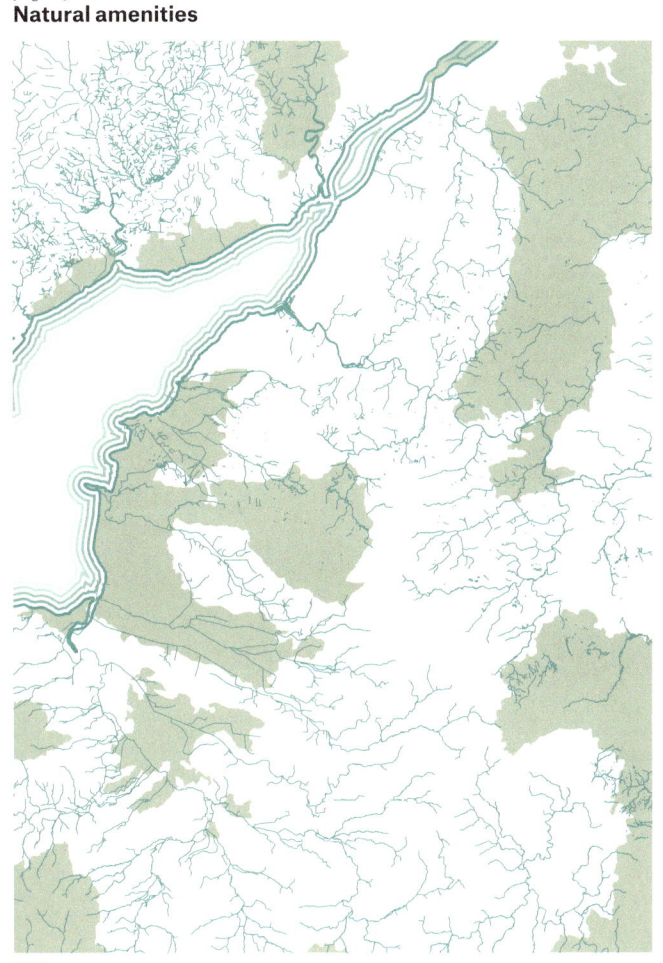

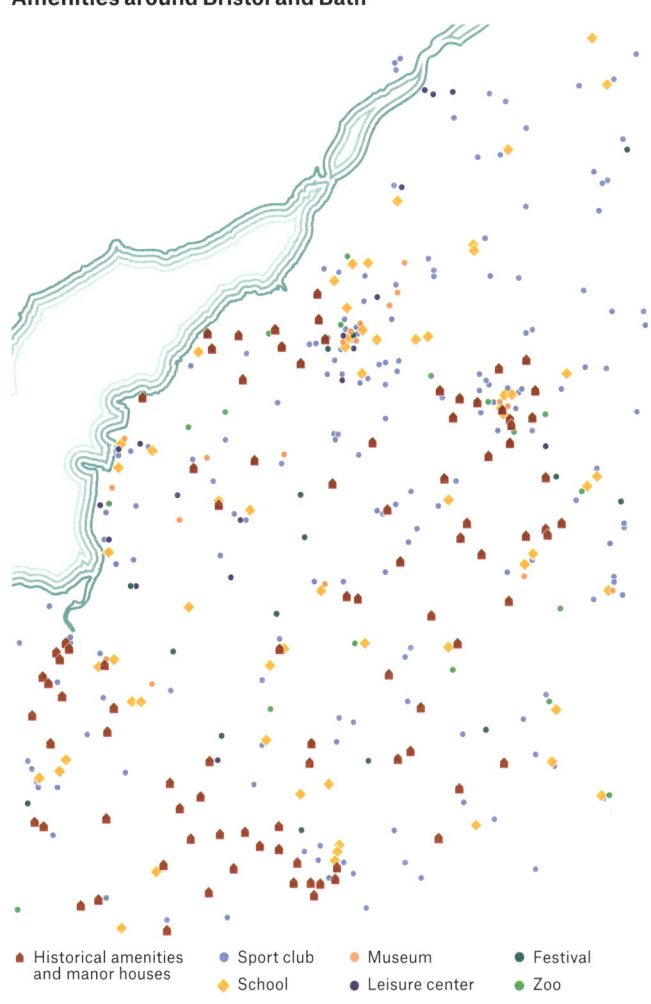

▫ Natural reserves
— Rivers and creeks

▲ Historical amenities   ● Sport club   ● Museum   ● Festival
  and manor houses   ◆ School   ● Leisure center ● Zoo

Territory: Avon Green Belt   39

[Fig. 22]
Avon Green Belt—Constitution: A resilient network of towns

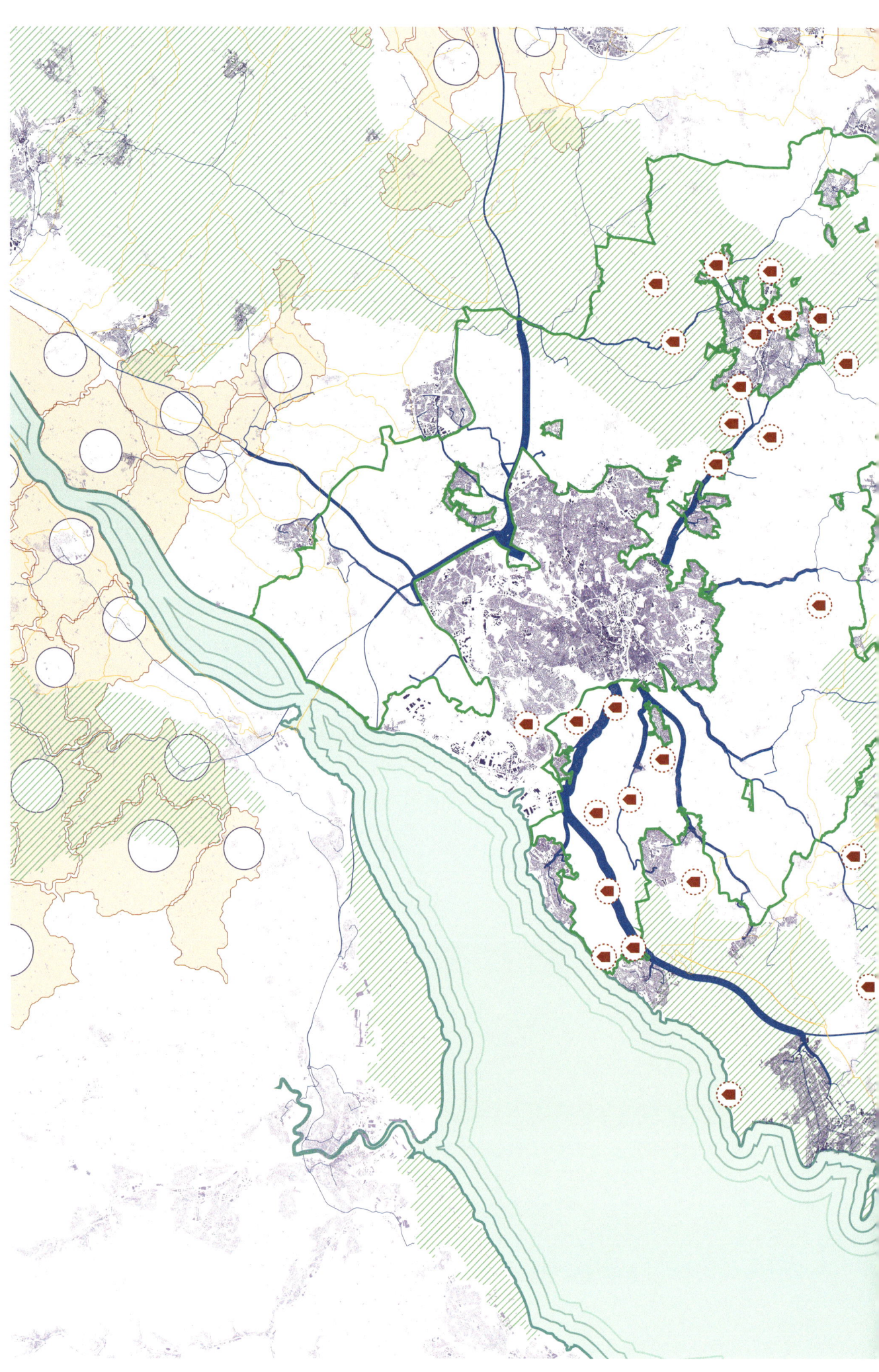

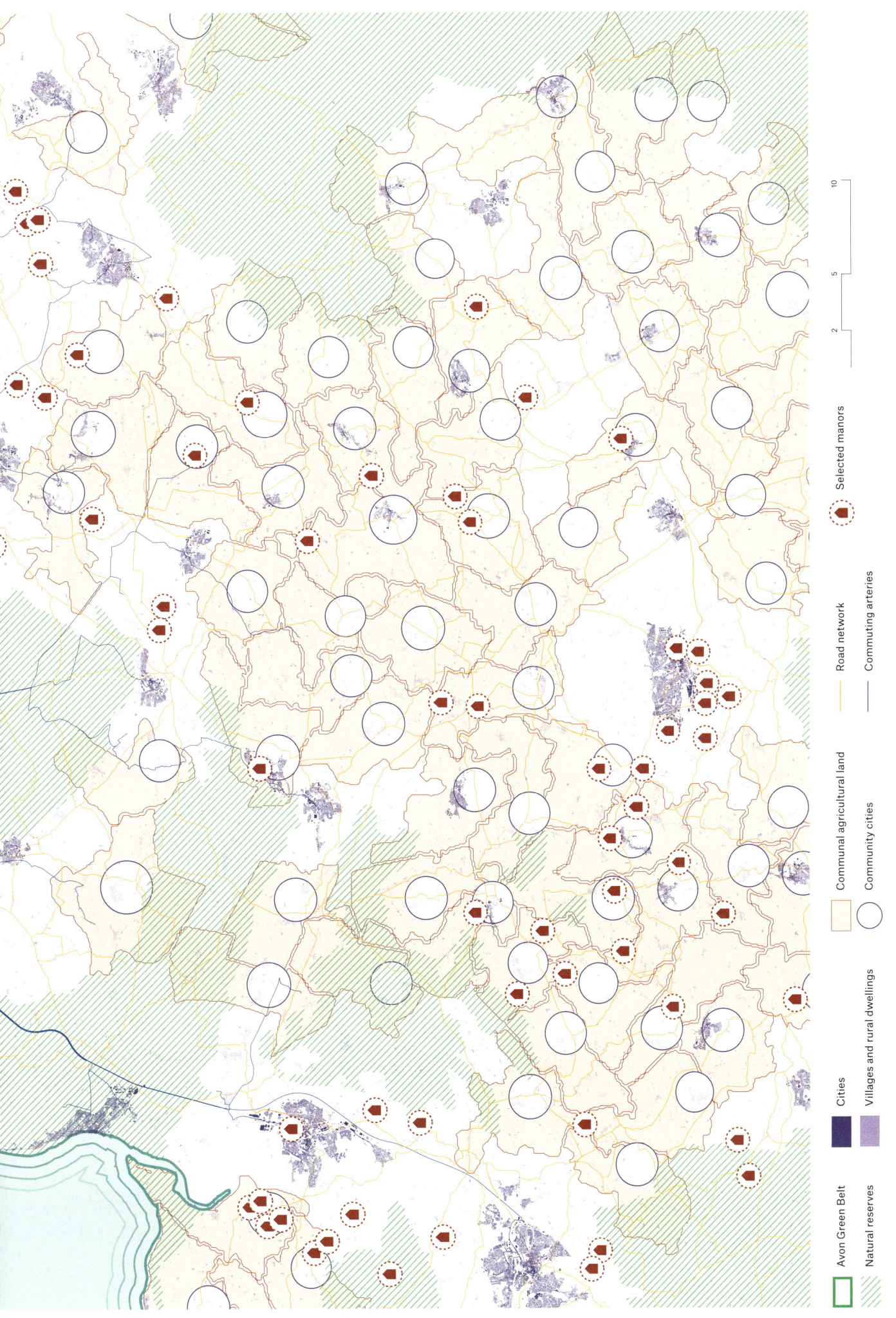

Territory: Avon Green Belt

Territory

Dorset Coast: Area of Outstanding Natural Beauty
    1. A Protected Territory   43
    2. The Politics of Regional Development   47
    3. Constitution: From Manors to Community Land Trusts   50

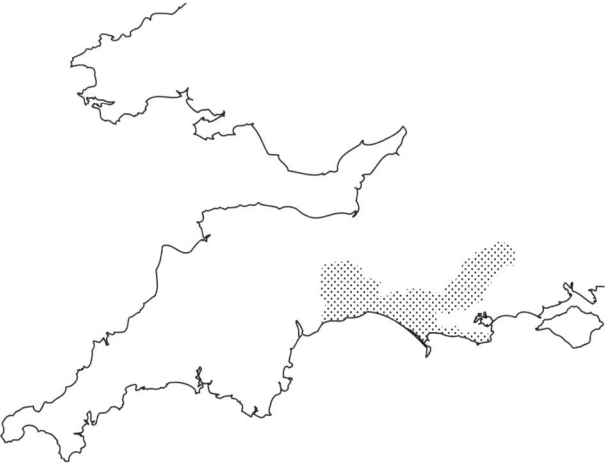

Dorset Coast: Area of Outstanding Natural Beauty

With the majority of its coastline protected under law due to its national significance as a place of beauty and tranquility, the local coastal economies are strained by the tensions between progress and preservation. Government proposals to reform the regulation of these landscapes allow us to analyze the consequences for the communities who reside within them. Among the multiple planning processes taking place inside the protected area, the present study has identified one particular scheme that benefits the territory in various ways.

1. A Protected Territory

An Area of Outstanding Natural Beauty (AONB) is land protected by law in order to conserve and enhance its natural beauty. The organizations which manage these landscapes have certain roles, rights, and responsibilities toward them as set out in the Countryside and Rights of Way Act 2000. As part of a continuing drive toward localism in British politics, the power given to these organizations is currently under review.[1]

Thirty percent of land in the South West of England is AONB with the percentage even higher in Dorset at 44 percent. *[Fig. 1–3]* The county of Dorset contains no cities,[2] its centralized administration taking place from the Dorset Council based in Poole, Christchurch, and Bournemouth. Towns inside the protected area do not exceed 12,000 inhabitants, and most of the population lives in rural areas. *[Fig. 4]* Primary needs such as housing development in these protected areas have become major issues. Developers suffer from the high number of administrative levels they have to encounter before actually achieving a project. Local inhabitants do not identify with, or simply cannot afford the new dwellings, resulting in a younger population drain.

World Heritage Site Golden Cap *i*

1.1. Areas of Outstanding Natural Beauty

> Its condition is recorded therein as that of heathy, furzy, briary wilderness—"Bruaria." ... "Overgrown with heth and mosse," says Leland of the same dark sweep of country.
> — Thomas Hardy [3]

Cliff along the Jurassic Coast *ii*

In 1949 the Campaign to Protect Rural England, responsible for the implementation of the Green Belt Policy, also ran a successful initiative to designate parts of the British countryside as National Parks. Many areas considered not large or cohesive enough to form a National Park were designated as Areas of Outstanding Natural Beauty, which now account for 15 percent of land in England including many stretches of coastline.

Unlike the National Parks who have their own administration, the AONBs are under the control of local government councils. There are

34 of these similarly protected areas in England yet they form a fragmented network of parts whose commonality derives only from their given name.⁴

1.2. National Landscapes

> Our country is changing fast. It is becoming more diverse. More urban. Much busier. New forms of farming, carbon emissions, the sprawl of housing, new technology and social shifts have changed the relationship between people and the countryside, and left nature and our climate in crisis.
> — David Glover⁵

In early 2018 the government commissioned an independent report on the national protected landscapes of England as a response to the "25 Year Environment Plan" policy paper. Informally known as the Glover review, it was released in September 2019. The board visited every protected landscape in England and analyzed their management and funding structures. The report finds much to be praised, yet identifies moments within the structural, organizational, and individual management of these protected landscapes that fall short of their founding missions.

Pastoral Interlude, Artwork by Ingrid Pollard, 1988 *iii*

The publication does not shy away from some glaring management concerns such as the fact that board members of AONBs are overwhelmingly male, white, and of retirement age. *[Fig. 5]* For the governance of a national resource funded by taxpayers, available and open to all, to be made up of such a small and unrepresentative section of society is clearly wrong.⁶

There are invisible social and historical boundaries faced by ethnic minorities in rural Britain, which have been foregrounded by artists such as Ingrid Pollard. Her photographic works *Pastoral Interlude and The Cost of the English Landscape* explore the tension between the symbolic representation of "quintessential Englishness" and the reality of multicultural identity in postcolonial Britain. She works with the familiar traditions of landscape painting, placing Black figures in quintessentially British landscape settings in order to challenge the conventional narrative that Black British culture is fundamentally urban. Pollard's works were created in the late 1980s, yet the composition of the boards for National Landscapes are indicative of the situation's stagnancy.

1.3. Rural reform

Undulating farmland of the Dorset AONB *iv*

The Landscapes Review recommends that the disparate and dispersed AONBs as well as the National Parks should be brought under the same structure and renamed "National Landscapes." The former National Parks will retain their current individual branding and funding, while the AONBs will be given a much greater level of control over their management and development. The board for each National Landscape will be evaluated in terms of its gender, age, and ethnic constitution. The boards will also be encouraged to increase the natural beauty and biodiversity of the region, rather than simply maintaining and preserving the status quo.⁷

[Fig. 1]
Areas of Outstanding Beauty (AONB)
Form 15% of the total land area of England

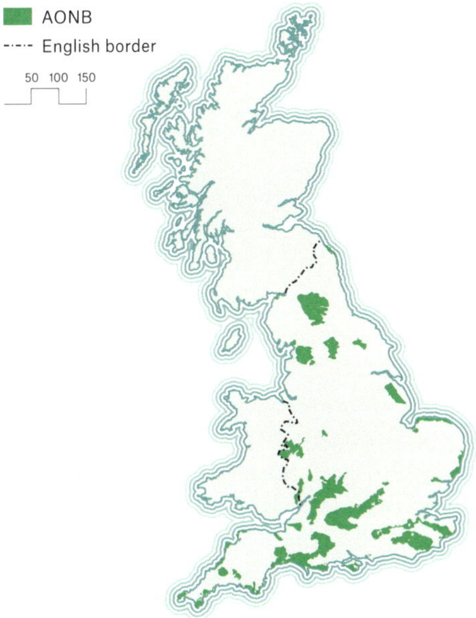

AONB
English border
50 100 150

[Fig. 2]
AONBs in the South West
Form 30% of the total land area

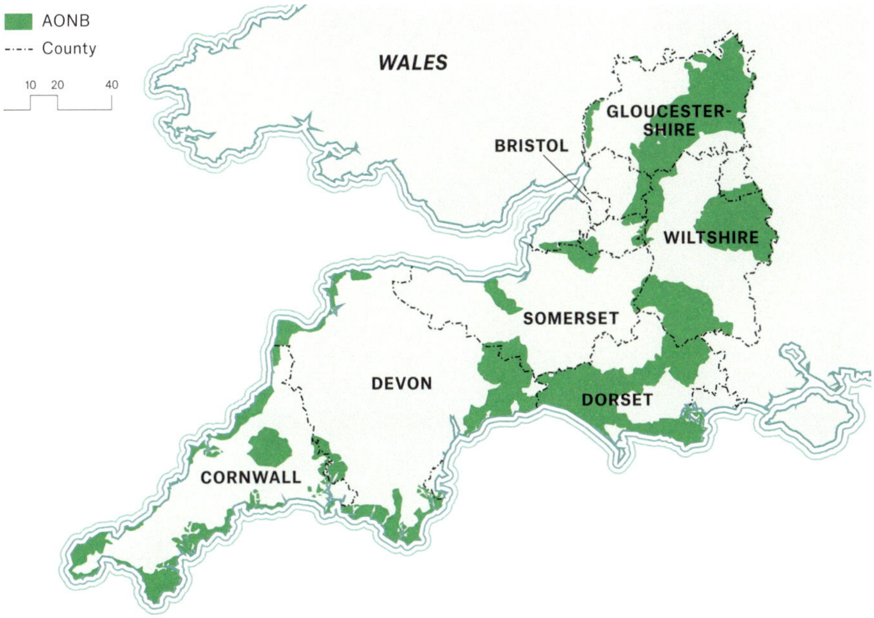

AONB
County
10 20 40
WALES
GLOUCESTER-SHIRE
BRISTOL
WILTSHIRE
SOMERSET
DEVON
DORSET
CORNWALL

[Fig. 3]
AONBs in Dorset
44% of Dorset total land area is designated as an AONB

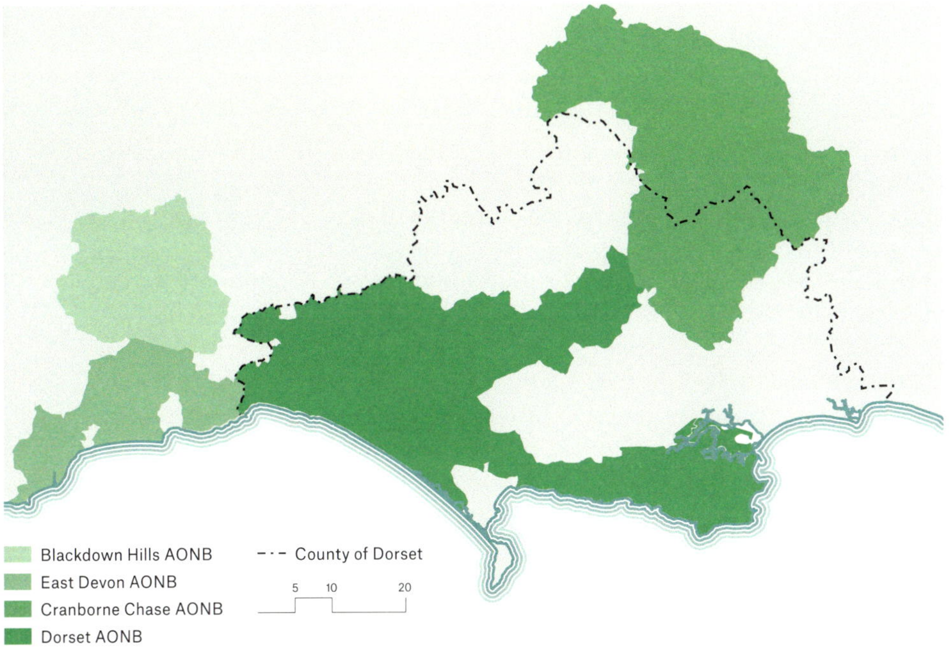

Blackdown Hills AONB
East Devon AONB
Cranborne Chase AONB
Dorset AONB
County of Dorset
5 10 20

[Fig. 4]
Population density
per square kilometer

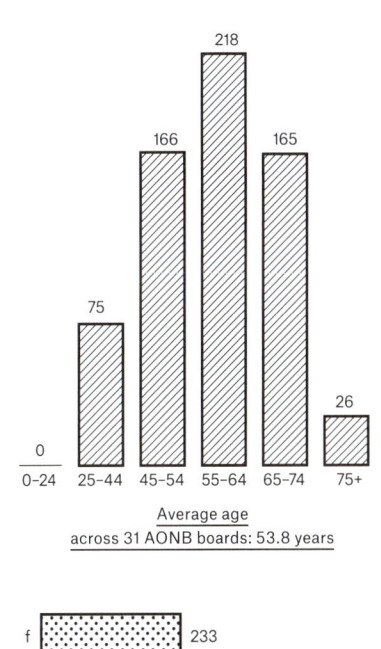

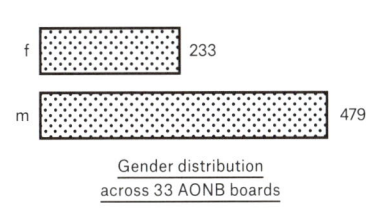

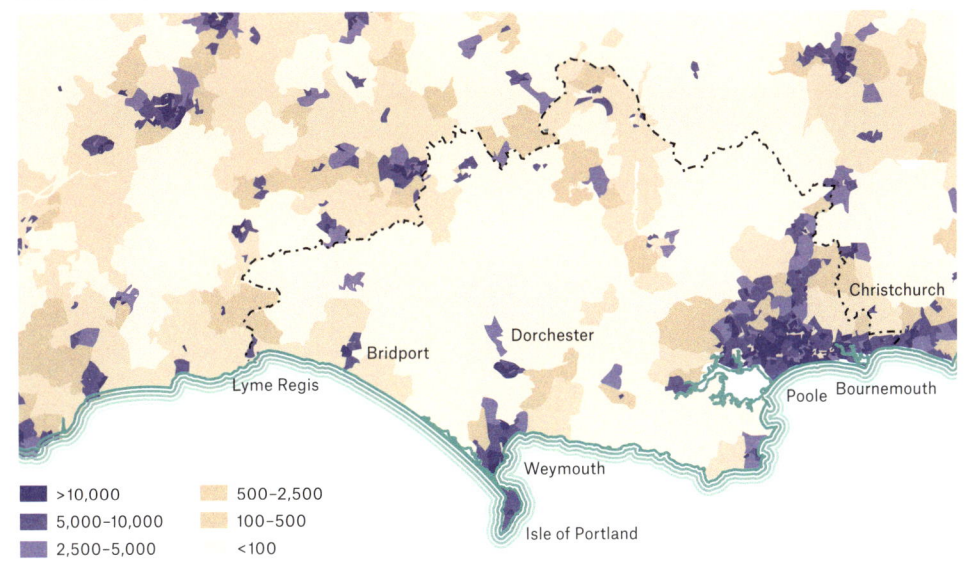

Christchurch
Dorchester
Bridport
Lyme Regis
Poole
Bournemouth
Weymouth
Isle of Portland
>10,000
5,000–10,000
2,500–5,000
500–2,500
100–500
<100

[Fig. 5]
Lack of diversity in boards of AONBs
Board members of AONBs are overwhelmingly male, white, and of retirement age

0
75
166
218
165
26
0–24
25–44
45–54
55–64
65–74
75+
Average age
across 31 AONB boards: 53.8 years
f
233
m
479
Gender distribution
across 33 AONB boards

Rural road in Dorset *v*

Two of the five categories of reform proposed by the report present great opportunities for the local governance of Dorset. Given the large proportion of AONB land and the increase in funding and control over decision-making recommended by the report, it is possible to imagine substantial rural reform.

1.4. Living landscapes

Most of the UK's protected landscapes have been inhabited by humans for centuries. The communities living on the land form part of the living tradition of the place, but they are not immune to the contemporary pressures of tourism and development. Interviews reported multiple accounts of rising house prices due to holiday lets and second homes, with little to no affordable housing schemes. Government housing development initiatives, while available for rural communities, are seen as being focused on the pressing needs of more populated areas.

Wishing to strengthen local communities, the new National Landscapes are required to foster the social and economic well-being of those communities who live on the designated land. Management decisions would therefore need to consider all current local economic activity including small businesses, agriculture, and tourism.

Secondly, a new National Landscapes Rural Housing Association will be formed specifically in order to build affordable homes for rent within these protected territories.[8]

Workshop building at Hooke Park *vi*

Robotically fabricated wood chip barn at Hooke Park *vii*

1.5. New ways of working

Perhaps the boldest and most radical set of proposals within the report come under the subheading "new ways of working." Identifying the barriers to renewal within the current system including a lack of coherence, ambition, and collective challenge, the suggestion is for central government to cede substantial control in the decision-making process to the boards of the National Landscapes. Devolving power in terms of planning and budgetary spending would empower those who live and work on the land itself.

The position of the former AONBs within the law would be strengthened, giving the governing boards statutory consultee status for all planning applications submitted on National Landscapes land. Former AONBs would be asked to create strengthened Management Plans to direct development and land use, devolving more control over future progress to the boards.

More funding would be made available to the former AONBs including direct funds to farmers for environmental services through the Environmental Land Management Scheme. With greater funding and responsibility comes the expectation that the governing bodies would become more enterprising. Responsible for their own ambitious fundraising campaigns, the National Landscapes would also be expected to enter into commercial partnerships and to improve efficiencies. Disguised as an increase in governmental support for these landscapes, a danger of the commercialization of these nationally protected territories is present in these new proposals.

2. The Politics of Regional Development

Rural sites tend to interest larger developers less than urban or semi-urban areas due to smaller plot sizes and a reduced potential customer base. Those sites in particularly beautiful tracts of the British countryside are even more unlikely to be developed with affordable units due to the pressures of holiday houses and second homes. *[Fig. 6]* Looking specifically at West Dorset we can witness both top-down and grassroots development strategies trying to meet the housing, infrastructure, and employment quotas passed down from central government.

Coastal town of Charmouth *viii*

2.1. Planning policy

Planning policy in Britain is a complex chain of hierarchy, the allocation of power ever shifting between the national, regional, and local governments. What began in 1947 as the nationalization of decisions on land development was transformed by 2004 into a hierarchical filter system. *[Fig. 7]*

A drive toward the idea of a "Big Society" during the coalition government saw large-scale cuts to central government services and the transfer of power back to local communities. The intermediate level of the Regional Assembly was dissolved in 2010, handing all planning powers directly to Local Authorities. Without the intermediate bridging guidance of a spatial strategy at a regional scale, a great chasm opened up between central government and Local Authorities, who were often under prepared and underfunded for the preparation of planning documents. The only guidance currently available to authorities having to draw up plans for their own jurisdiction is a paper known as the National Planning Policy Framework (NPPF). The framework specifies that the duty and responsibility for complying with national policy and for regulating local development lies solely with Local Councils.[9]

Reorganizations of the law and redrawing of Local Authority boundaries has resulted in a patchwork of planning documents across England. Many Local Authorities do not have an adopted plan and others have out-of-date plans dating from the old system. *[Fig. 8]* Furthermore, each plan has its own logic and terminology making cooperation and comparison problematic.[10]

2.2. Bridport's top-down development

Despite attempts at a localization of the planning system by handing decision-making control to Local Authorities, Local Plans (LP) drawn up today tend to be oversimplifications of the rich complexities of the spaces that they regulate. Especially in rural districts where Local Authorities are responsible for directing multiple dispersed and diverse communities who may have little in common other than the same rubbish collection service. The geographic consolidation of rural territories has been used to help order and organise these unique and ever changing semi-rural settlements. *[Fig. 9]*

Busy main street in Bridport *ix*

Bridport hosts a population of around 8,000 inhabitants and is the main service, retail, and social center for a large adjoining rural territory. It is located entirely within the AONB and boasts a unique industrial heritage as a site of rope making at least as far back as Roman times. [Fig. 10] The entire center of the town is a Conservation Area, within which sit hundreds of listed properties.[11] Despite the layers of protection bestowed on Bridport, it is offered no immunity to development, and as the second largest town in West Dorset, the Local Authority sees Bridport as an important site to provide much-needed new affordable housing and workspace. [Fig. 11]

The Local Plan sets out a vision for Bridport in 2031 where sustainable development has led to employment opportunities and affordable housing to meet the needs of the community. The hope being that a younger generation will be persuaded to remain in the area. The plan describes how the development proposals will preserve surrounding nationally designated landscape, views, and green spaces as well as the town's character, while strengthening the cultural, retail, social, and other amenity offerings serving the rural hinterland. The plan looks optimistically toward a sustainable town built on its reputation for local produce and tourism, where the car plays a decreasing role.

By 2031 a total of 945 new homes will have been constructed, the majority of these in one single development at Vearse Farm, a site directly adjoining the town to the southwest. An example of a top-down approach, the whole site was planned and submitted to the council for approval within one application, granted by the council in 2019 after a 4-year process of statutory and community consultation. The proposal has met with contention, with critics pointing out that the development would result in an estimated 25 percent increase in Bridport's population and would constitute the largest ever development to occur within an AONB. Despite a lengthy consultation process, residents and local service providers have registered comments on the application stating their concern at the sudden expansion of the town and at the minimal agency of local residents to meaningfully affect the future of the development.

Walkway at Vearse Farm ˣ

2.3. Rural exceptions

A loophole written into planning law allows for smaller sites that border existing development but are currently not designated for housing to be used for affordable housing in perpetuity. These "Rural Exception Sites" seek to address the needs of the local community by accommodating households who are either current residents or have an existing family or employment connection. Small numbers of homes may be permitted on non-development sites at the Local Authority's discretion, and this exemption has been used by community groups to purchase and develop former agricultural land on semi-rural sites.[12]

2.4. The potential of the Community Land Trusts (CLTs)

CLTs are set up and run by members of a community to develop and manage homes as well as other assets important to that community. There is an assumption in a CLT development that the trust will take a long-term formal role in the stewardship of the spaces it helps to develop, often retaining ownership of the freehold. CLT homes provide

[Fig. 6]
Proportion of second homes

1%
England

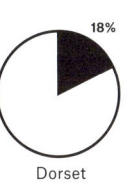
18%
Dorset

[Fig. 7]
UK planning system
Hierarchy of planning guidance documents pre and post localism bill

	2004–2011	Post 2011 Localism Bill	
Central Government	Planning Policy Statement (PPS) 1500 pages setting out national planning policy by theme	National Planning Policy Framework (NPPF) 50 pages of general guidance	
Region (Welsh Assembly, Scottish Parliament, 9 English Regions)	Regional Spatial Strategy Documents establishing a spatial strategy for each region based on the PPS, including quotas and targets		
Local Planning Authorities	Local Development Framework	Local Plan	Development Plan
		Neighbourhood Plan	

[Fig. 8]
Local Plan status in England 2019

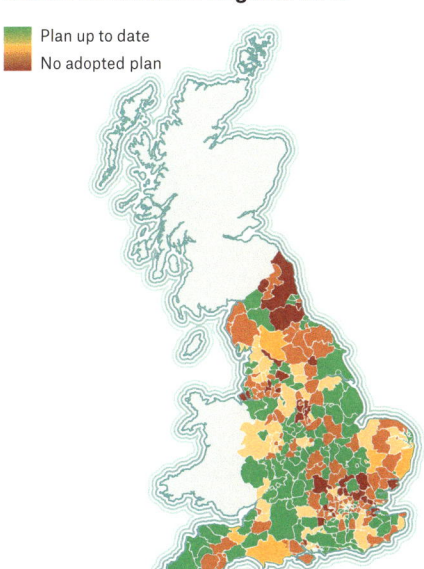

- Plan up to date
- No adopted plan

[Fig. 9]
Infrastructure in Dorset

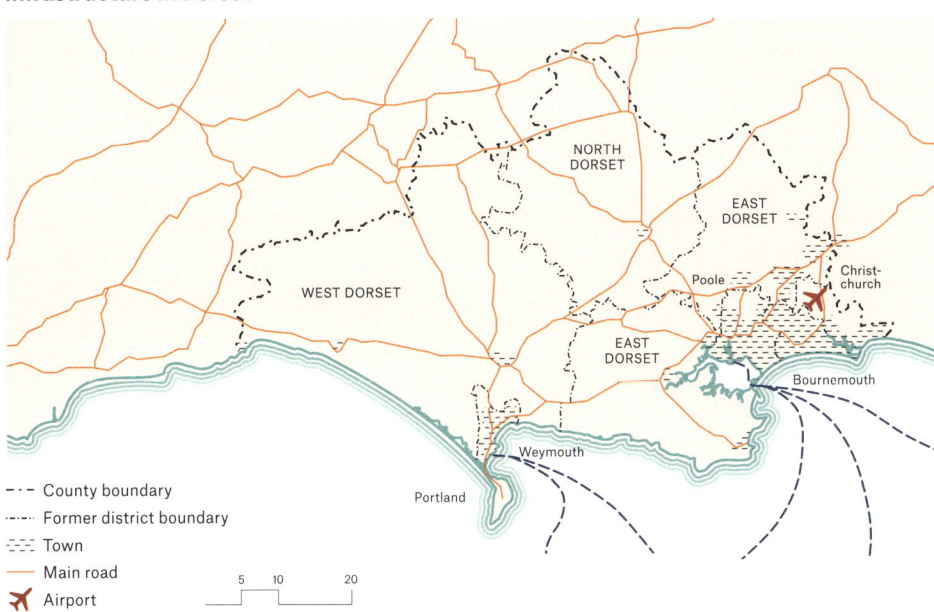

- --- County boundary
- -·-·- Former district boundary
- ::::: Town
- ——— Main road
- ✈ Airport

[Fig. 10]
Strategic development diagram
West Dorset, Weymouth, and Portland Local Plan 2015

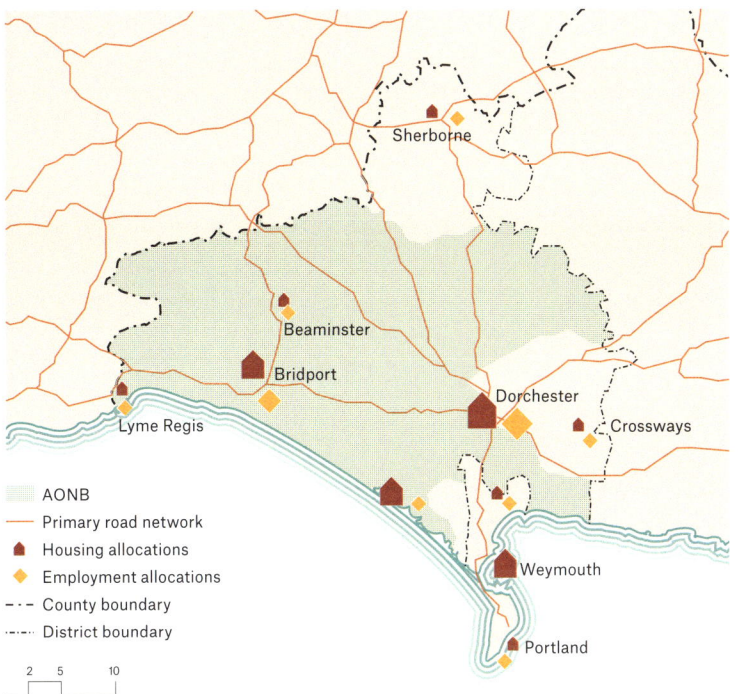

- AONB
- ——— Primary road network
- 🏠 Housing allocations
- ◆ Employment allocations
- --- County boundary
- -·-·- District boundary

Territory: Dorset Coast   49

New town of Poundbury on the outskirts of Dorchester *xi*

Buttermarket in Poundbury *xii*

long-term sustainable solutions to local housing needs as they remain genuinely affordable—prices are based on what people actually earn in their area—and are not open to the Right to Buy scheme.[13] *[Fig. 12]*

2.5. Wessex Community Assets

The South West has a strong culture of alternative economic and political thinking. The chapter on the South Hams looks at towns such as Totness that have taken control of local politics in order to become a Transition Town, committed to ecological and developmental sustainability. Groups such as arts and environmental charity Common Ground have for the past 30 years used the county of Dorset as a kind of laboratory for their projects.

Since 2007 Wessex Community Assets has connected over 100 of these community benefit societies, providing support in achieving their aims. They also provide comprehensive support to groups wishing to establish CLTs and develop local affordable housing.

Numerous CLT groups have developed small plots of land using the Rural Exception Site policy into clusters of affordable housing; however, they are often based on the familiar planning and architectures of low-density models such as Letchworth and Poundbury and in the worst case, the repetitive forms of the mass home builders Barret and Wimpy.

In Bridport a joint stakeholder group between Wessex Community Assets, Bridport Town Council, and Common Ground commissioned London-based art and architecture practice Assemble to investigate alternate spatial possibilities for grassroots developments. The work imagines CLT home building at a greater scale and with more ambitious typologies and tenures, while questioning the current accepted density of rural developments. Scaling up of ambition allows for a realistic conversation to take place around the use of local labor and materials, which would support the development of local industries. Housing such as this with a genuinely high standard of living, which is at the same time produced in an efficient enough way to make it genuinely affordable, may prompt a radical rethinking of the accepted spatial model of rural development.

3. From Manors to Community Land Trusts

In the chapter "Avon Green Belt," we looked at *Garden Cities of Tomorrow* in terms of its foundational ideas about the green belt system. The majority of Howard's book, however, does not concern itself with the well-known spatial diagrams of new cities. Instead, Howard talks in great detail about how city settlements self-organize and self-govern. Described by Lewis Mumford as a "bold rectification" of the conditions of the city as a private commercial venture,[14] Howard proposed a settlement that would hold and manage the land, meaning rents could be set by local government. This idea was a new form of liberalism poorly translated into real-life examples, but it has found synergies at a smaller scale within the land management and development structure of the CLT model.

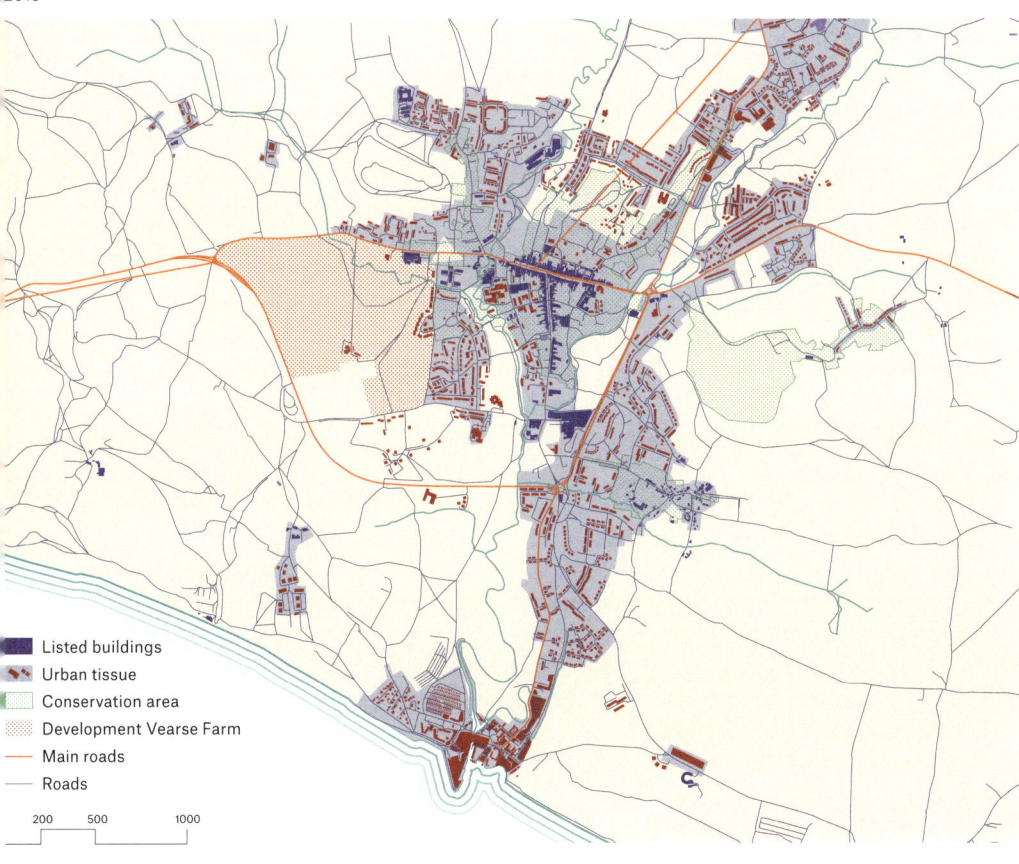

[Fig. 11]
Bridport development plan
2015

- Listed buildings
- Urban tissue
- Conservation area
- Development Vearse Farm
- Main roads
- Roads

200   500   1000

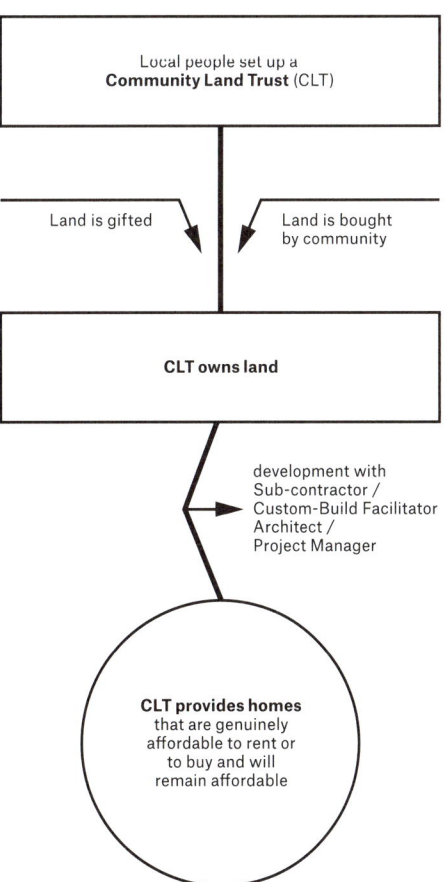

[Fig. 12]
Structure of a Community Land Trust development
CLT remains long-term steward of homes and assets

Local people set up a **Community Land Trust** (CLT)

Land is gifted | Land is bought by community

CLT owns land

development with
Sub-contractor /
Custom-Build Facilitator
Architect /
Project Manager

CLT provides homes
that are genuinely
affordable to rent or
to buy and will
remain affordable

Territory: Dorset Coast   51

3.1. Bio regionalism

Unlike eco regionalism which defines boundaries based on the physical conditions of the earth, flora, and fauna, bio regionalism attempts to take human communities and political administration into account. Developed in the 1970s as a method for improving environmental policies through an increased understanding of the way human geography interacts with the natural world, it can be used at a variety of scales as an agent for change. [Fig. 13]

The boundaries of AONBs could be considered as micro bio regions, areas of land bound together not by municipal boundaries but through a combination of identifiable physical characteristics and systems of governance. Bio regionalism could be thought of as a new developmental paradigm. [Fig. 14]

3.2. Neighborhood unit

In his discussion of a type of territorial planning via neighborhood units in the suburbs of cities, Lewis Mumford described these communities as an "organizing social nucleus, which provided the necessary facilities for working and co-operating in all manner of neighbourly activities."[15] There is the potential for small-scale local governance such as Bridport Town Council and community groups such as CLTs to propose and deliver small- to medium-scale projects within which they have genuine agency. With larger organizations such as the Wessex Community Assets providing legal and methodological advice, there are opportunities for governmentally driven localism to be capitalized upon.

The nucleus described by Mumford can be conceptualized both metaphorically and physically. The distribution of manor houses across the territory [Fig. 15] can be imagined as physical manifestation of these organizing social spaces. Examples such as Hooke Park, Dartington Hall, Schumacher College—all socially orientated educational arts facilities based in historic houses and grounds—display a tendency toward the reuse of these historic objects as community assets.

Wraxhall Manor, Higher Wraxhall, Dorset *xiii*

3.3. Community-controlled landscapes

Local governance should be re-localized by redefining the administrative boundaries based on bio regions. New powers divested by central government via AONBs and Neighborhood Plans should be exploited by village- and town-scale self-organized democratic governance. Given the power to decide where and how development should take place, and the means of its execution, the communities dwelling within AONBs could become their own developers. New developments should center around the historic manor houses, using these protected sites of heritage as social nuclei.

Dorset Coast: Constitution Map [Fig. 16]

[Fig. 13]
Physical characteristics

- Blackdowns
- Mashwood Vale
- South Purbeck
- Dorset Downs
- Weymouth Lowlands

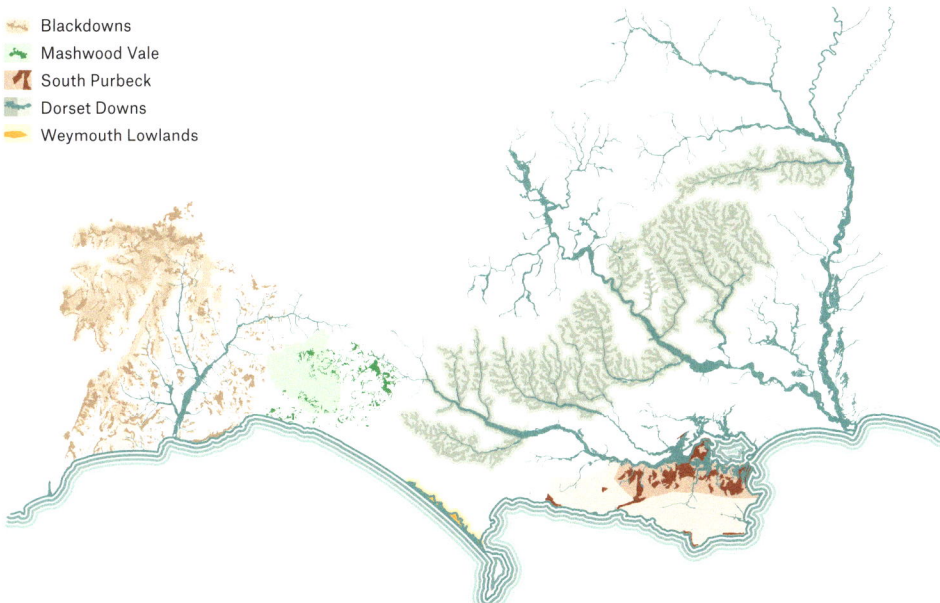

[Fig. 14]
Proposed new bio regional boundaries based on NCAs and AONBs

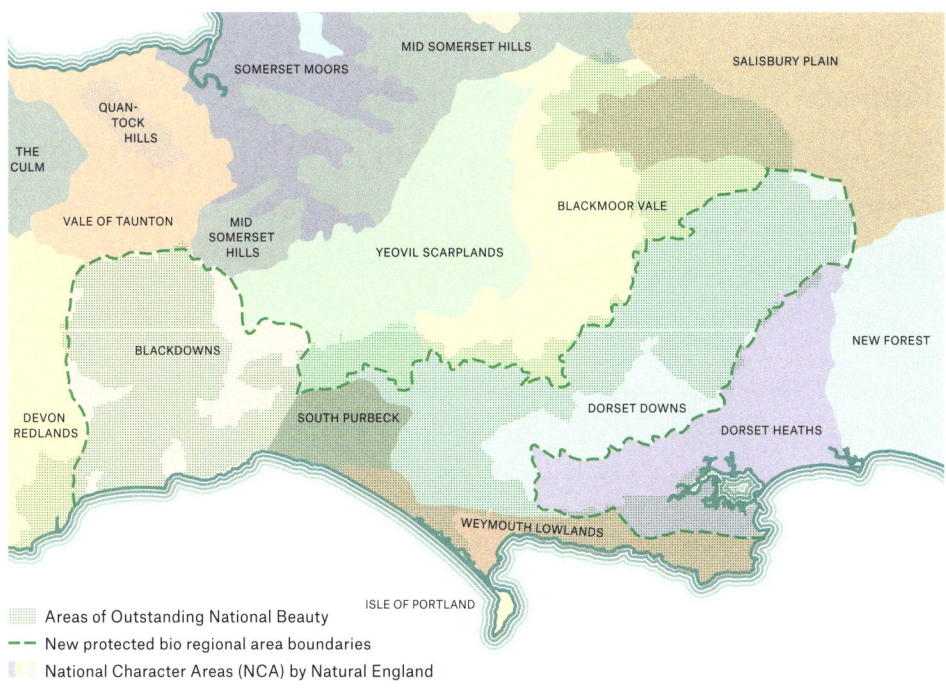

- Areas of Outstanding National Beauty
- New protected bio regional area boundaries
- National Character Areas (NCA) by Natural England

[Fig. 15]
Manor house distribution

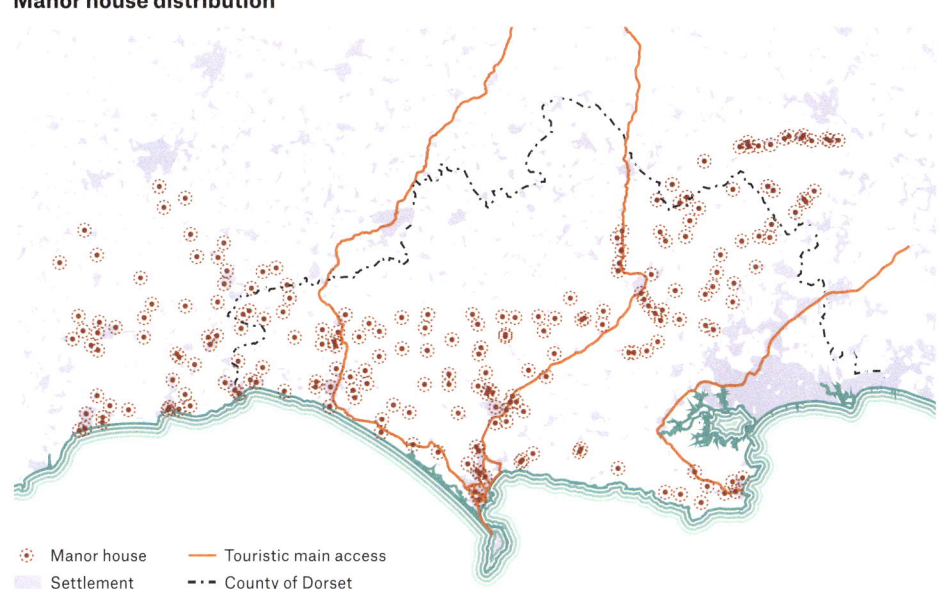

- Manor house
- Settlement
- Touristic main access
- County of Dorset

Territory: Dorset Coast 53

[Fig. 16]
Dorset Coast—Constitution: From Manors to Community Land Trusts

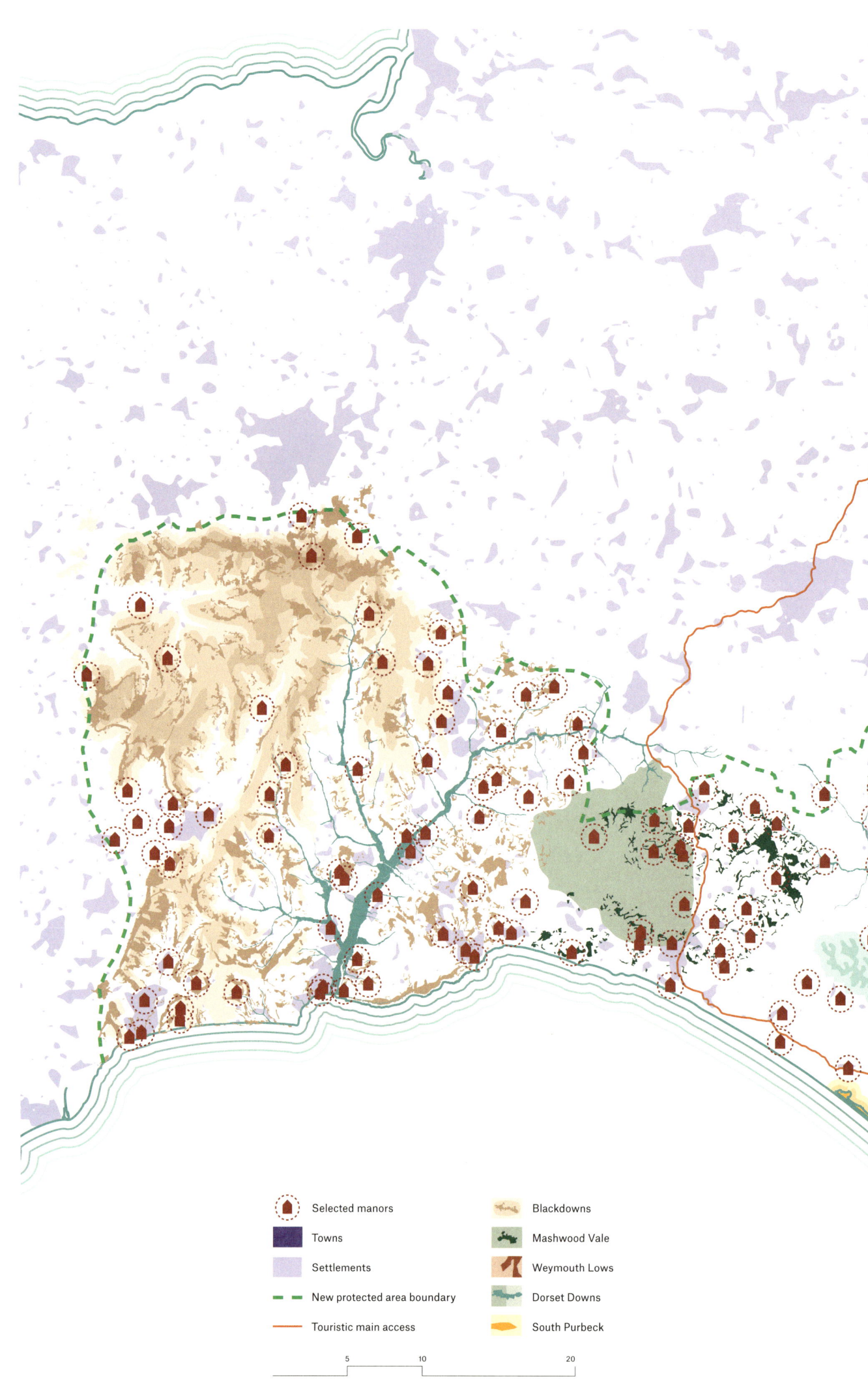

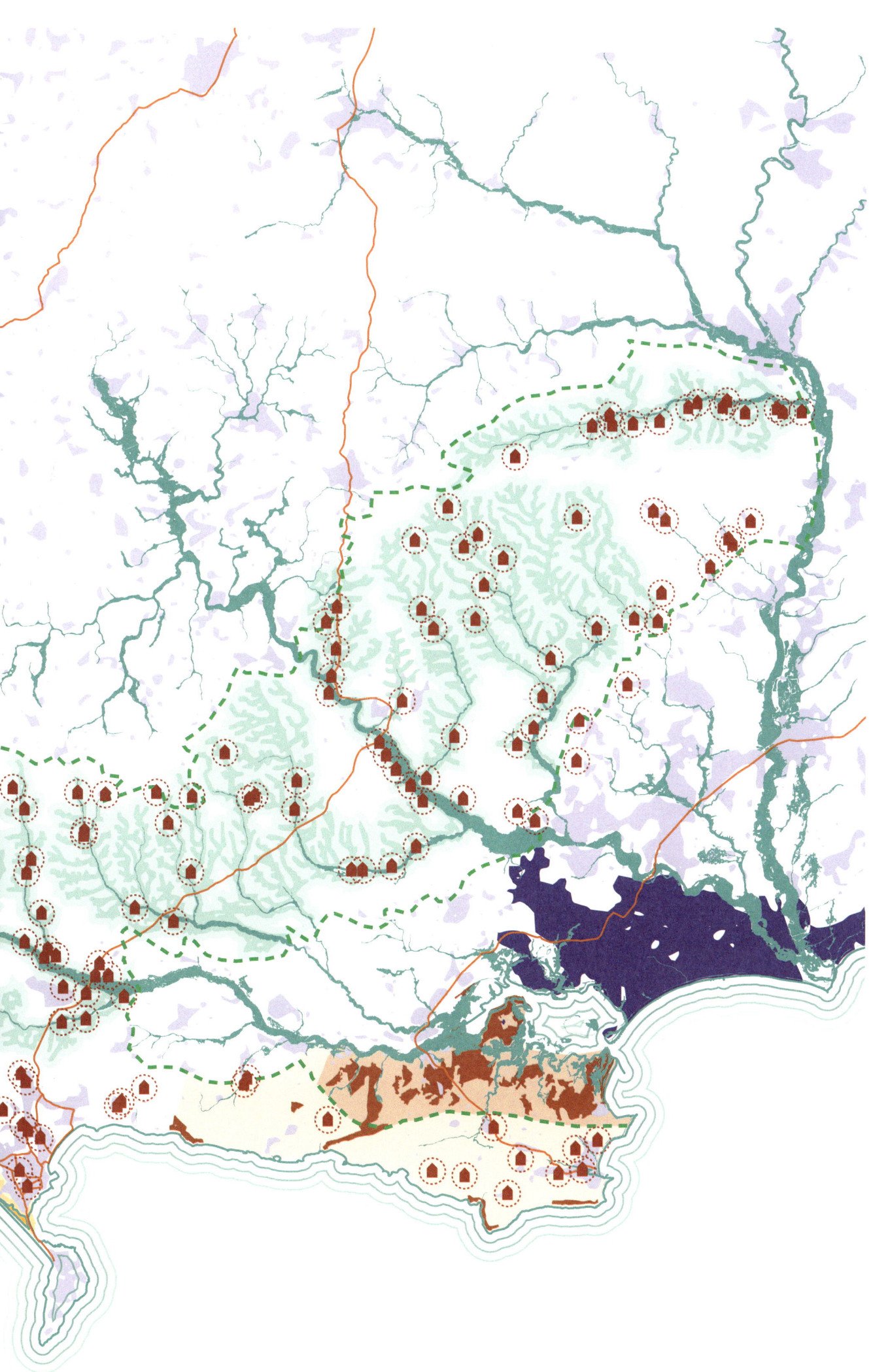

Territory: Dorset Coast

Territory

South Hams: Town-Country-Magnet
1. Moorland Maritime 57
2. A Contested Agricultural Territory 58
3. Constitution: Manors Maintaining the Town-Country-Magnet 62

South Hams: Town-Country-Magnet

This region of South Devon has important landscape features, such as Dartmoor National Park to the north, the coast to the south, and the rivers that fall from the moor, draining the territory into the English Channel. The fertile river valleys have proved fruitful testing grounds for alternative and ecologically minded new businesses.

1. Moorland Maritime

A coast characterized by cliffs and coves rises sharply through rich agricultural valleys to the high and barren land of Dartmoor, which causes heavy sea air blowing in off the coast to settle on the high ground as mist and clouds. The cross section of landscapes across the territory makes tourism and agriculture the main economic driving forces of the area.

1.1. Dartmoor

Imagining a north-south geological section though southern Devon would reveal a great thrust of granite rising up through the coal-rich sedimentary rocks.[1] [Fig. 1] Harder than the sandstones and mudstones surrounding it, the granite eroded at a much slower pace; high and less hospitable, the granite thrust formed the unique microclimate and atmosphere of Dartmoor. Great rocky outcrops known locally as "tors" rise up from the peat bogs forming peaks of up to 300 meters high. John Leland described the area in the 1540s as "of very greate compace, and is suche a wilde morisch and forest ground as Exmore is."[2] High ground and sea air blowing in give the moor its character as a misty, cloudy, and rainy landscape, [Fig. 2] inspiring famously mysterious legends and tales. Arthur Conan Doyle's *The Hound of the Baskervilles* is set on the moor, inspired by legends of a great black dog who roamed the uplands. Wet weather and acidic soils have prevented any kind of intensive farming of the lands, leaving tracts of forest and bog, rich in species of lichen, moss, birds, and insects. Although mostly privately owned land, Dartmoor has National Park status and has been designated as "Access Land" with no restrictions on movement. [Fig. 3]

Wild horse in Dartmoor National Park *i*

1.2. Linear infrastructure

Human settlements are dotted around the land surrounding the National Park, those sandwiched in the crescent of land between the moor and the coast being the largest. The coastal towns of Plymouth, Exeter, and Torquay, founded as ports and boosted by the tourism economy, are strung together by the linear infrastructure of the M5 and the A38, known as the "holiday route" connecting the three coastal poles. [Fig. 4] The Great Western Railway connects London directly to the South

Exeter-Plymouth line—part of the Great Western Mainline *ii*

Devon coast in three hours, making Exeter and Plymouth accessible and available holiday destinations for London and the South East of England. [Fig. 5] Only small sections of the South Devon shore have not been designated as an Area of Outstanding Natural Beauty, adding to its appeal for summer vacationing. No fewer than six rivers drain from the moor toward the coastline, along valleys equally famed for their natural beauty. The Dart Valley's tidal riverbed connects Dartmouth with Totnes, the brackish ebbing and flowing water forming a unique wetland habitat for plants and wildlife. Hills overlooking the river are dotted with historic manor houses and castles profiting from the fertile soils, vantage points, and sheltered access to the sea via the inland estuary.

1.3. A new tourist economy

> The time seems near, if it has not actually arrived, when the chastened sublimity of a moor, a sea, or a mountain will be all of nature that is absolutely in keeping with the moods of the more thinking among mankind. And ultimately, to the commonest tourist, spots like Iceland may become what the vineyards and myrtle gardens of South Europe are to him now.
> —Thomas Hardy [3]

Brixham, a touristic coastal town with an idyllic harbour *iii*

Adapting to increased societal awareness of the environment, while catering to a market hungry for new and novel experiences, the South Devon tourist industry has embraced the immersive holiday. According to the Visit England annual survey of attractions in Britain, farms have recorded the largest increase in UK visitor admissions since 1989.[4] [Fig. 6] Devon Farms is a network of around 60 family-run agricultural establishments that offer holiday accommodations on their farms in the form of self-catering cottages, bed and breakfasts, and camping. [Fig. 7]

2. A Contested Agricultural Territory

The calm rural landscape of the South Devon countryside is also a farming frontline in the battle between food production and environmental concerns.

2.1. Productivism

Since World War II, Europe has made a concerted and conscious effort to produce surplus food reserves. Policies, formed to favor overproduction above all else, helped to replenish depleted food stocks and feed malnourished populations in the 1940s. The realization during wartime that individual countries who could no longer rely on the cross-border trade of foodstuffs were nowhere near self-sufficient in their own production capacities left a deep scar in political memory. The attitude followed by the EU and many national governments after World War II was one of productivism: the conception of farming's sole role and responsibility being the production of food and fiber. The policies which followed

[Fig. 1]
Geological cross section

- Rermo Triassic sedimentary rocks, Permian sedimentary rocks
- Early Carboniferous rocks, Holsworthy Group Teign Valley Group
- Devonian rocks, Devonian sandstones, conglomerates and mudstones
- Lundy Island granite, Cornubian batholith
- Lizard Complex
- Ordovician and Silurian sedimentary rocks

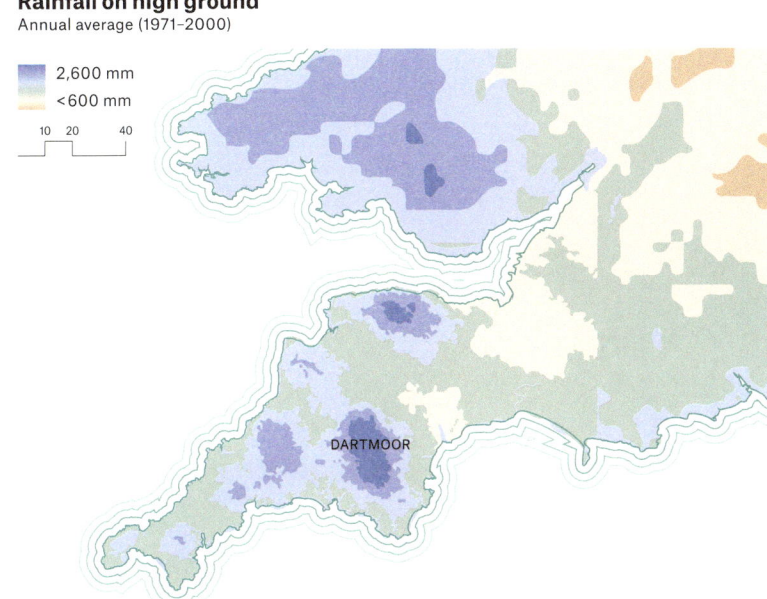

[Fig. 2]
Rainfall on high ground
Annual average (1971–2000)

- 2,600 mm
- <600 mm

[Fig. 3]
Landscape features

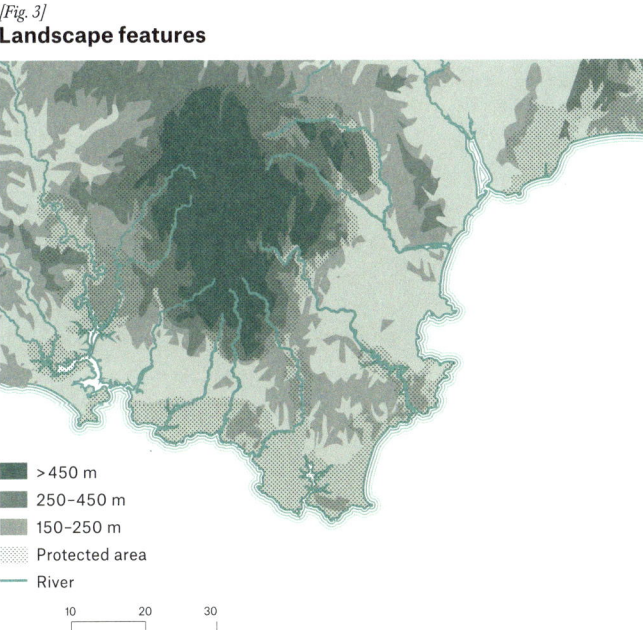

- >450 m
- 250–450 m
- 150–250 m
- Protected area
- River

[Fig. 4]
Population density
per square kilometer

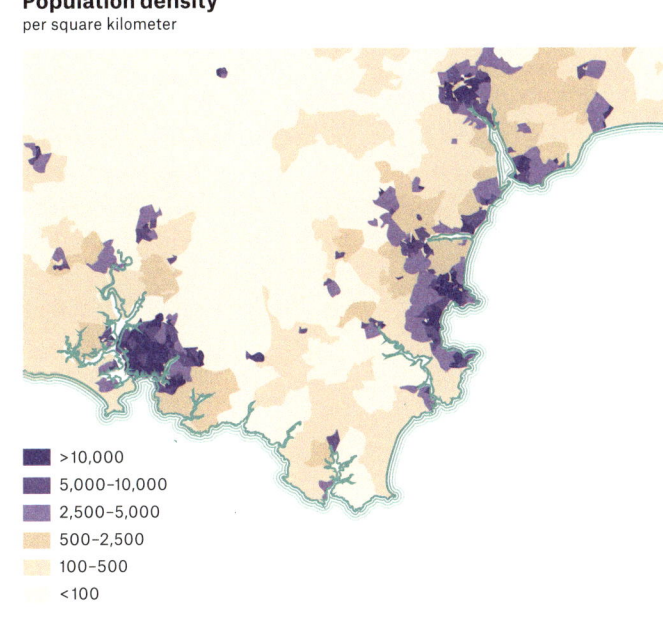

- >10,000
- 5,000–10,000
- 2,500–5,000
- 500–2,500
- 100–500
- <100

[Fig. 5]
Infrastructure network

- Settlement
- Railway
- Roads

Territory: South Hams   59

incentivized large-scale and intensive agricultural organizations and rewarded production over method. Productivist farming is characterized by concentration, intensification, and specialization.[5]

2.2. Common Agricultural Policy (CAP)

Introduced in 1962 the CAP provides funding and subsidies to the agricultural sector in Europe, attempting to increase productivity through technology, while ensuring a comfortable standard of living for farmers. By 1984 the CAP made up 73 percent of the total EU budget and led to farms becoming so productive that they grew more food than needed, sparking a series of reforms reevaluating the purpose of the policy. *[Fig. 8]*

Schumacher College, international college for ecological studies *iv*

In 2003, after 19 years of discussion and reform, the EU decided to cut the direct link between subsidies and production, with farmers from then on only receiving income support on the condition that they fulfill some basic food safety, environmental, and animal health and welfare standards. In 2018 the EU supported farmers with 58.82 billion Euros, 41.71 of which went directly to income support.[6]

In Devon, the results of the CAP's drive toward production, prior to the 2003 reforms, are evident in the mega farms concentrated on the arable land surrounding the M5. *[Fig. 9]* As a county, Devon has the 6th highest number of indoor reared dairy cows and the 3rd highest number of intensively reared egg hens in the UK. The effect on the rural landscape of central Devon can be seen from the motorway, the vast barns and feed silos of animal agriculture, alongside fields growing crops for their feed.

The grain of the landscape has also been affected by the production-orientated policies. Larger fields with fewer hedgerows are more efficient for large-scale industrial machinery, and the diverse habitat of the hedgerow and the grass siding has slowly been destroyed to make way for more field area. Most of Devon's open field systems were already enclosed in medieval times,[7] yet the size and shape of these fields were still insufficiently large and regular for the modern combine harvester, and a new expansive grid of fenced enclosures has superseded many of the hedge-lined smaller fields.

2.3. Polarized production

Despite the increase in the number of intensive farming units since 2003,[8] the average dairy herd per holding is still only 82 cows. Numbers of dairy farms in the South West of England decreased 61.19 percent between 2005 and 2013, yet the number of cows in the region has only dropped 9.14 percent over the same period of time. These two statistics point to an industry increasingly marked by a split between large-scale intensive farms and small holdings, pointing to a polarization within the industry.[9] *[Fig. 10]*

The motivation behind intensification is clear: economization, government subsidies, and catering to monopolized production and processing plants. Small- and medium-sized farmers have been forced to rethink business models to remain competitive in a market whose prices

[Fig. 6]
Growth of farm tourism
Sectors outperforming vs. market

in % of visits by attraction categories

(Farms, Gardens, Visitor / Heritage Centers, Country Parks, Museums / Art Galleries)

[Fig. 7]
Members of Devon Farms

• Member of Devon Farms

[Fig. 8]
Common Agricultural Policy (CAP)
As the single most important policy of the EU budget

EU budget in 1985
73% CAP **27%** Other EU's policies

EU budget in 2017
37% CAP **63%** Other EU's policies

[Fig. 9]
Intensive farming in Devon concentrated around the M5
Mega farms have more than 40,000 birds, 2,000 pigs, or 750 breeding sows

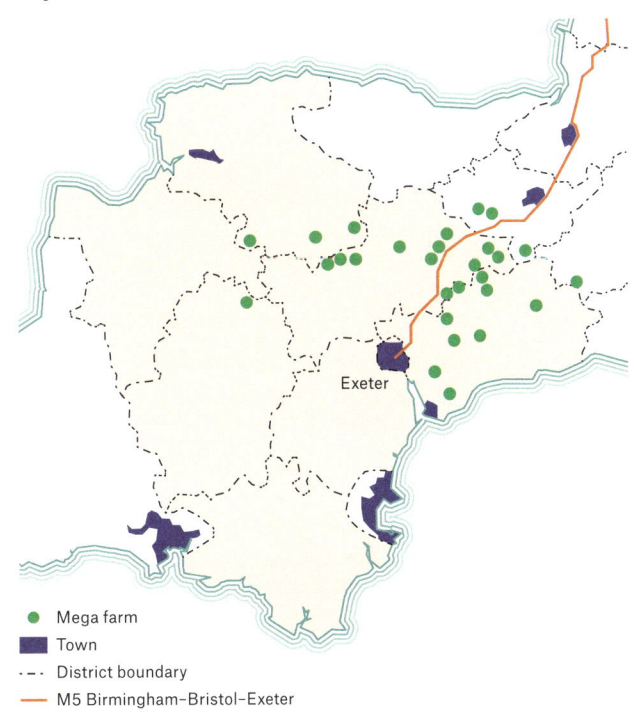

• Mega farm
■ Town
-·-· District boundary
— M5 Birmingham–Bristol–Exeter

[Fig. 10]
Dairy farming statistics
Reduction of dairy producers, holdings, and cows in the South West is proportionally less than the UK as a whole

☐ England
■ South West total

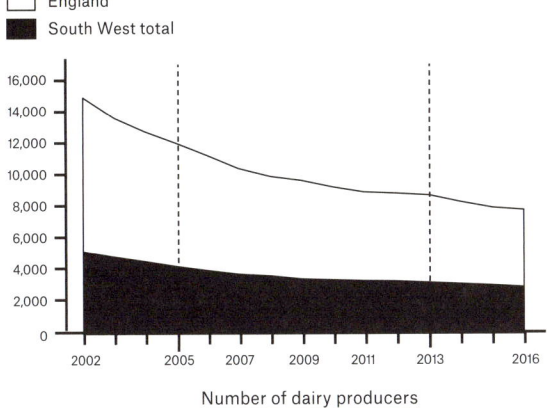

Number of dairy producers

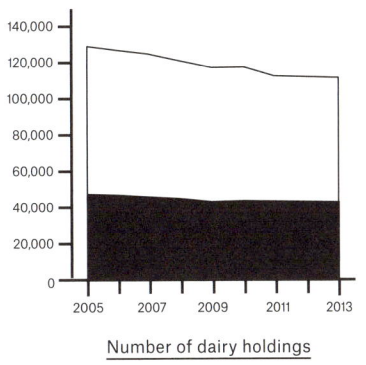

Number of dairy holdings

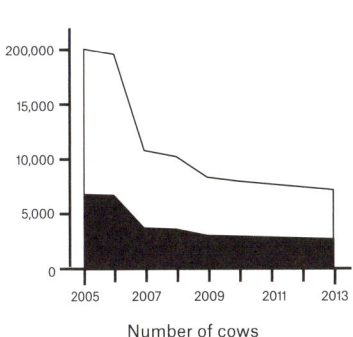

Number of cows

Fowlescombe Farm v

Whitehall Farm vi, vii

are entirely controlled by the four biggest supermarkets that sell the vast majority of their products. Diversification has been key to survival for many, with farmers venturing into the tourism market, yet also catering to a portion of society who like to use their buying power to support gentler ways of working with the land.

2.4. Agri-ruralism

Smaller producers have turned their focus to organic farming and traditional techniques, which reduce the deployment of fertilizer, pesticides, fungicides, and herbicides on the land. The government is recognizing many of these measures as worthy of subsidy, and farmers can now receive payments for replanting hedgerows, using sustainable horticultural techniques, and for leaving fields fallow to reinvigorate the soil's natural fertility. With less focus on scale and efficiency, the agricultural landscape can witness an increase in natural biodiversity, yet farmers must also come to terms with lower yields and higher price points. A differentiated approach saw many small holders go part time on their farming activities, while they explored diversification into other sectors including agritourism. [Fig. 11]

3. Constitution: Manors Maintaining the Town-Country-Magnet

Looking back at Ebenezer Howard's three magnets diagram, the country magnet has been drawing young families and former city dwellers back to the countryside. Devon's connectivity to larger cities, such as Bristol and London, along with its idyllic rural setting and proximity to the coast, make it a prime location for those wanting to transition to a slower pace of life and a more profound connection to the land. Urban flight as a phenomenon can be seen in working age populations, yet it is far more pronounced in those of retirement age, especially in the towns and villages along the south coast. Desired locations for people aged 65 and over do not necessarily match those of the working age, and a geographically disbalanced migration leads to significantly older coastal populations. [Fig. 12–13]

    Seasonal tourism coupled with a large portion of retired individuals makes for an unstable and fluctuating economy. Desire to own a holiday home or to retire to the Devon coast has inflated house prices in certain seaside areas, [Fig. 14] and resulted in 14 percent of the housing in South Hams to be second homes, holiday accommodations, or standing empty. [Fig. 15]

    Towns such as Totnes have, however, gathered momentum as a center for environmental innovation and activism. In 2006, Totnes, an inland market town on the River Exe, became the first transition town, an experimental grassroots model aiming toward self-sufficiency, in order to reduce the potential effects of climate destruction and its associated economic instability. An inspiration for countless other transition towns, urban neighborhoods, islands, and cities across the globe, Totnes has become not only a magnet for people longing to live somewhere

[Fig. 11]
Areas of organic farming land
In thousand hectares

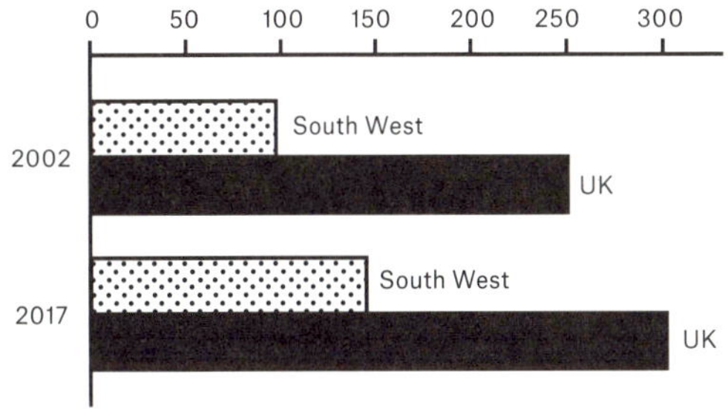

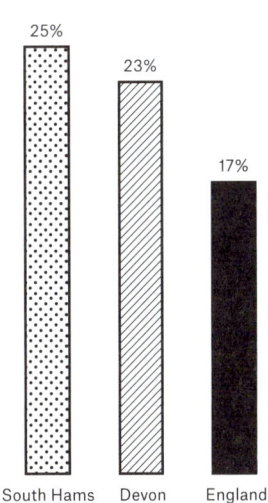

[Fig. 12]
Percentage of population aged 65+ in South Hams

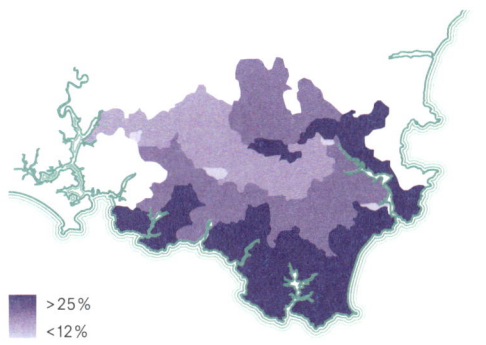

> 25%
< 12%

[Fig. 13]
Percentage of population aged 65+
2013

25% 23% 17%

South Hams   Devon   England

[Fig. 14]
Average property prices in South Hams
2012

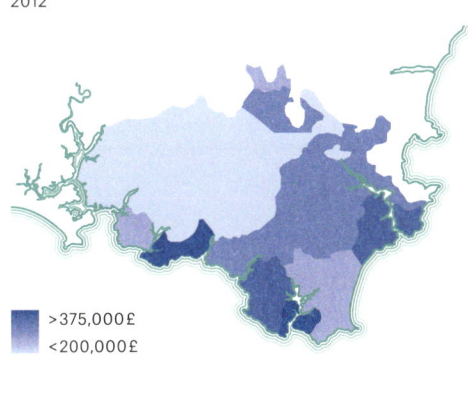

> 375,000 £
< 200,000 £

[Fig. 15]
Percentage of second homes in South West England and Wales
2011

> 9%
< 2%

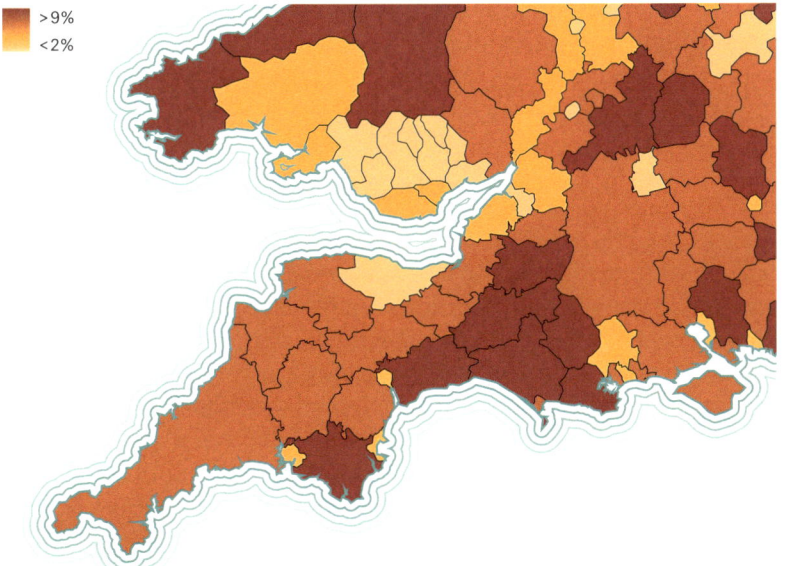

Territory: South Hams   63

taking climate issues in their daily lives seriously, but also a touristic location for the same reasons.

3.1. Post-productivism

Standing in opposition to the capitalistic ideas of productivism, a movement with its roots in the 1970s New Age wave of the counterculture, the post-productivism ideology has a different reading of the land. The broad concept is based on the idea that the agricultural sector, especially in developed economies such as the UK's, is small and run inefficiently, propped up by government funding.

The countryside can and should have other uses than the uneconomically viable production of food, and could be an accessible landscape for all. Strands of environmentalism and aestheticism run through ideas within the model, but it could be generalized as a movement toward a multidimensional reading of the countryside, with its use as a commodity in itself, coupled with its use in the production of commodities.

Historically the views of post-productivist actors have provoked strong reactions from communities whose own history and livelihood have stemmed from the agricultural use of the land. Seen as a direct attack on, and a misunderstanding of, a rural way of life, tensions between newcomers and historical farming communities characterized the rural paradigm in the 1970s and 1980s. Formally seen as stewards of a bucolic landscape, farmers saw themselves demonized by counter-cultural groups attempting to share the same rural space.

Abandoned quarry in Dartmoor National Park *viii*

3.2. Overcoming opposition

The idea of a "contested countryside" has been woven into the fabric of the UK's rural biography, yet what was seen, in the 1990s, as tension between post-productivists and agri-ruralists, has softened. Both top-down and grassroots movements have bridged the gap between farmers and middle-class activists. Local and national governments offer support for diverse and sustainable economic activity on agricultural land, and new generations of farming families, willing and compelled to explore other methods of operation, have embraced small-scale local production and distribution networks.

3.3. Testing grounds

Towns inland from the coast benefiting from lower land value because of reduced pressure from coastal tourism, such as Totnes, Kingsbridge, and Ivybridge, have become hotspots for micro businesses. *[Fig. 17]* Situated between the coast and the National Park along river valleys, these settlements benefit from the pull factors of Howard's country magnet—the beauty of nature, an abundance of water and fresh air, and low rents—have attracted a working age population. Market towns such as these have historically, and continue to, act as hubs for the surrounding countryside.

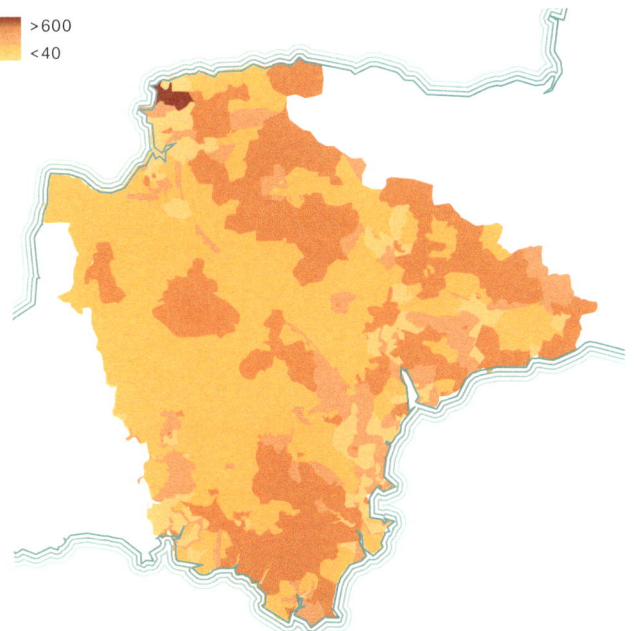

[Fig. 16]
Concentration of micro businesses in Devon
By local authority, in 2010

>600
<40

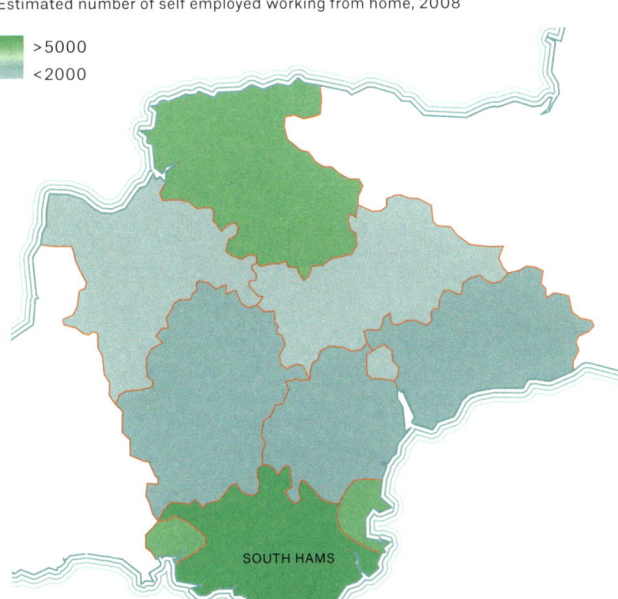

[Fig. 17]
Density of self-employment
Estimated number of self employed working from home, 2008

>5000
<2000

SOUTH HAMS

[Fig. 18]
Rates of self-employment
In 2017

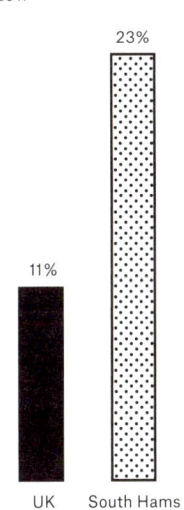

23%
11%
UK   South Hams

Territory: South Hams

Fleet House, Holbeton, South Devon *ix*

The market has responded to the desire for a greater quantity of flexible, collaborative, low cost work spaces for new business enterprises, with many work hubs opening up in the above-mentioned towns. As such, the rate of self-employment in South Hams is also far above the national average. *[Fig. 17–18]*

3.4. Constellation network

A horizontal network connecting small-scale producers and new business enterprises already exists in part. Farmers' cooperatives and schemes, such as Devon Farms, have fostered collaboration between agribusinesses across Devon as a whole.

Equally, the market towns are already acting as epicenters for exchange for the self-employed in the rural landscape. Market towns sit on vectors of production and tourism at the hinge point where valleys cross transport arteries. Each valley contains a subtly different touristic and horticultural attribute, from the maritime to the moorland. *[Fig. 19–20]*

A system of manor houses overlays the territory with a loose relationship to both the pastoral situation and the town communities. Their historical locations were the center of an open field system, meaning that their physical locations do not necessarily correlate with today's conurbations. It is proposed that these existing manor houses act as an overlay network that bridges the larger settlements with remote agrarian locations. Impregnated with new programs, centered around sustainable rural life, the invigorated manor houses act as poles along the river valley production axes. *[Fig. 21]*

The manor houses—a support infrastructure that fosters communities interested in the cultivation of rural society—have the potential to bring agronomy, education, tourism, and economy together.

South Hams: Constitution Map *[Fig. 22]*

[Fig. 19]
Settlement poles between Dartmoor National Park and the sea

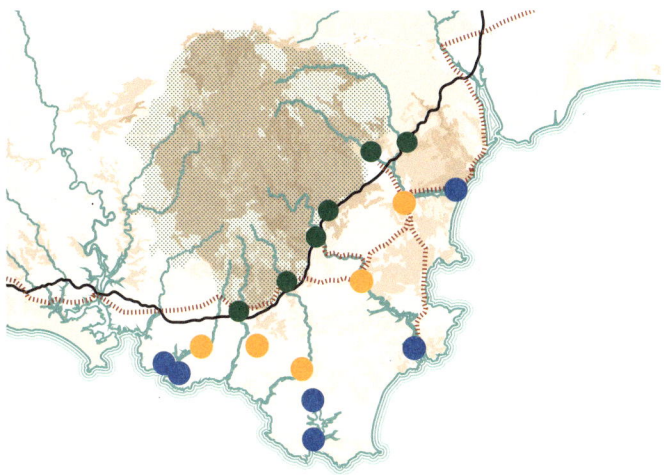

[Fig. 20]
Settlement poles along the main infrastructure

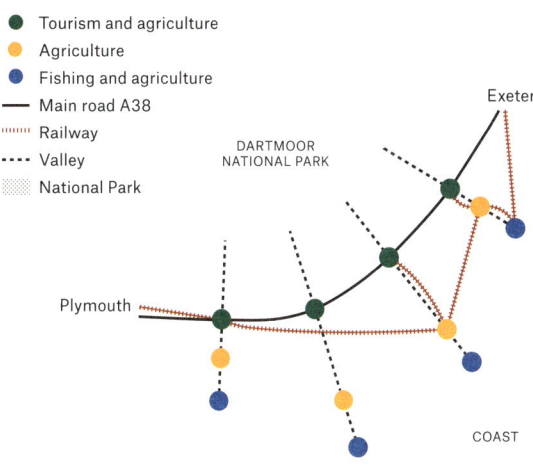

[Fig. 21]
Constellation network of manors along the valleys

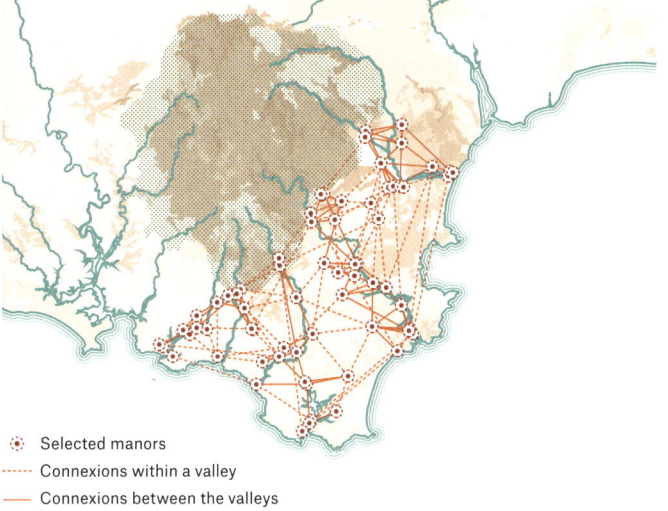

Territory: South Hams 67

[Fig. 22]
South Hams—Constitution: Manors maintaining the town-country-magnet

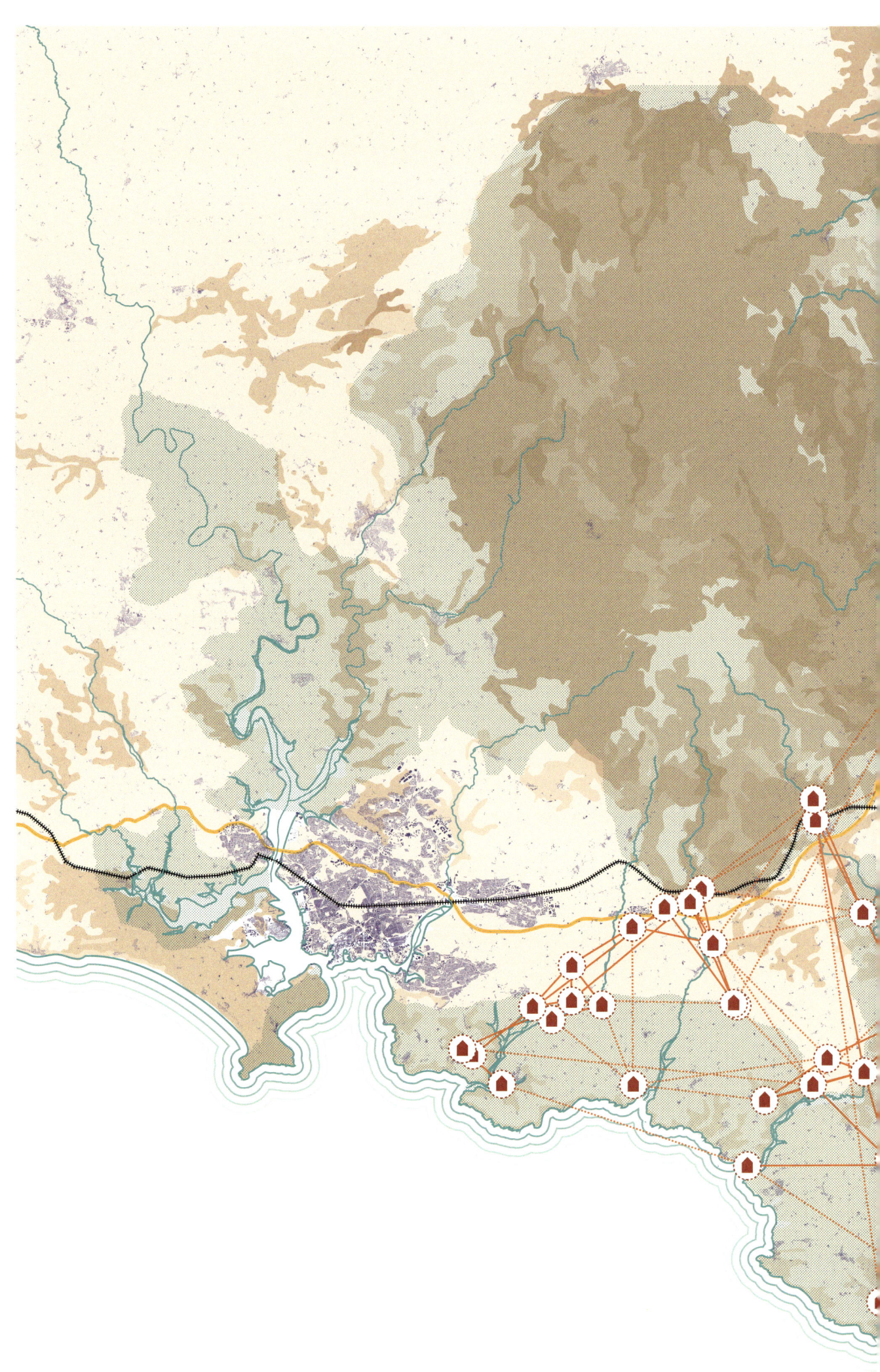

Territory: South Hams

Territory

Taw & Exe Valley: Remote Communities
- 1. A Remote Valley Territory — 71
- 2. Higher Education — 74
- 3. Constitution: New Commons — 76

Taw & Exe Valley: Remote Communities

Two river basins bisect the county of Devon, each ending in their respective coastal municipalities of Barnstaple and Exeter. The valleys split the peninsula in two, with Exmoor, Somerset, Bristol, and Bath to the northeast, and Dartmoor, South Devon, and Cornwall to the southwest. The valley landscapes between the metropoles suffer from a rural youth exodus and low levels of economic growth, challenges facing many remote yet idyllic places in the UK.

1. A Remote Valley Territory

The settlements at the mouths of the Rivers Exe and Taw are the economic poles of the region. Conversely, the connecting countryside between Barnstaple and Exeter could be described as demographically and economically peripheral. The valley system exists as a void between the coastal centers, with sparse and dispersed provisions for amenities, education, and services.

1.1. Idyllic landscape

The valley system epitomizes the English rural idyll. With the viewfinder of a camera separating the image from the reality, small hamlets scattered across rolling hills form an image of a quiet and contented life. First defined in the late 1980s, the concept of the rural idyll as a happier, healthier, and more neighborly place with fewer problems than urban areas[1] has some basis in the realities of life outside cities and towns. Small communities tend to be closer knit, and the likelihood of knowing local service providers personally is fairly high. The rural idyll also points, however, toward a misunderstanding of the everyday hardships of living in remote communities.

View across the Exe Valley. Near Silverton, Devon [i]

1.2. A valley system

Water draining from the high wetland moors of Dartmoor and Exmoor has formed a transversal rift across the peninsula, and the manifold tributaries feeding streams and rivers have shaped the topography into gentle rolling hills. [Fig. 1] The majority of this land has been designated as Grade II or III agricultural land: rich pasture for livestock and dairy. The flatlands around Exeter and Tiverton in the southeast offer the only grade 1 agricultural land suitable for cropping.

1.3. Urbanized poles

What was once a feudal agrarian landscape network spread across the valley system has gone through a process of slow littoralization. The

Cathedral church of St. Peter in Exeter *ii*

settlements along the north and south coastlines have seen a steady increase in population, services, and built urban fabric leaving a sparsely populated hinterland peppered with the physical remains of the former agrarian communities. *[Fig. 2]* The manor houses and churches, which were once the hearts of feudal communities, today often find themselves disconnected from contemporary rural settlements. Grand manor houses which were, centuries ago, the court house, tax office, and warehouse for a community living off the land, transformed their status. Through the privatization of the lands they ruled over they became seats of power and symbols of status. This societal separation of the landed gentry and the working class has manifested itself physically in the disconnect between the manor house and the local village.

1.4. A connective spine

The main transport infrastructure follows the two principal fluvial courses linking Barnstaple to Exeter. *[Fig. 3]* Train line and A-road share the easier route adjacent to the two riverbeds, leaving B-roads and country lanes to meander through the undulating landscapes between remoter settlements across the territory. *[Fig. 4]* In this situation the car becomes an essential tool to enable access to services and amenities for those living away from the connective transport spine.

1.5. Economic periphery

Productivity in Devon is poor when considered in relation to the UK as a whole. Gross value added (GVA) per filled job stands at 77 percent of the UK average and GVA per hour work at 82 percent, with both of these figures declining in relative terms.[2] This may correlate with an increase in part-time work and self-employment, pointing to more informal and unpredictable patterns of work. These alternative work arrangements often represent the two extremes of economic stability: on the one hand precariousness and on the other hand privilege.[3]

Exeter is a clear exception to the trend; its GVA per capita sits well above the UK average. *[Fig. 5–6]* Being a university city with good physical connections to London and the South East, it has attracted investment from larger companies such as Balfour Beatty, Coutts & Co. and EDF Energy.

When measured by GVA, the rest of Devon has low economic productivity. Governmental drives toward increasing productivity, especially in preparation for leaving the European Union, has lead councils in rural areas to review local economic systems. In practice, however, Devon's economy cannot be understood through the one-dimensional narratives of growth and the standardized methods of measurement. The ideas behind improvement, as well as their intentions, are manifold, yet a Devon Council Report in 2018 suggested that increasing the skills profile of the Mid and North Devon population would increase both productivity and social mobility in these areas. The report also noted the dominance of Exeter in the knowledge economy, as well as its overall economic performance, suggesting that these two factors could be linked.

[Fig. 1]
Taw & Exe Valley between the National Parks

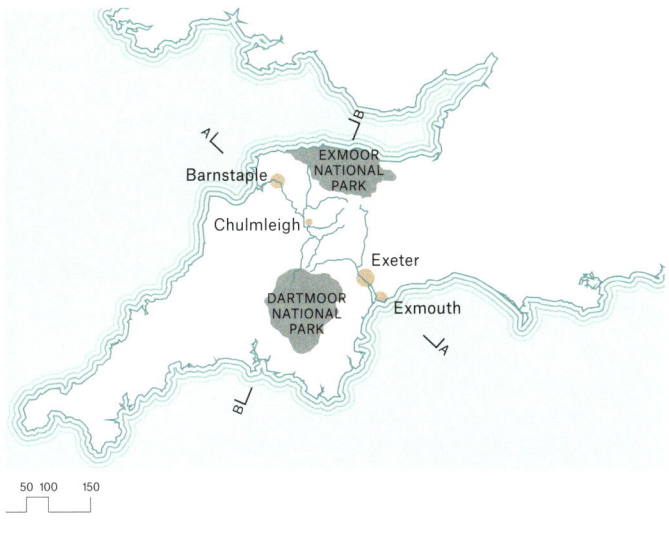

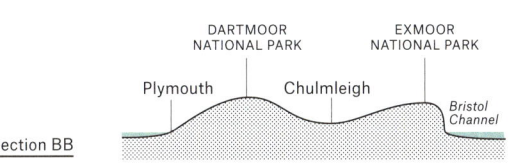

[Fig. 2]
Topography and urban settlements

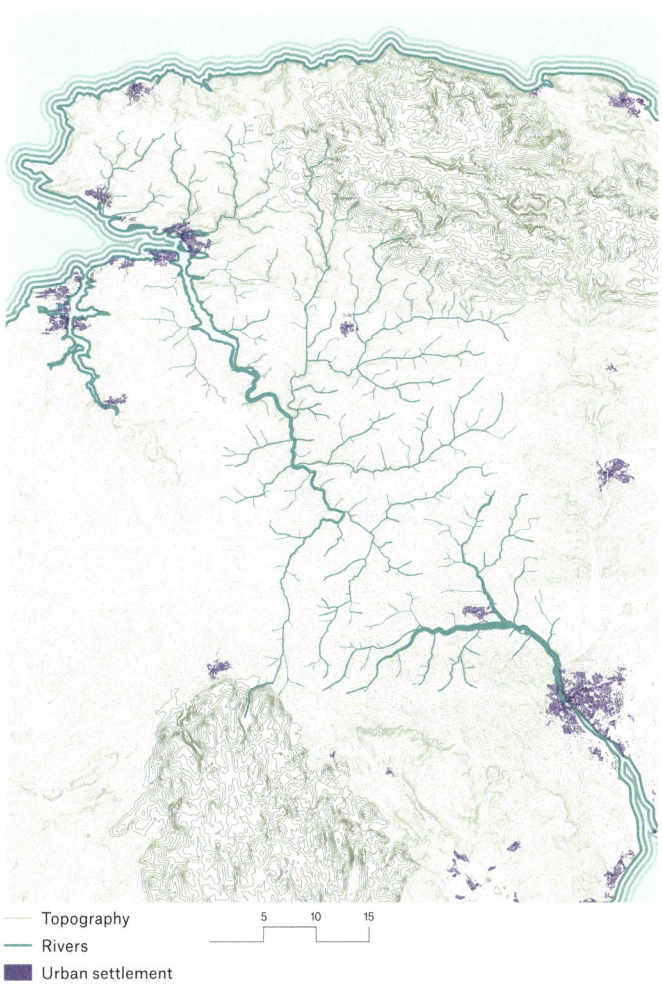

- Topography
- Rivers
- Urban settlement

[Fig. 3]
Rail infrastructure

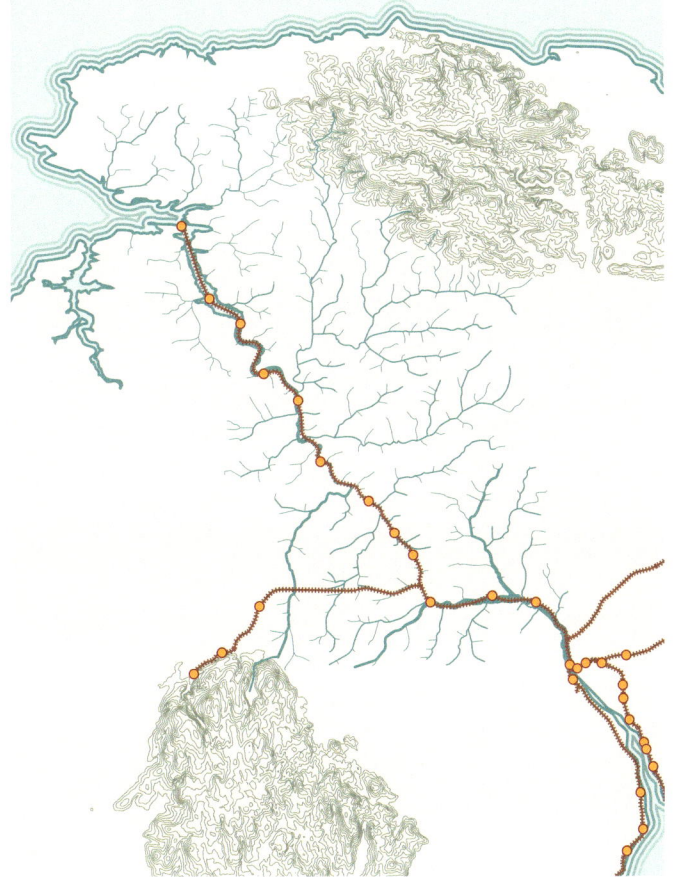

- National Park
- Railway
- Railway station

[Fig. 4]
Network of roads

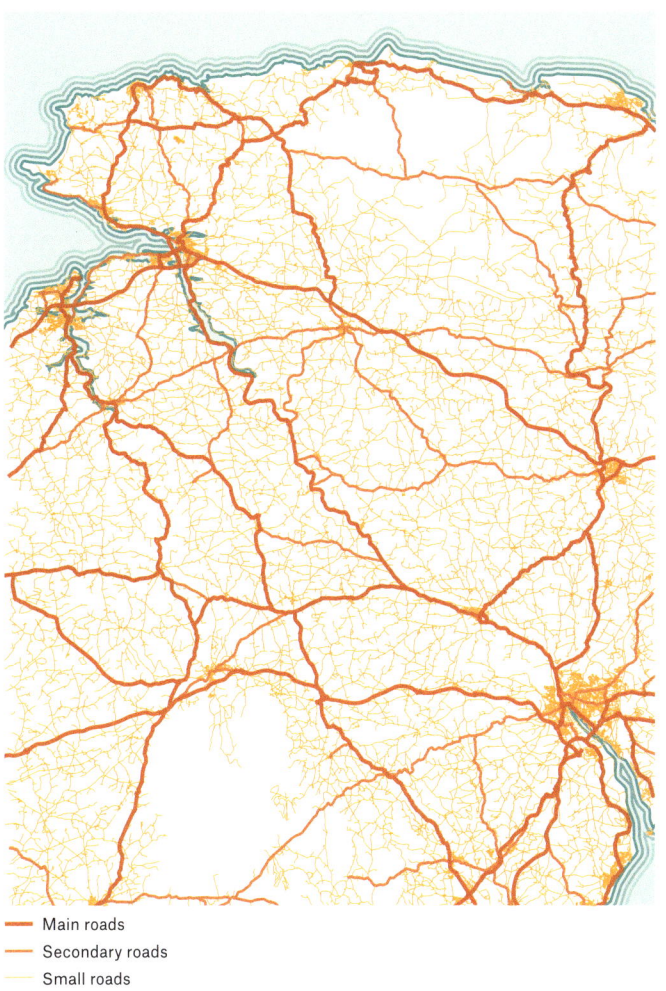

- Main roads
- Secondary roads
- Small roads

Territory: Taw & Exe Valley 73

2. Higher Education

The lack of higher education opportunities drains the rural South West of its youth population. Young minds flock to university towns and cities where edification and employment are easy to find, leaving their hometowns skipping the beat of a generation. And yet a sprinkling of alternative education opportunities for young people sitting parallel to the standard university system has begun to offer an alternative future.

2.1. Youth exodus

Castle Hill *iii*

All districts apart from Exeter and Plymouth see a net outward migration of 18–23-year-olds caused by young people moving away for their higher education. The two university towns show a spike in the student age population with a subsequent and almost equivalent dip in 22–25-year-olds indicating that although young people move to Exeter and Plymouth for university, the majority do not stay long term. *[Fig. 7]*

Neither do the graduates who left the rural areas seem to move back after completing their studies, the net migration only rising over the 0 line above the age of 40. Generally, the youth out-migration is more pronounced in the rural districts of East, Mid, and North Devon.

2.2. Shrinking local revenues

Arch Castle Hill *iv*

Local Council budgets are funded roughly 50 percent by central government with the remaining revenue being drawn locally from taxes on households and businesses. *[Fig. 8–9]* A stable or shrinking population in rural areas, which is also aging, leaves Local Councils with less revenue through both of these local sources and yet more demand on local services.[4]

2.3. Brain drain

Manorial garden at Castle Hill *v*

The problem of the youth exodus and aging populations in rural areas is multifaceted, resulting in a reduced labor force and breaks in continuity of family-run businesses, farms, and industries. Another major issue facing the rural Taw & Exe valley system is proportional loss in those young people with higher education qualifications—a loss of brain-power. Tony Blair's Labour party famously won over voters in the 1997 general election by stating his top three priorities as: "Education, education, education."[5] In the following years university degree courses were expanded and funding models developed to make attaining a higher education more accessible to a wider range of people. The proportion of the population in Great Britain with the equivalent of a university degree rose from 22.5 percent in 1999 to 40.3 percent in 2019.[6] *[Fig. 10]* Education increases geographic mobility. The young people who move away from rural areas tend to be the highest educated, gravitating toward the university cities and towns in which they studied, or to urban centers where job prospects are more varied, which creates a "brain drain" for the communities they leave behind.[7]

[Fig. 5]
Gross Value Added (GVA) per head
in £

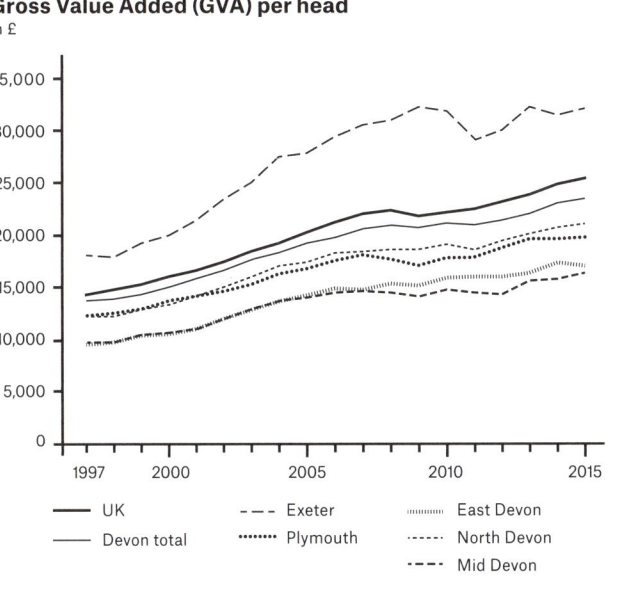

[Fig. 6]
GVA per district
in millions £

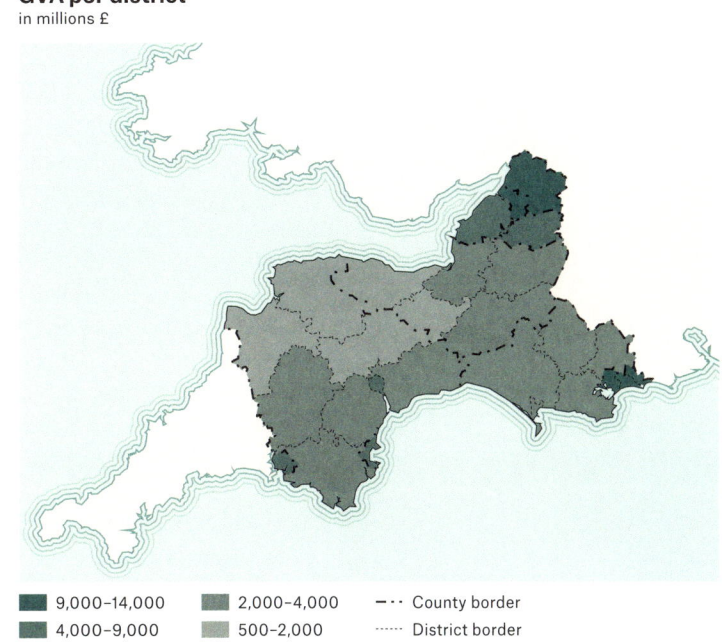

[Fig. 7]
Net migration per age

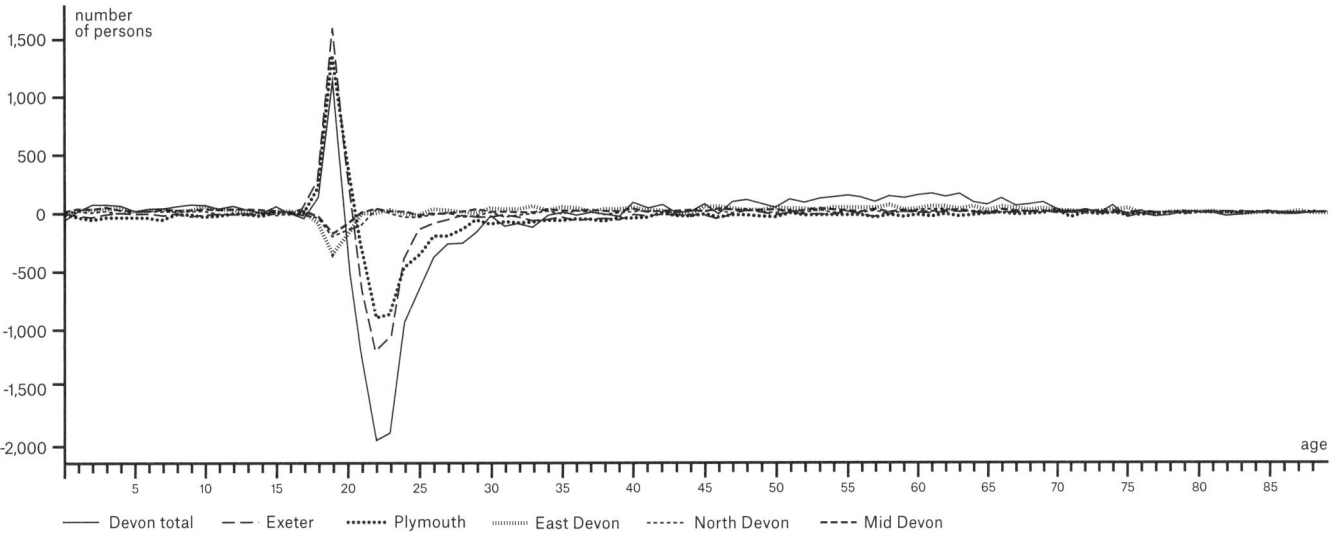

[Fig. 8]
Expenditure by Local Authorities
England average

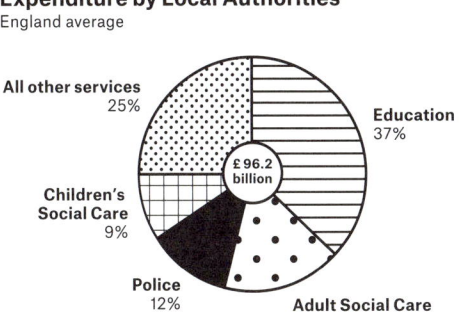

[Fig. 9]
Financing of Local Authorities
England average

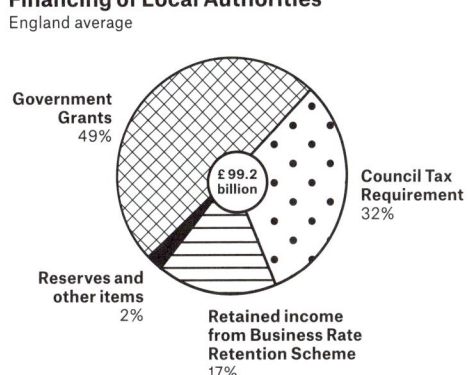

[Fig. 10]
Education in Great Britain
Population aged 16–64 with a degree level qualification or higher

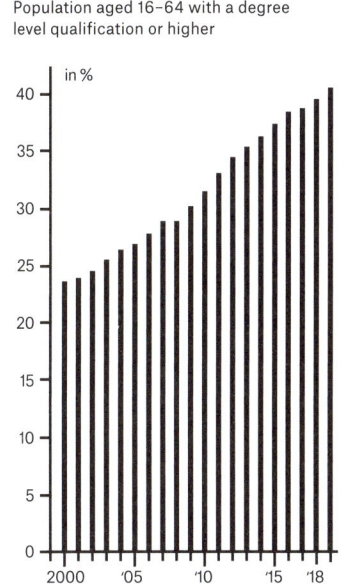

Territory: Taw & Exe Valley   75

2.4. Learning on the land

The notion of reengaging with nature as a fundamental part of education has been a recurring theme in different guises since the Industrial Revolution. Most recently the French philosopher Sébastian Marot has been advocating for architects to align themselves more closely to agriculture. Discussing the historical proponents of the land, he highlights some of these actors such as anthropologists studying remote self-governing communities in Southeast Asia, the Ruralists of the late 19th century, the environmental counterculture movement of the 1970s, and exiled monastic communities.[8]

Eggesford House, Devon [vi]

The monastic communities of the Middle Ages set up places of prayer and study in self or imposed exile. In remote rural or forested areas they reconnected with the cultivation of both knowledge and plants, undisturbed. In isolation they developed a range of agricultural, architectural, and scientific techniques. One could draw a comparison between these remote islands of education and a more recent "Back to the Land" movement focusing on alternative higher education courses offered outside towns and cities. Examples such as Hooke Park in Dorset, Schumacher College in Devon, and further afield the Graduate School of the Environment at the Centre for Alternative Technology in west Wales are offering graduate and post graduate courses in remote rural locations.

3. Constitution: New Commons

The manor houses of the Taw and Exe River Valleys, historically a status symbol of agrarian life, are now disconnected from local settlements, yet retain their status as focal points in the collective memory of the community. In *Taking the Country's Side*, Marot argues for a cross fertilization between architecture and agriculture,[9] and if we imagine the manor houses and their grounds as the symbolic remains of this agricultural history, then their reuse could bring their neighboring residents closer to this shared memory.

3.1. Finding a common ground

Buildings with a historical or social significance act as focal points for rural communities; the village shop, the schoolhouse, the church, and the local pub are at once wayfinding devices and social hubs. These spaces can be seen as a type of common ground, space for community meetings, social gatherings, and exchange with tourists and visitors.

Many of these rural village typologies, such as the village hall, are under pressure from the multiplicity of function, while others are suffering economically from a lack of demand. Local shops are finding it increasingly difficult to remain economically viable in the age of online shopping and home delivery, primary schools are suffering from lower attendance demanding further travel distances for rural children, and numbers of pubs in rural villages have been declining steadily for the past 20 years.

[Fig. 11]
Chulmleigh in the Taw Valley

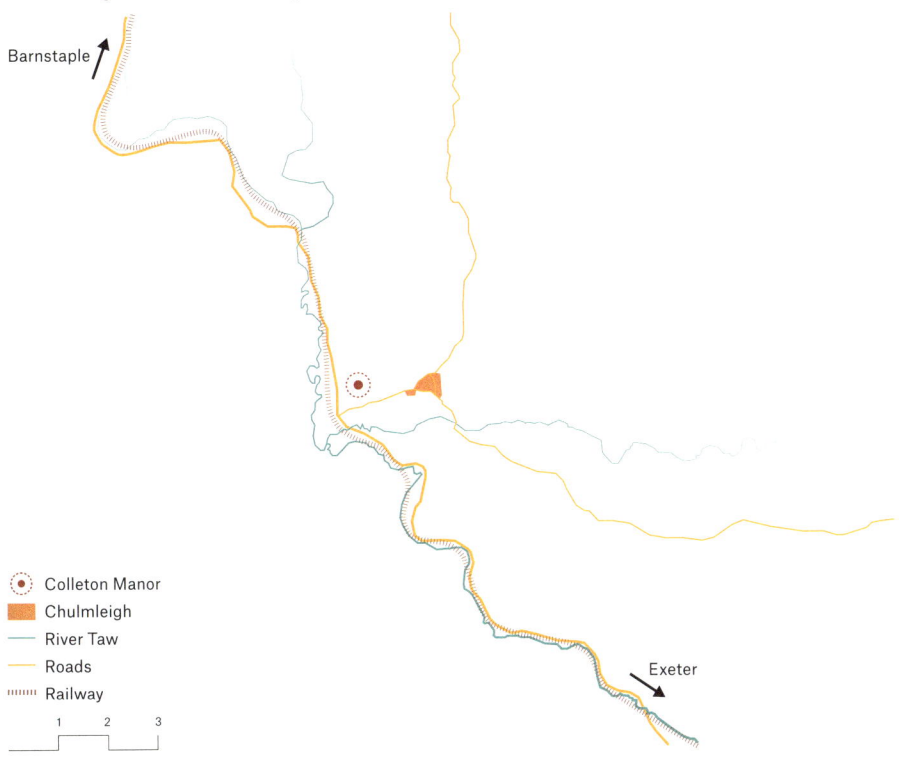

- ⊙ Colleton Manor
- ▮ Chulmleigh
- — River Taw
- — Roads
- ⋯ Railway

Barnstaple ↗
Exeter ↘

[Fig. 12]
Colleton Estate and Chulmleigh Village as seperate entities
Colleton nowadays

[Fig. 13]
Colleton Manor as public estate
Colleton Estate as gateway and point of historical and social reference

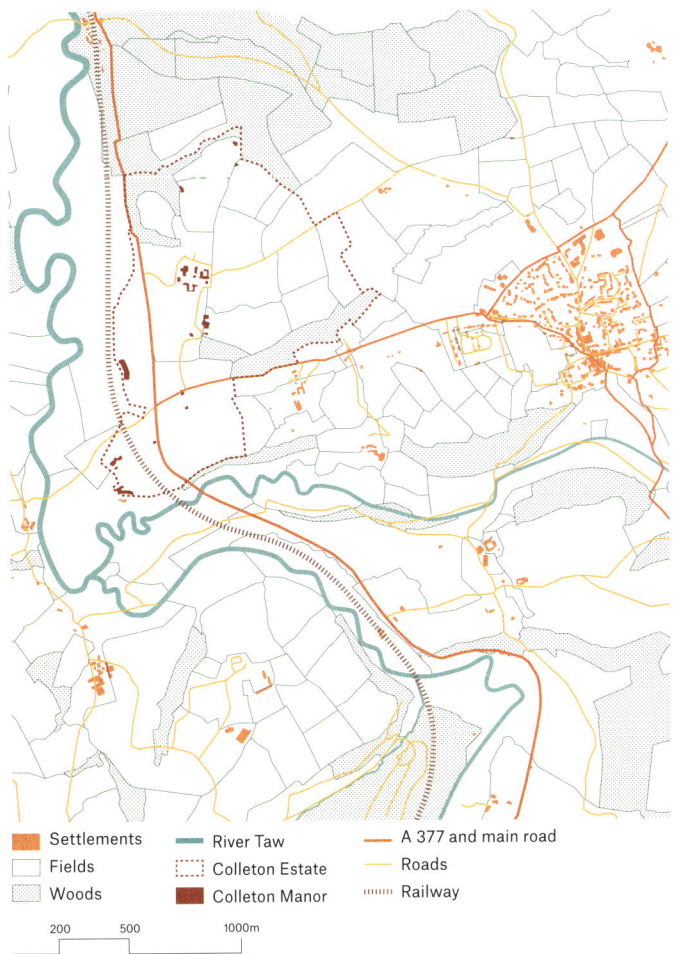

- ▮ Settlements
- ☐ Fields
- ▨ Woods
- — River Taw
- ⋯ Colleton Estate
- ▮ Colleton Manor
- — A 377 and main road
- — Roads
- ⋯ Railway

- ⋯ Colleton Estate
- ▮ Colleton Manor
- ▮ Manor Park
- ☐ Common fields
- ▨ Common woods
- — Road Colleton–Chulmleigh
- ▮ New train station

Territory: Taw & Exe Valley 77

3.2. Colleton and Chulmleigh

Using the example of Colleton, an agricultural hamlet complex, and its neighboring village Chulmleigh, we can witness the disconnect often seen between modern rural settlement and historic estate. What would once have been a singular entity now has two distinct borders, with little exchange between the owners of Colleton and the residents of Chulmleigh. Colleton, however, is located on the prime agricultural land next to the river and sits geographically nearer to both road and rail infrastructures. [Fig. 11]

As a speculative exercise, if Colleton was to become integrated into community life through new uses, it could be seen as an entry point or gateway to the village beyond, visible from afar it could act as a symbol of village life. Public rights of way historically used to travel between dwellings in the village and work on the land could be reopened, strengthening this connection between village and manor. [Fig. 12–13]

Colleton Manor *vii, viii*

3.3. Remote learning

Small higher education institutions located in the countryside would help to prevent the drain of young skilled workers out of this rural valley system. Historical models of monasteries and more contemporary examples of construction, landscape, and agricultural colleges based in historical buildings in remote places are a prototype for this new kind of remote learning.

3.4. Reusing built heritage as a commons

The return of built heritage to communal use would address the current problem of remote communities scattered across the countryside, struggling to maintain their local services and amenities, superimposed with a network of historic houses whose maintenance bills outweigh their revenues. [Fig. 14] Sites for alternative higher education would also invite younger people to the rural valley system while attracting investment from businesses. A reintroduction of local pubs, community shops, and sites of commerce and exchange could generate revenue to help maintain the historic buildings they occupy as well as promote their use by the public. This proposal recommends that remote communities reestablish their connections to these sites of collective memory, injecting new uses and vitality by sustained use, rehabilitating heritage sites into community life. [Fig. 15]

Taw & Exe Valley: Constitution Map [Fig. 16]

[Fig. 14]
Manor estates in the Taw & Exe Valley

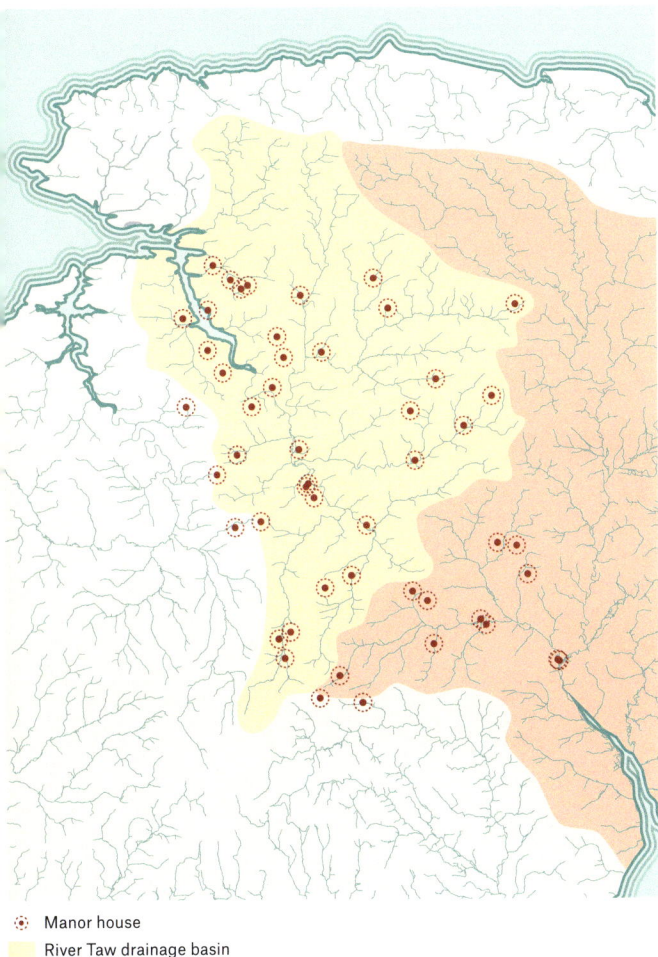

- Manor house
- River Taw drainage basin
- River Exe drainage basin

[Fig. 15]
Taw & Exe Valley spine

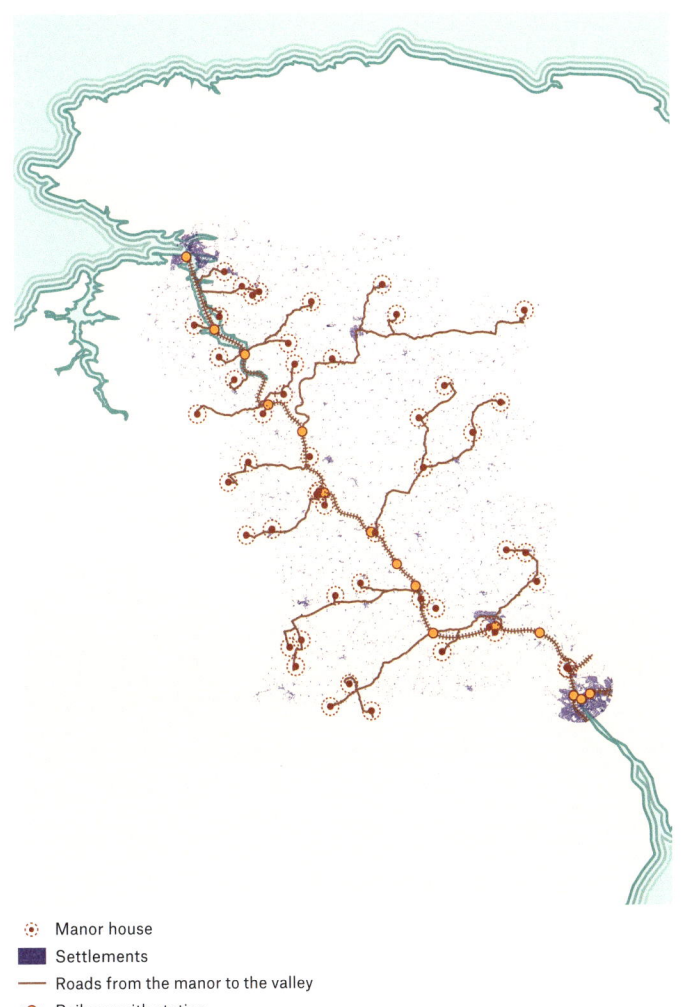

- Manor house
- Settlements
- Roads from the manor to the valley
- Railway with station

Territory: Taw & Exe Valley   79

[Fig. 16]
Taw & Exe Valley—Constitution: New Commons

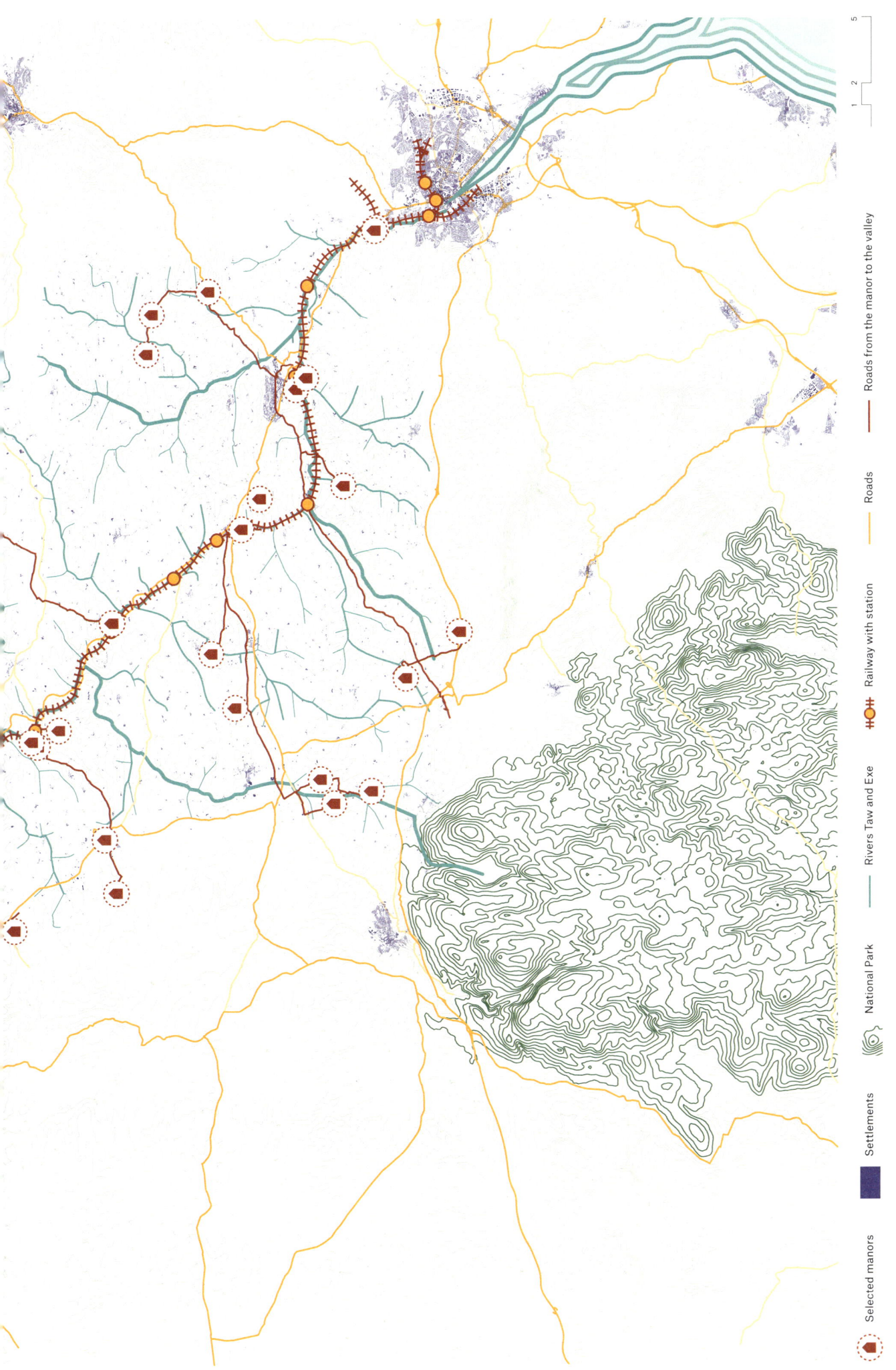

Territory: Taw & Exe Valley

Fowlescombe Farm, Ivybridge, Devon

Dyrham Park, near Bath, Gloucestershire

Creech Grange, Steeple, Dorset

Newark Park, Wotton-under-Edge, Gloucestershire

Lacock Abbey, Chippenham, Wiltshire

Drawing Matter, Shatwell, Somerset

The Circus, Bath, Somerset

Minchinhampton Common, Stroud, Gloucestershire

Eggesford House, Chulmleigh, Devon

Knightshayes Court, Tiverton, Devon

Lacock, Wiltshire

Dartmoor National Park, near Haytor Rocks, Devon

Dartmoor National Park

Dartmoor National Park, former granite quarry

Creech Grange, Steeple, Dorset

Powerstock, Dorset

Newark Park, Wotton-under-Edge, Gloucestershire

Hauser & Wirth, Bruton, Somerset

Radić Pavilion, Hauser & Wirth. Garden design by Piet Oudolf

Newark Park, Wotton-under-Edge, Gloucestershire

Parnham House, Beaminster, Dorset

Eggesford House, Chulmleigh, Devon

Dartington Hall, Totnes, Devon

A Territorial Constitution

The 11 student projects presented in this chapter act as critical syntheses and proof of concept for the territorial constitutions (see "Territory" chapter). As such the individual projects form, in their totality, a meta project and are to be considered that way. In order to allow for this proposed reading, the projects are presented to render their interrelated character obvious and easy to detect, the projects being grouped by the four territories investigated: Avon Green Belt, Dorset Coast, South Hams, and Taw & Exe Valley.

The three projects related to the Avon Green Belt (Nos. 1–3) provide a perfect example to explain our strategy of presentation. In one way or another, all of these projects support the territorial strategy proposed. That strategy, taking decentralization as a model for the future growth of the area, reimagines the territory surrounding Bristol and Bath as a system of smaller and denser urban nodes with an expanse of agricultural land sufficient for its alimental and recreational needs. All three projects aim to contribute to this overarching goal.

For example, the *Intergenerational Co-Housing at Westwood Manor* (No. 1) addresses the urgent need for alternative forms of housing. It does so by activating and extending the manor house, while at the same time creating a new centrality for Westwood parish with the associated health center.

The *Mendip Quarries Visitor Center* (No. 2) aims at attracting visitors not only from the region but from all over UK and abroad by reactivating the disused quarries with a wide range of adapted leisure activities.

Finally, the *Orchards Cooperative at North Cadbury Court* (No. 3) proposes the revival of local fruit growth and transformation by extending the community orchard and installing a process plant right next to the court building, tying back together the court estate with the village and its community.

These short descriptions show how all of the projects engage in the territory, adapting and reconfiguring their milieu simultaneously. It is only through these architectural projects that the territorial constitutions are rendered comprehensive and tangible.

1 Westwood Manor
Clara Brun / Alix Houlon
> p. 130

2 Southill House
Raphaël Vouilloz
> p. 136

3 North Cadbury Court
Ombline Heili
> p. 142

4 Parnham House
Juliette Armanet / Marina Garlatti
> p. 148

5 Kingston Maurward Manor
Paul Trellu
> p. 154

6 Creech Grange Manor
Romain Barth / Sébastien Friess / Solène Hoffmann
> p. 160

7 Sharpham House
Lucas Bastos Vieira / Elie Tournier
> p. 166

8 Sharpham Marsh
Vincent Bianchi / Raphael Delmuè
> p. 172

9 Nettlecombe Court
Marion Aubert / Océane Perrone
> p. 178

10 Colleton Manor
Alexis Corre / Tanguy Mulard
> p. 182

11 Eggesford House
Camille Ehrensperger / Tania Versteegh
> p. 188

1	Intergenerational Co-Housing Clara Brun / Alix Houlon	130
2	Mendip Quarries Visitor Center Raphaël Vouilloz	136
3	Orchards Cooperative Ombline Heili	142
4	Woodworking School Juliette Armanet / Marina Garlatti	148
5	Student Housing Paul Trellu	154
6	Institute of Architecture Romain Barth / Sébastien Friess / Solène Hoffmann	160
7	Eco-Communal Housing Lucas Bastos Vieira / Elie Tournier	166
8	Inhabited Path Vincent Bianchi / Raphael Delmuè	172
9	Refuges for Hikers Marion Aubert / Océane Perrone	178
10	Public House Alexis Corre / Tanguy Mulard	182
11	Student Housing Camille Ehrensperger / Tania Versteegh	188

TAW & EXE VALLEY

SOUTH HAMS

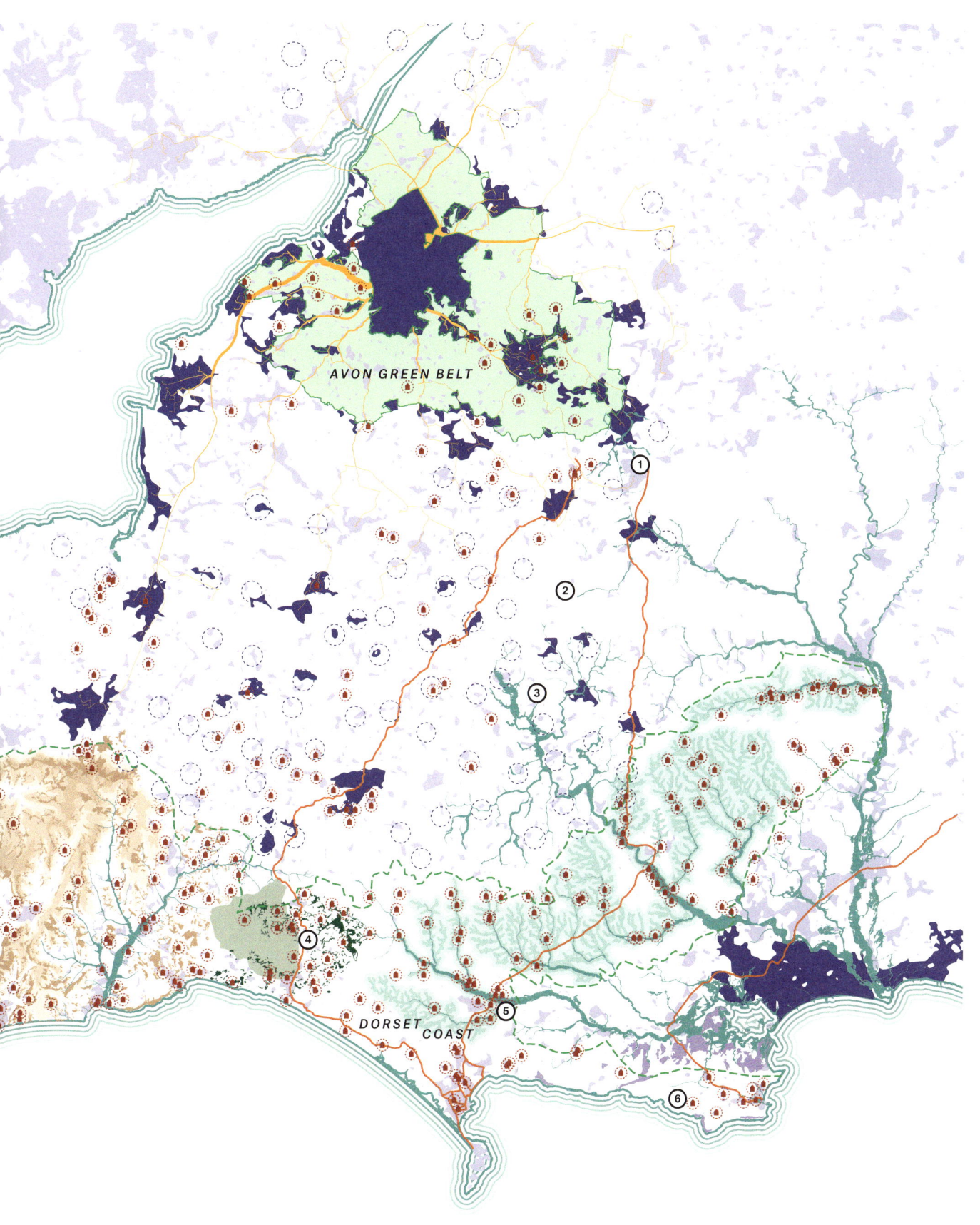

1 Westwood Manor—Intergenerational Co-Housing

Clara Brun / Alix Houlon

Location: Bradford-on-Avon, Wiltshire
Owner: National Trust
Architect: unknown
Date: Late 15th century
Area: 59 acres
Landscape architect: unknown

Westwood Manor

This compact, L-shaped house of local limestone was built in the late 15th century with early 16th-century and Jacobean additions. Thomas Horton, a prosperous local clothier, acquired the lease by 1518 and altered many of the interiors. John Farewell, who lived here between 1616 and 1642, pulled down part of the medieval work, leaving the present compact L-shaped house.

In 1911 Edgar "Ted" Lister brought Westwood Manor back to its 17th-century glory, giving much attention to restoring medieval, Tudor, and Jacobean details. After Lister's death, the National Trust acquired Westwood Manor in 1956, and it was listed as a Grade I building shortly after. The property has since been partially occupied by tenants who administer it on behalf of the National Trust. A total of six rooms are open to the public but only a few days a week during the summer.

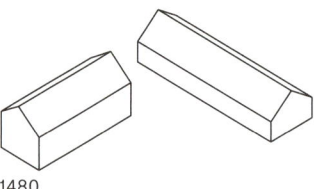

1480
Thomas Culverhouse

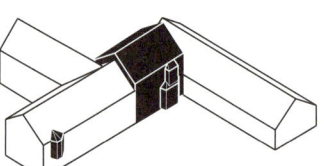

After 1518
Thomas Horton

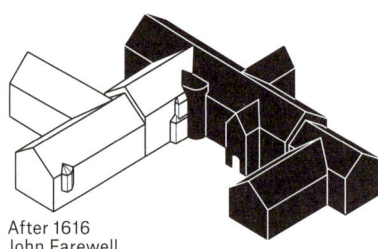

After 1616
John Farewell

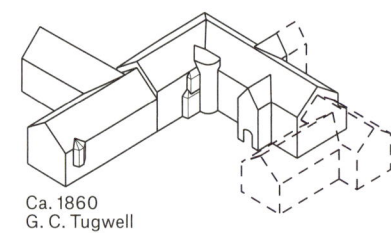

Ca. 1860
G. C. Tugwell

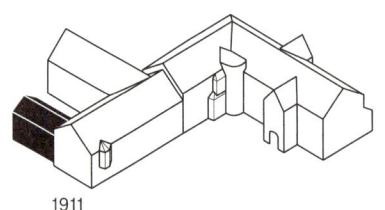

1911
Edgar Lister

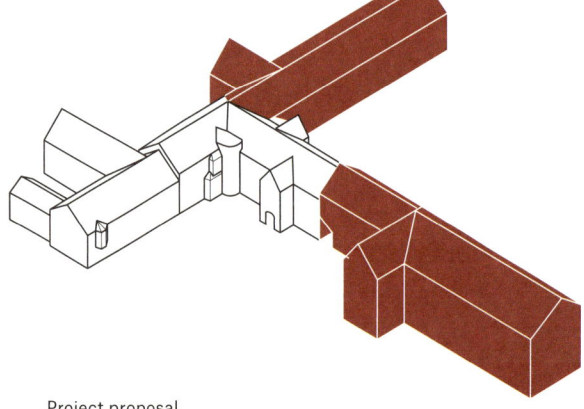

Project proposal

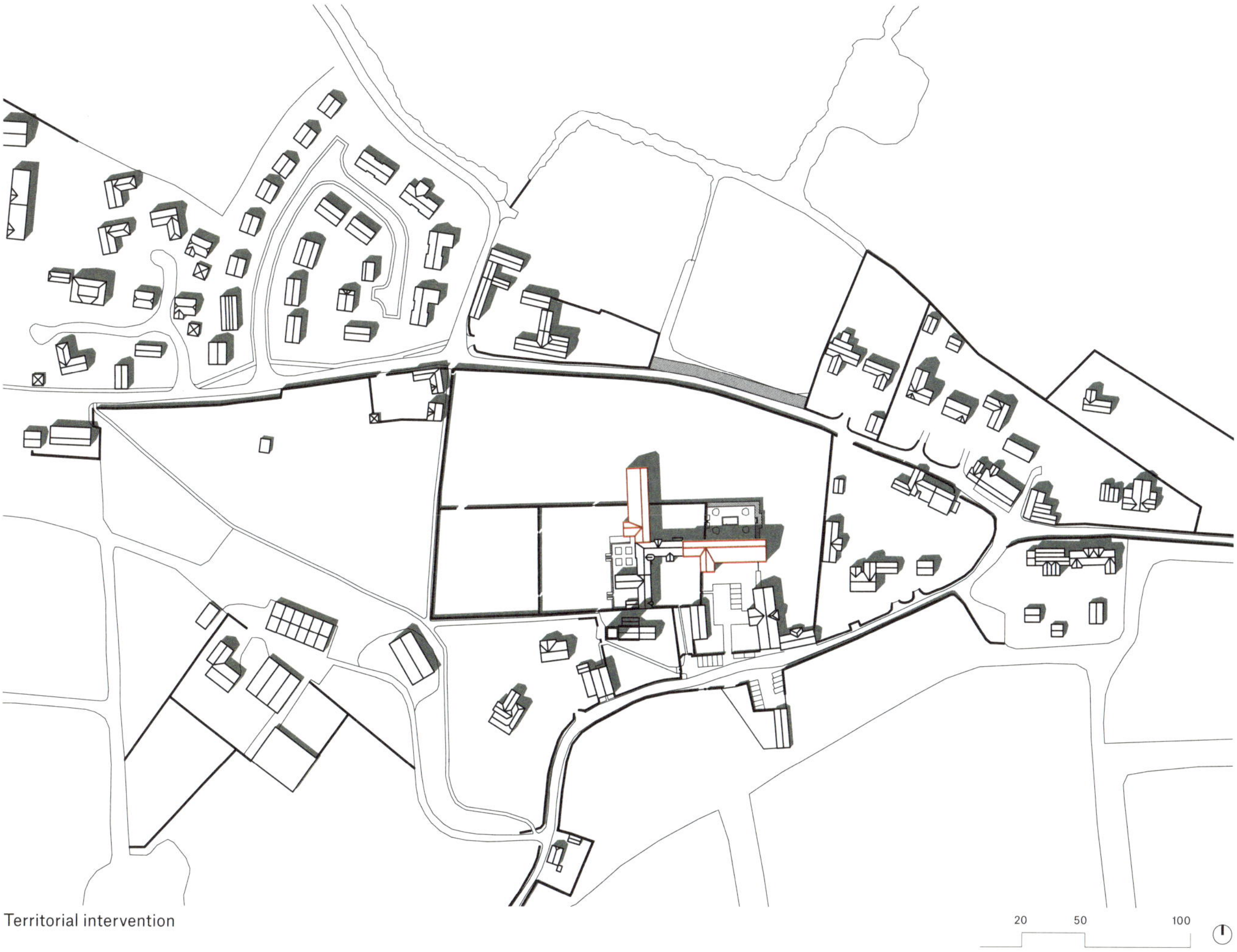

Territorial intervention

Axonometry of the project

Architecture: Avon Green Belt 131

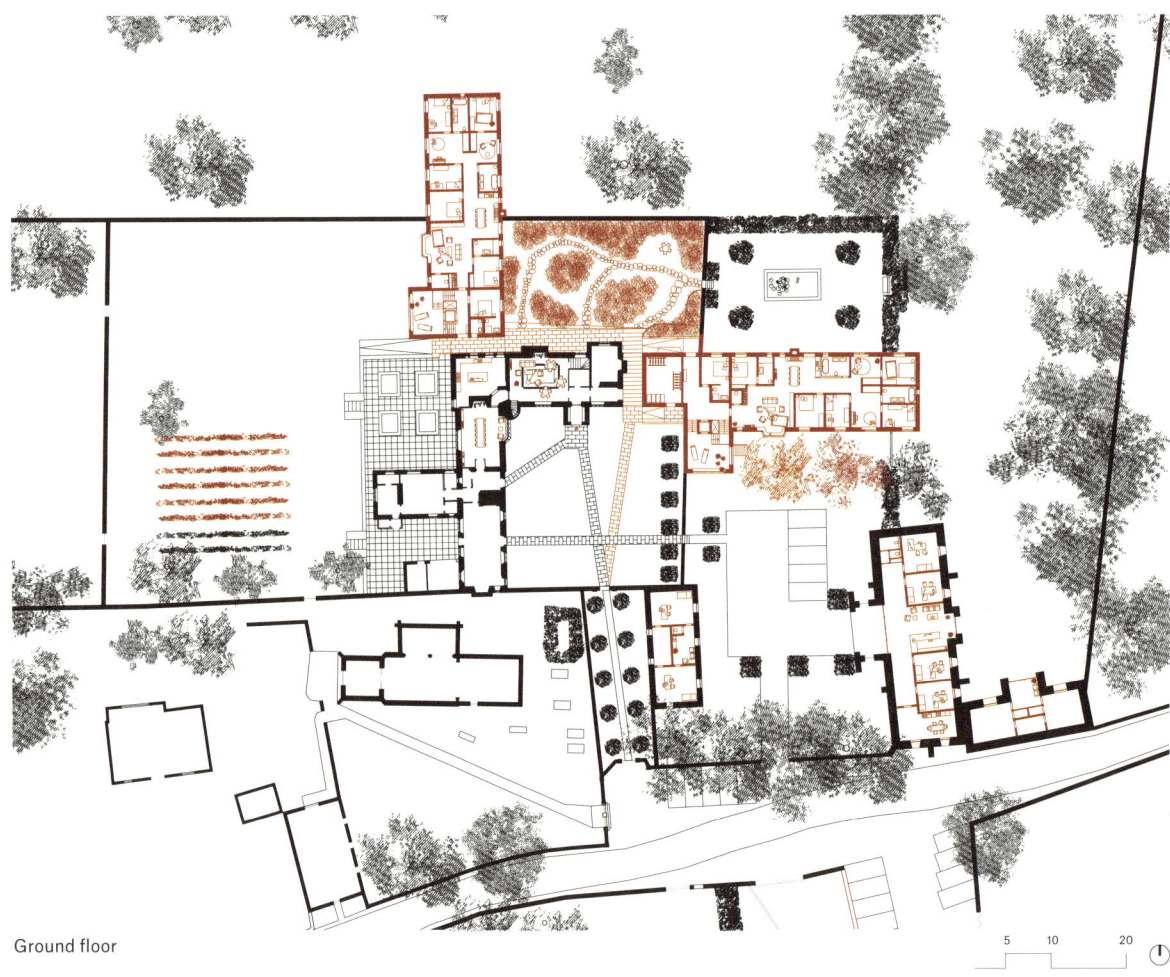

Ground floor

Intergenerational Co-Housing

Westwood Manor has changed considerably since its first incarnation in the 1400s. Over the years, different families have added to—and removed—different parts, leaving their permanent mark on its fabric and structure. What is seen today was built in the 15th century, extended in the 16th century, considerably refitted in the 17th century, and restored and refurbished in the early 20th century. The manor became part of the National Trust in 1956, which made it accessible to the public. Flanked by walled gardens, the manor house has since been partially occupied by tenants who administer the summer visits on behalf of the Trust.

Open only a few days a year, this exceptional site should preserve its great historical attractiveness while finding a more collective use for the community. The local attractiveness of the place, its walking distance to Westwood Village, the extent of the site, and the existing non-used outbuildings are the main elements considered for another conversion of the manor.

The National Trust presents an opportunity as it holds properties of universal heritage already outside the market system and is willing to support England's local communities. Indeed, Westwood parish currently needs new affordable homes to meet the county's housing requirements. Elderly people and young families in Wiltshire are both facing a lack of appropriate housing at a decent price. This urges the creation of intergenerational housing schemes. Westwood's underused manor house with its large empty outbuildings has a strong collective potential and could be reused for the village's corresponding needs. Hence, in addition to its function as a museum, Westwood Manor could welcome an affordable, intergenerational co-housing scheme with an adjacent health center.

The two new housing wings follow the development logic of the manor house. They are joined directly to the main building, mirroring its volume and in conjunction with the existing walled garden consolidating the adjacent enclosed courtyards. The combined elements, old and new, are uniformly expressed. They function as a single organism avoiding the removal of any historic traces. The remarkable yet empty barn and stable are refurbished to provide a health center for local residents. The main purpose is to give a new sense of community to the place by integrating different groups on one site, and therefore interweaving different levels of privacy: public gardens and an orchard for ramblers, manor rooms either open for visitors or inhabited, and indoor gathering spaces for the inhabitants.

The proposed cluster apartments deliberately depart from the manor distribution and suggest contemporary ways of living, combining qualities of the small apartment and the shared household. Generous openings, treated as niches, enlarge the apartment rooms while providing a higher degree of domesticity. The façade seeks to capture the vocabulary and material qualities of the context, aiming at the same time for a contemporary architectural expression.

— *Clara Brun / Alix Houlon*

Topiary garden

Great courtyard and St. Mary's church

North façade

Barn and stable

Visualization: Shared living spaces

Architecture: Avon Green Belt 133

South façade

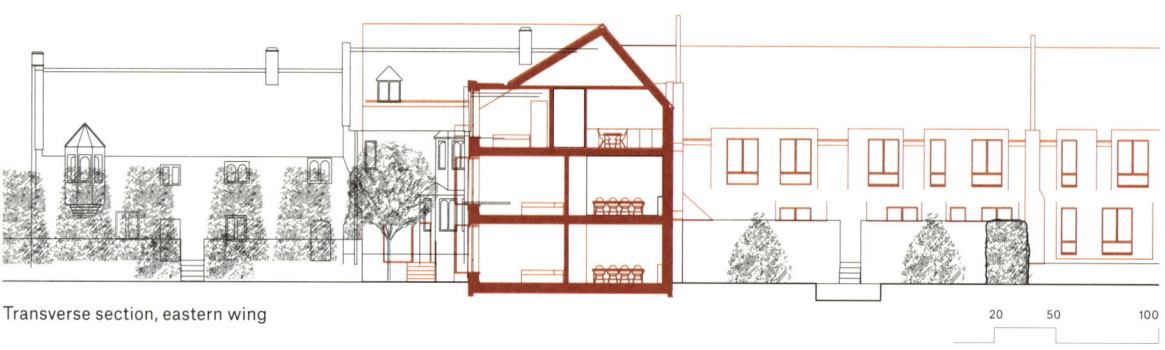
Transverse section, eastern wing

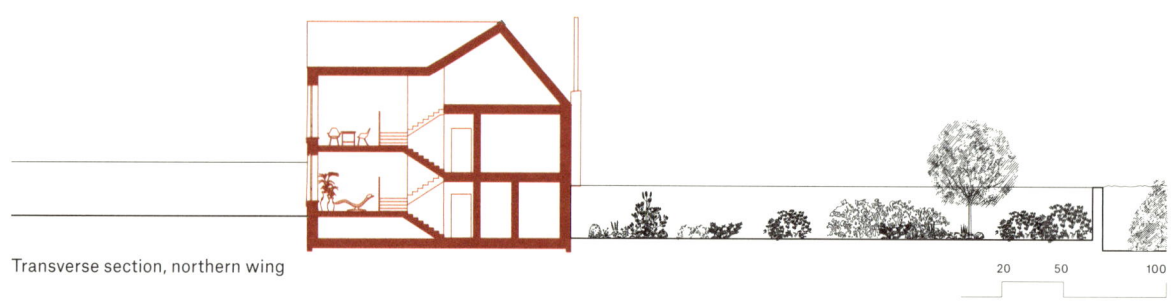
Transverse section, northern wing

Visualization: A shared space

Axonometry of the East wing

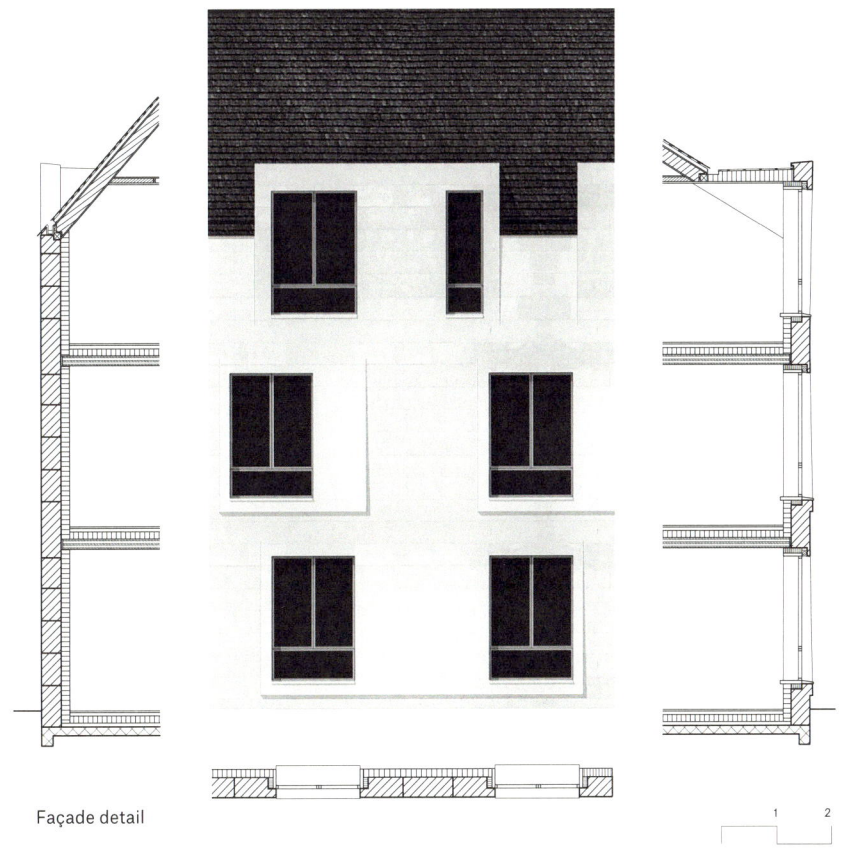

Façade detail

Architecture: Avon Green Belt

2 Southill House — Mendip Quarries Visitor Center

Raphaël Vouilloz

Location: Cranmore, Somerset
Owner: Mr. and Mrs. James Lambert
Architect: John Wood the Younger
Date: 1611
Surface: unknown
Landscape architect: unknown

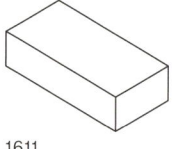

1611

1750

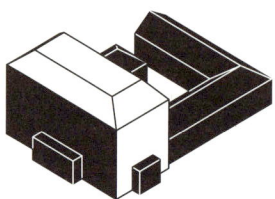

1820

Southill House

Southill House is an early 18th-century manor house in Somerset, designated as a Grade I listed building. It is situated in Cranmore, a village of 700 inhabitants, 23 kilometers south from Bath. The manor is built on a small hill outside the village, overlooking a beautiful valley of meadows that stretches to the south. Its gate is close to the house, but in the past, it was further north along the main road and encompassed the village of present-day Cranmore.

The main volume is rectangular and has been rebuilt on the existing cellars of the former house. On its west side, it was given an exceptional new façade by John Wood the Younger at the end of the 18th century. The west façade is a three-unit frontage with a giant Ionic order on twin end pilasters.

At the back of the main volume, two wings form a court. The western side of the south wing was rebuilt with a lot of charm at the beginning of the 20th century. For the rest, the architectural style is modest with many similarities to that of agricultural buildings. The volumes and purposes for the house have changed over time, including a garage and a school. More recently, an indoor swimming pool was proposed. The estate is nowadays privately owned as a country home by a family from London.

19th century

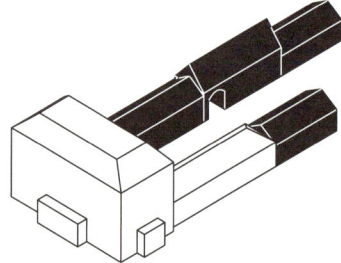

1920

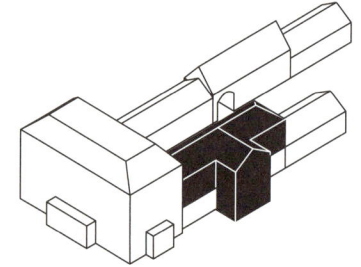

Project proposal

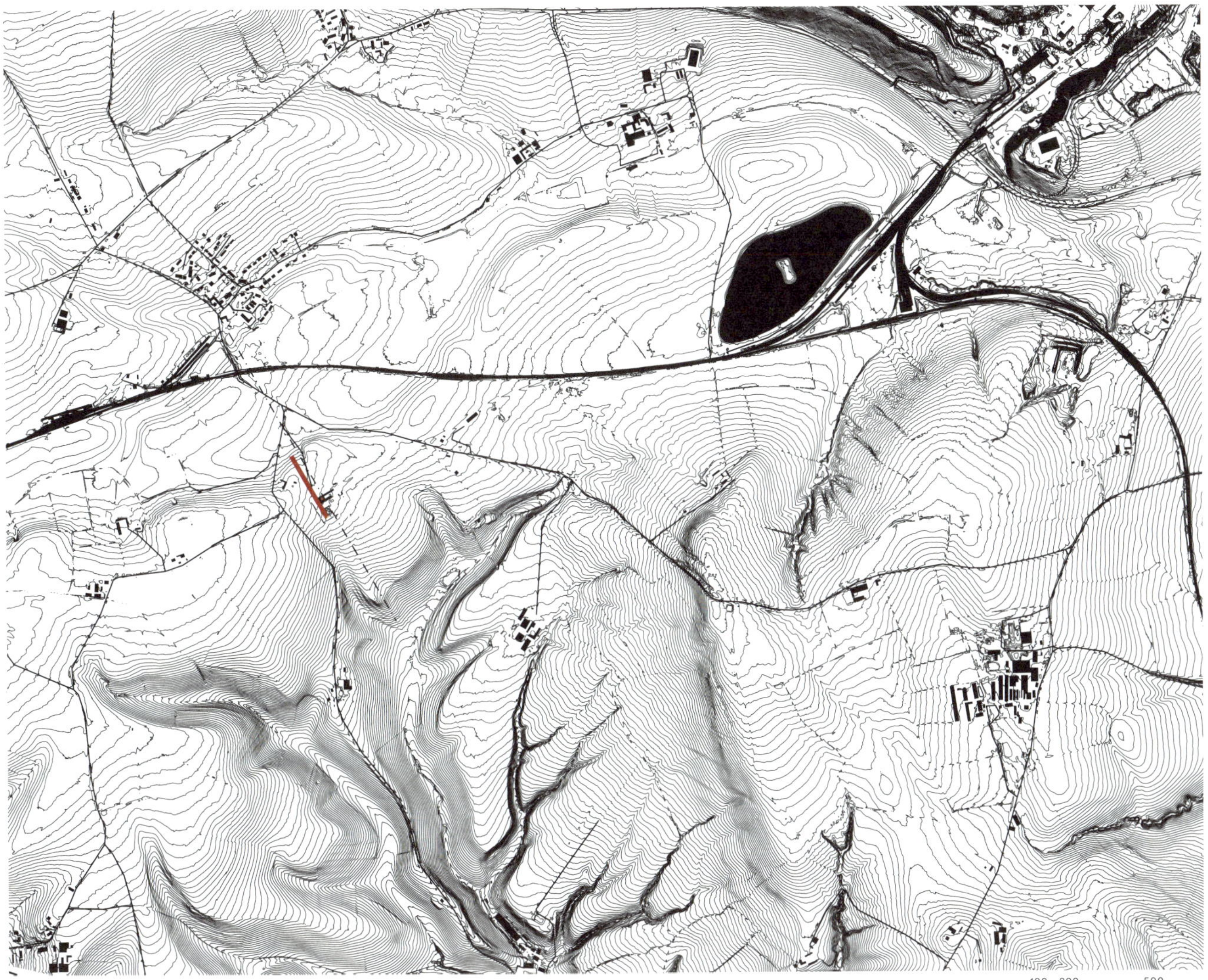

Territorial intervention

Detail of the trench

Architecture: Avon Green Belt 137

Cross section

Mendip Quarries Visitor Center

The project reflects on the strong centralization of the Bristol–Bath metropolitan aera. The closure of the local railway line is a direct result of this centralization process. It happened when the so-called *Beeching Cuts* took place which dismantled local railways all over the UK in 1965. The reopening of this railway line (of which the tracks still exist) is one of the goals of this project.

Within a six-kilometer radius around Cranmore, beside the Mendip Hills, the soil contains limestone of which the many disused quarries give testimony. A touristic resort is proposed in the former quarry, hosting sports, leisure, and cultural activities to attract visitors. Thus, a reopened railway would act as a direct connection between the resort and Bristol, and further afield. Ideally located 500 meters south from the Cranmore station, Southill House is thought to become the visitor center of such a resort.

The project, in a strong act of land art, cuts the hill through excavation, forming a new entry at the manor's western façade that evokes the nearby quarries. The rock exposed is "Fuller's earth rock," a yellow-colored limestone. The surfaces of the excavation will become overgrown, creating a new biotope in this unique space. The trench is carried out by shoring and underpinning, which are common civil engineering techniques. This new entrance, with its rough details and visible rock bolts, recalls the industrial character of the quarries and railways.

The magnificent panorama of the valley reveals itself as one advances along the trench. It leads to the manor's cellars. The imposing steel beams supporting the portico and the west façade embrace the visitor inside this dark grotto-like space. Shaped in gabion walls, just beneath the manor house, it becomes the entrance to the visitor center. Across the door, the staircase leads toward the light into a new distribution space at the back of the main house.

From here, all spaces are accessible, a departure hall for the quarries, the main courtyard, and finally a square at the foot of the main façade. The central volume is preserved as a physical monument to the house's history. The northern wing of the extension is transformed into a museum of the Mendip Quarries.

The excavation effort is part of a constructive logic of the *genius loci*. The excavated material is used to build the new walls in massive ashlar stones, and the rest of this highly prized rock will be sold. In this way the project intends to connect the built heritage of the region to one of its greatest landscape treasures, limestone quarrying.

— *Raphaël Voullioz*

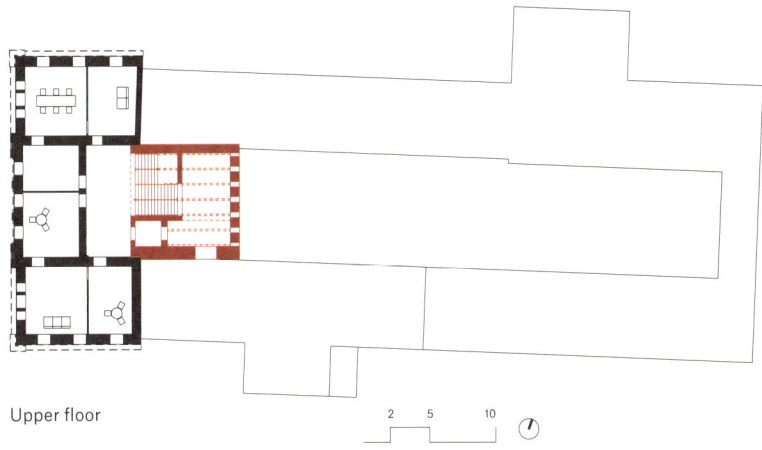

Upper floor

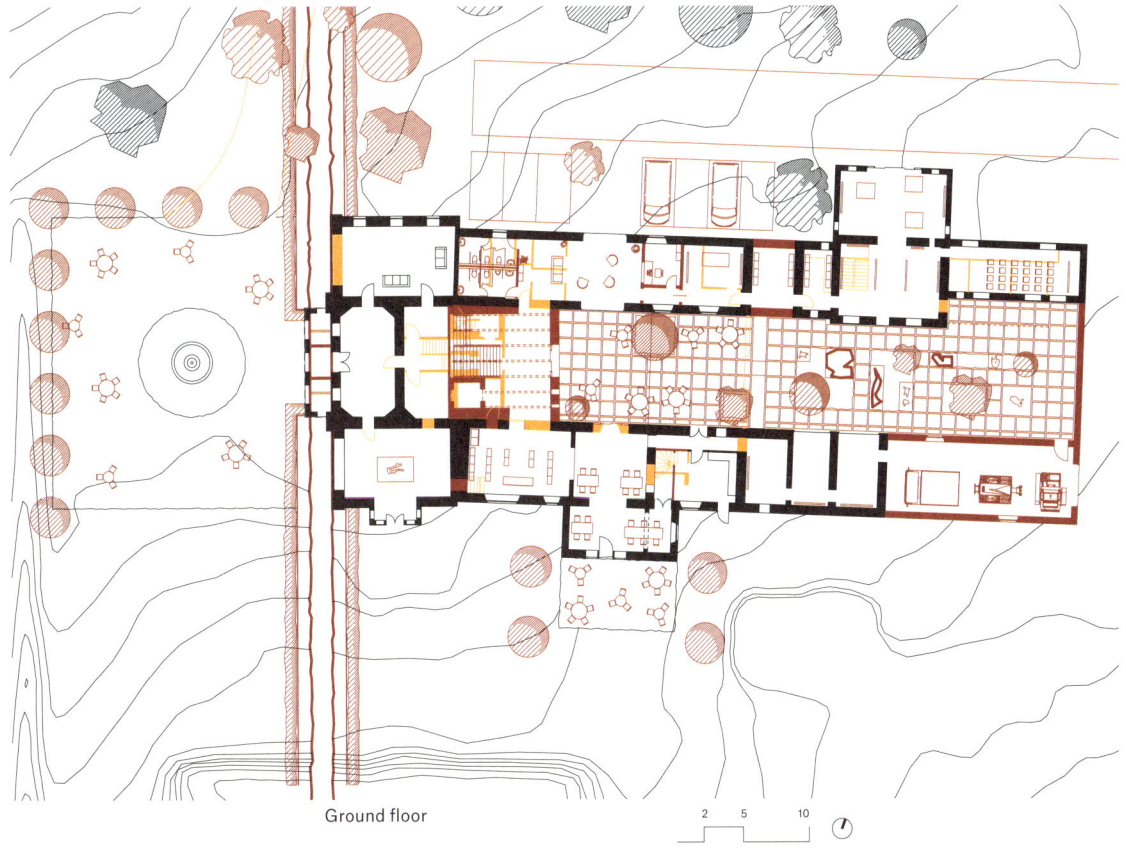

Ground floor

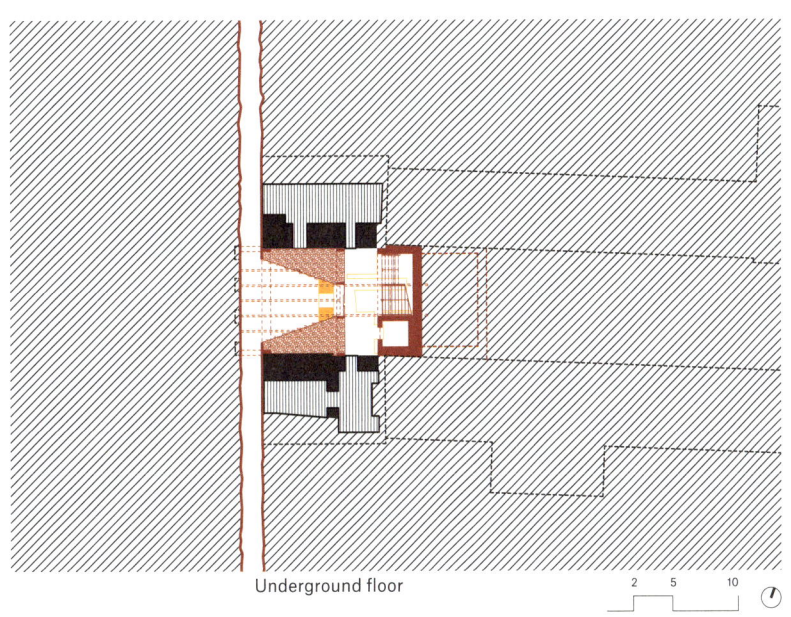

Underground floor

Architecture: Avon Green Belt 139

Elevation

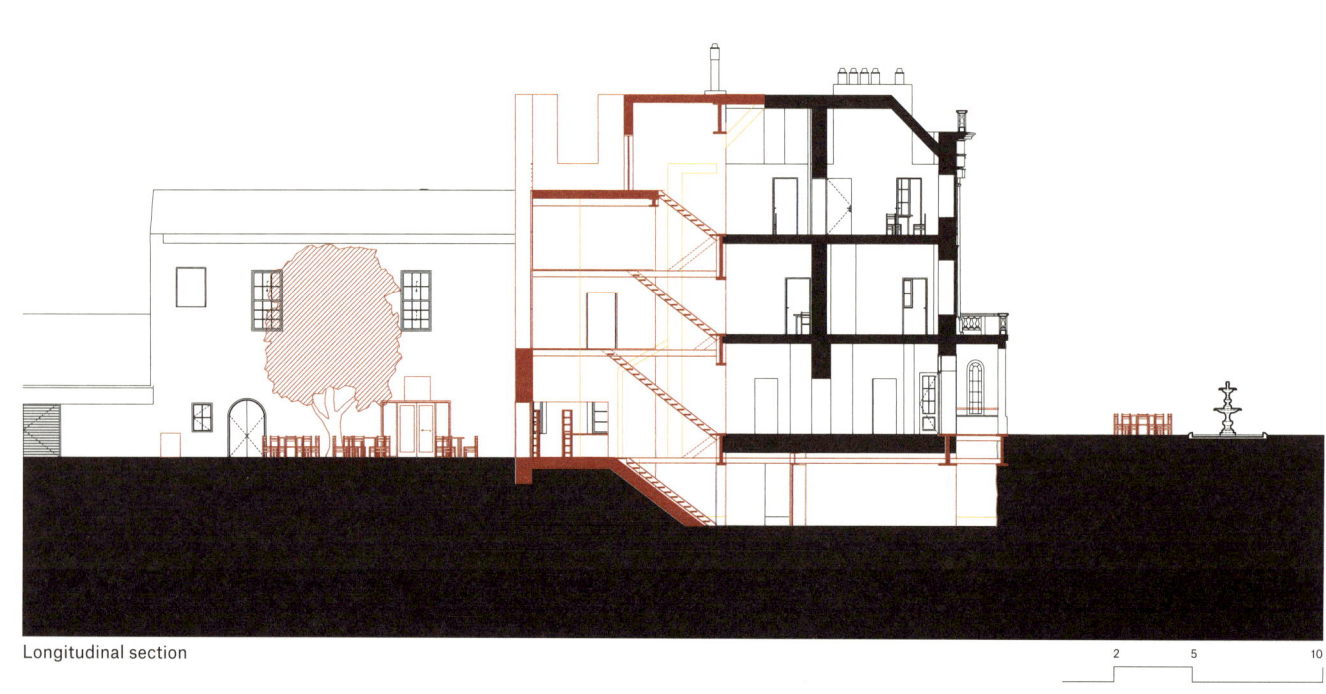

Longitudinal section

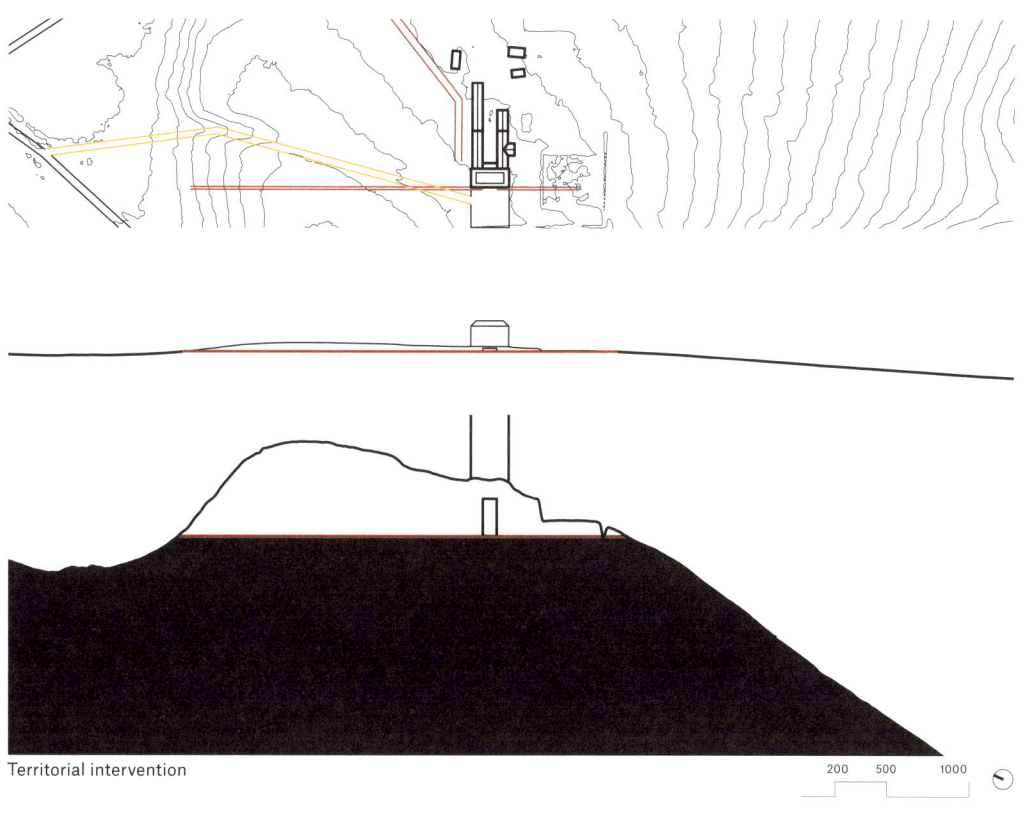

Territorial intervention

Visualization: View from the roof top

Architecture: Avon Green Belt 141

3 North Cadbury Court—Orchards Cooperative

Ombline Heili

Location: North Cadbury, Somerset
Owner: Archie Montgomery
Architect: unknown
Date: 14th century
Surface: 1,500 acres
Landscape architect: Thomas H. Mawson (1911)

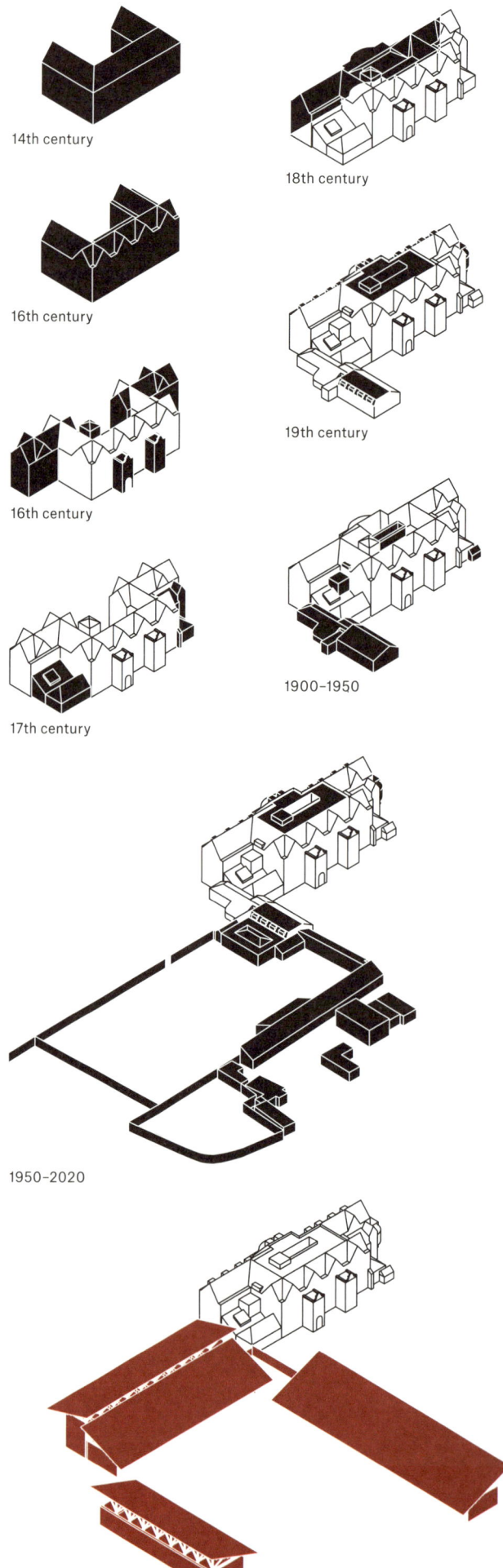

14th century
16th century
16th century
17th century
18th century
19th century
1900–1950
1950–2020
Project proposal

North Cadbury Court

North Cadbury Court is located at the border of North Cadbury village in South Somerset.

Its history dates back to the 14th century. On the top of a hill, it was first a medieval hall. The large Elizabethan mansion was added in the 16th century, and a ballroom and the Georgian style south façade followed in the 18th century. A few outbuildings were built to the east in the 20th century.

This family house welcomed new uses over time. During World War II, a London nursery was evacuated into the house. Between 1948 and 1966, a large part of it was lent to the YMCA, as part of a scheme to train underprivileged city boys who wanted to enter farming.

Archie Montgomery now owns North Cadbury Court, a family home for 100 years. The Court, a Grade I listed building, and its 1,500 acres has become an exclusive venue for weddings, corporate events, family holidays, and cheese tastings. The Montgomery family have been farming for three generations and are the makers of the renowned Montgomery's Cheddar Cheese.

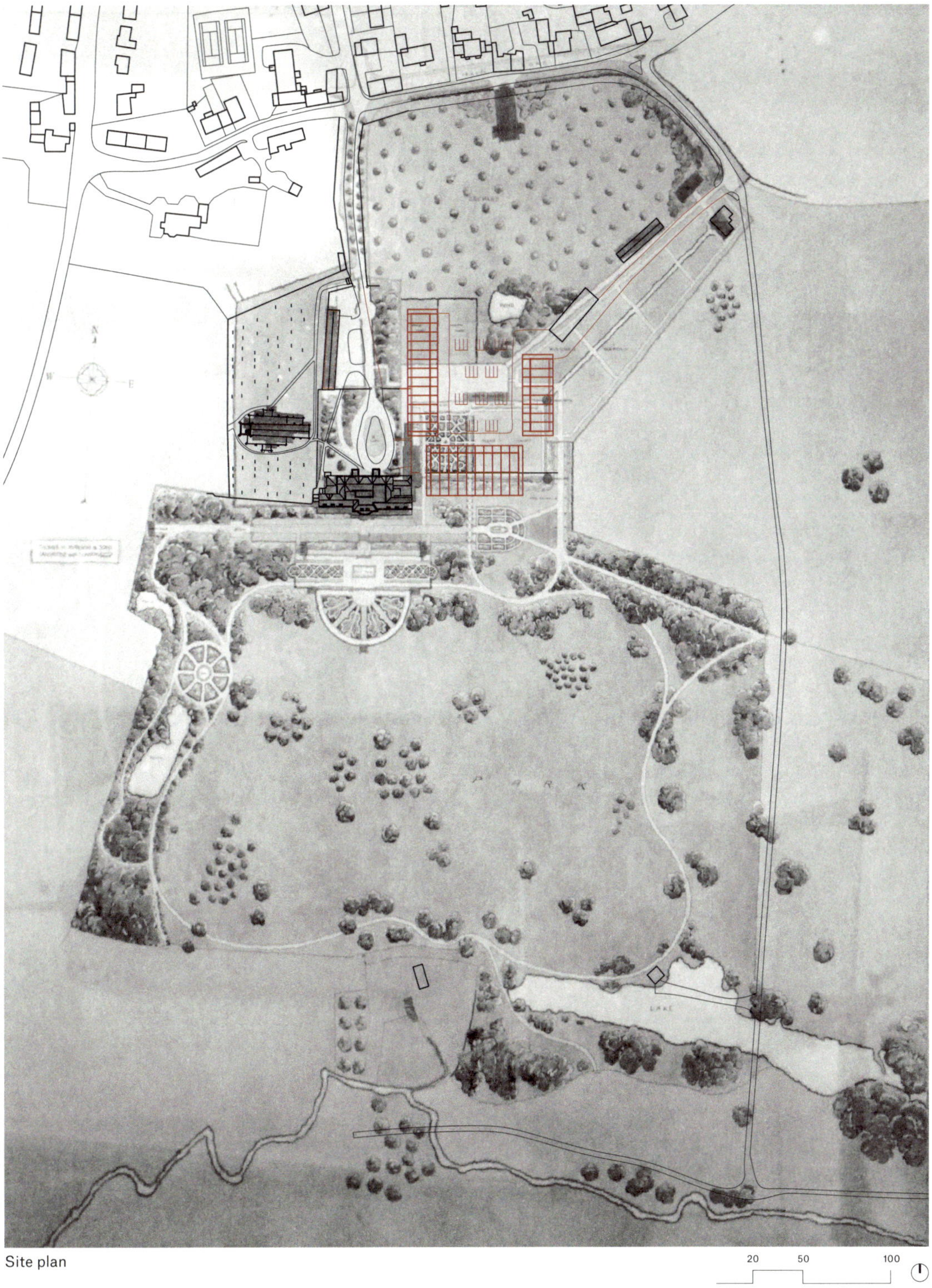

Site plan

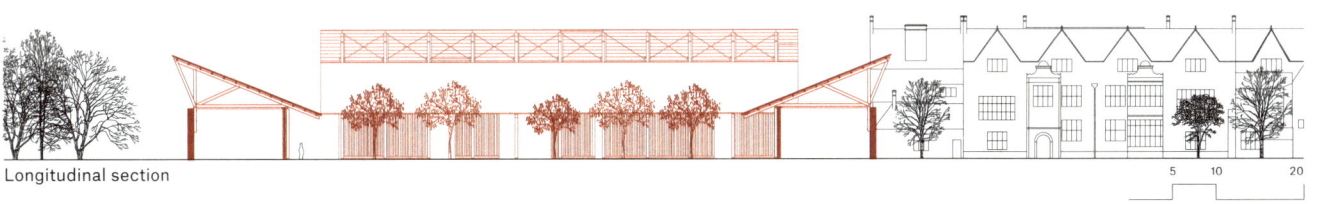
Longitudinal section

Architecture: Avon Green Belt 143

Orchards Cooperative

Currently, the 192 acres of orchards in the parish of Great Cadbury produce a wide variety of apples totaling around 780 tons a year. The project aims to revive an interest in local fruit growth and transformation. On the one hand, it is about making a community orchard: a communal asset for the whole parish including an open-air village hall. On the other hand, it is a place to process the fruit production of the whole community, coming both from orchards and isolated trees. In order to sustain such a production, the development of beekeeping is required for pollination reasons.

The orchard located between the village and North Cadbury Court seems ideal for the establishment of the main program linked to it: a light industry at the heart of village life, accessible by foot and open to the community. Accordingly, the project is shaped as an open cloister. The production is organized in its porticoes, with the fruit processing and fruit juice extraction chains in the west wing, honey production in the east wing, and cider fermentation in the south wing.

This implantation opens up northwards toward the village while the manor house opens onto its park to the south. All technical access is done by a secondary road while the main access of the site remains the historical axis to the manor house. The existing courtyard, now a public space, allows an engagement with the history of Cadbury dating back to the 13th century. The old stables are transformed into a shop/restaurant, while the Church remains a socially active place for the village.

An expressive punctual structure is fixed to the surrounding massive walls, supporting a floating roof. It is inspired both by the structural form of fruit trees and by the principles of assembly found in tree grafting.

The wooden structure is hooked to the existing or rebuilt brick walls, reusing the material from the dismantled buildings. On the cloister side, wood pillars support the light metal sheet roof. Sliding cladding doors are suspended on that side. As a sole monumental exception, the cider fermentation vats are facing the park, forming a higher volume but having a similar structure as the other wings. A wood façade contrasts with the Georgian one and offers a seating area on the side of the manor to admire the park.

— *Ombline Heili*

Visualization: The pathway from the village to the manor

Visualization: The south façade

Visualization: A glimpse of the wooden structure

North elevation

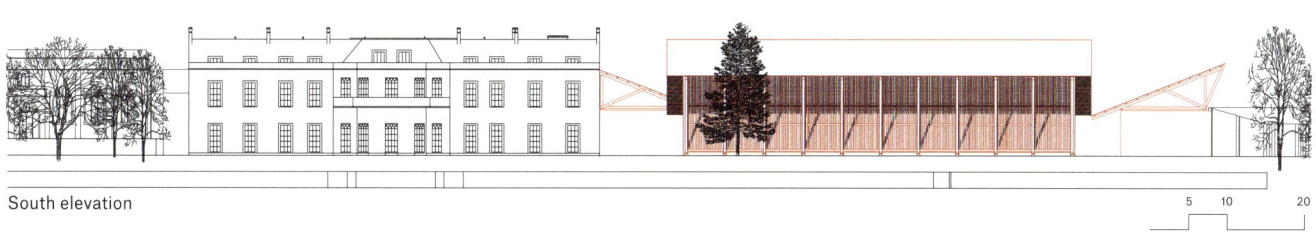

South elevation

Ground floor

Architecture: Avon Green Belt 145

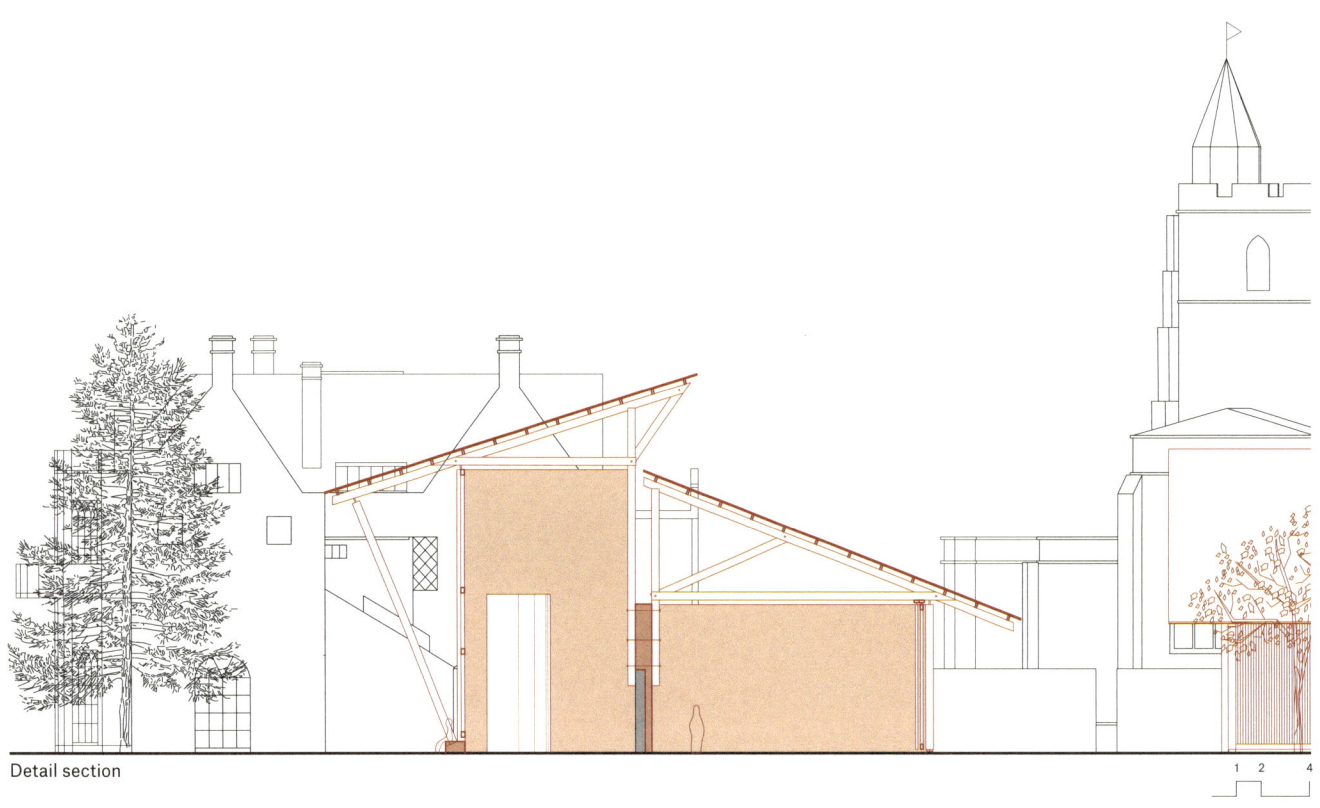
Detail section

Visualization: View of the church from the cooperative courtyard

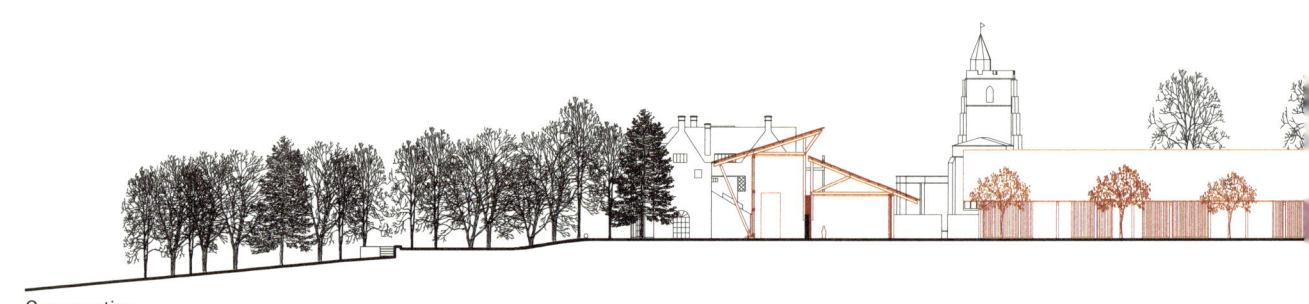
Cross section

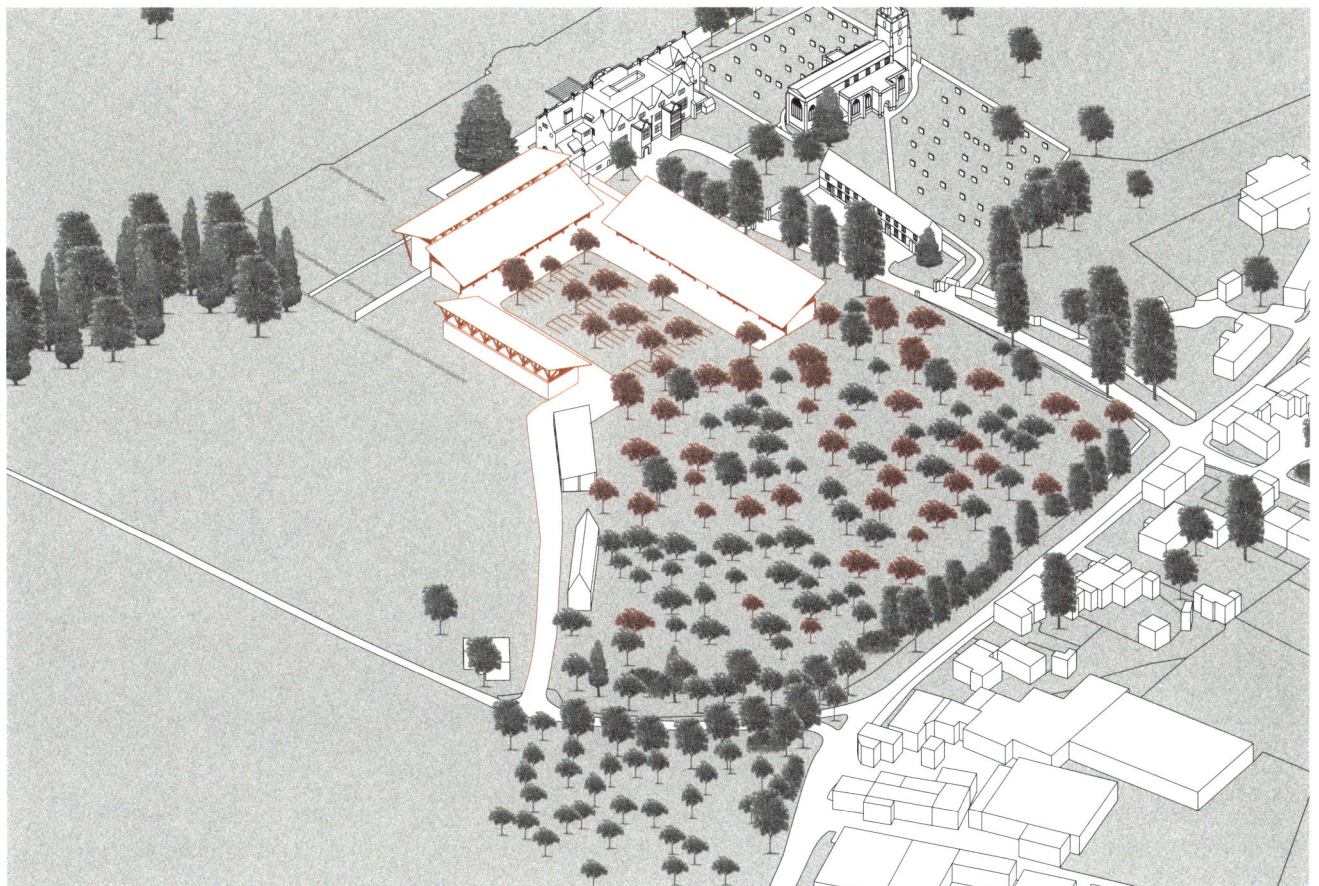
Axonometry of the project

Visualization: The new façade from the park

Architecture: Avon Green Belt 147

4 Parnham House—Woodworking School

Juliette Armanet / Marina Garlatti

Location: Beaminster, Dorset
Owner: Unknown
Architect: John Nash and other
Date: 16th century
Surface: 107 acres
Landscape architect: Francis Inigo Thomas

Parnham House

Parnham House is an Elizabethan stone-built manor house, a Grade I listed building since 1953. It is located in the Dorset Area of Outstanding Natural Beauty. The estate is composed of the manor house, several outbuildings, a formal garden, and a deer park.

The manor house was first built in the 15th century. It was restored several times throughout the centuries, including a restoration by John Nash in 1810. In World War II it was requisitioned by the US army. John Makepeace, a well-known designer specializing in working with wood, purchased the house in 1976 to set up the School for Craftsmanship in Wood, also known as Parnham College.

Despite several extensions and purposes, the manor house kept its coherence until a fire in summer 2017 destroyed two-thirds of the manor house, leaving only external walls.

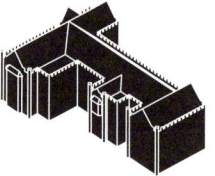
16th century

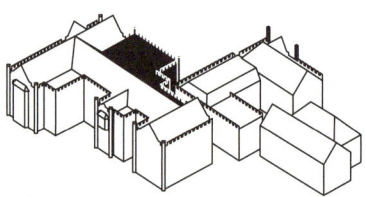
17th–18th century

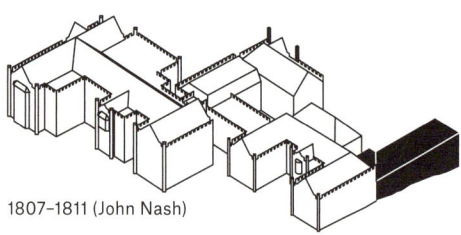
1807–1811 (John Nash)

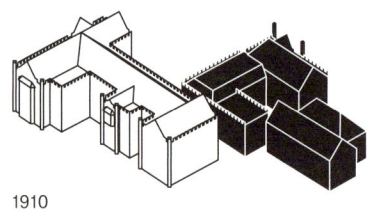
1910

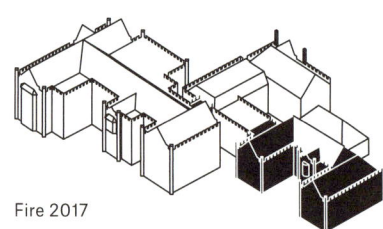
Fire 2017

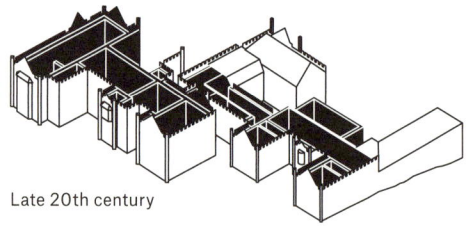
Late 20th century

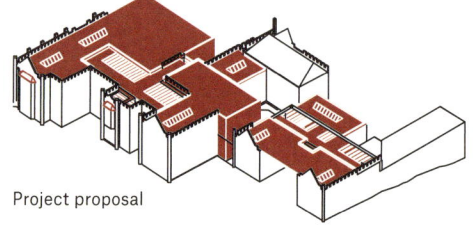
Project proposal

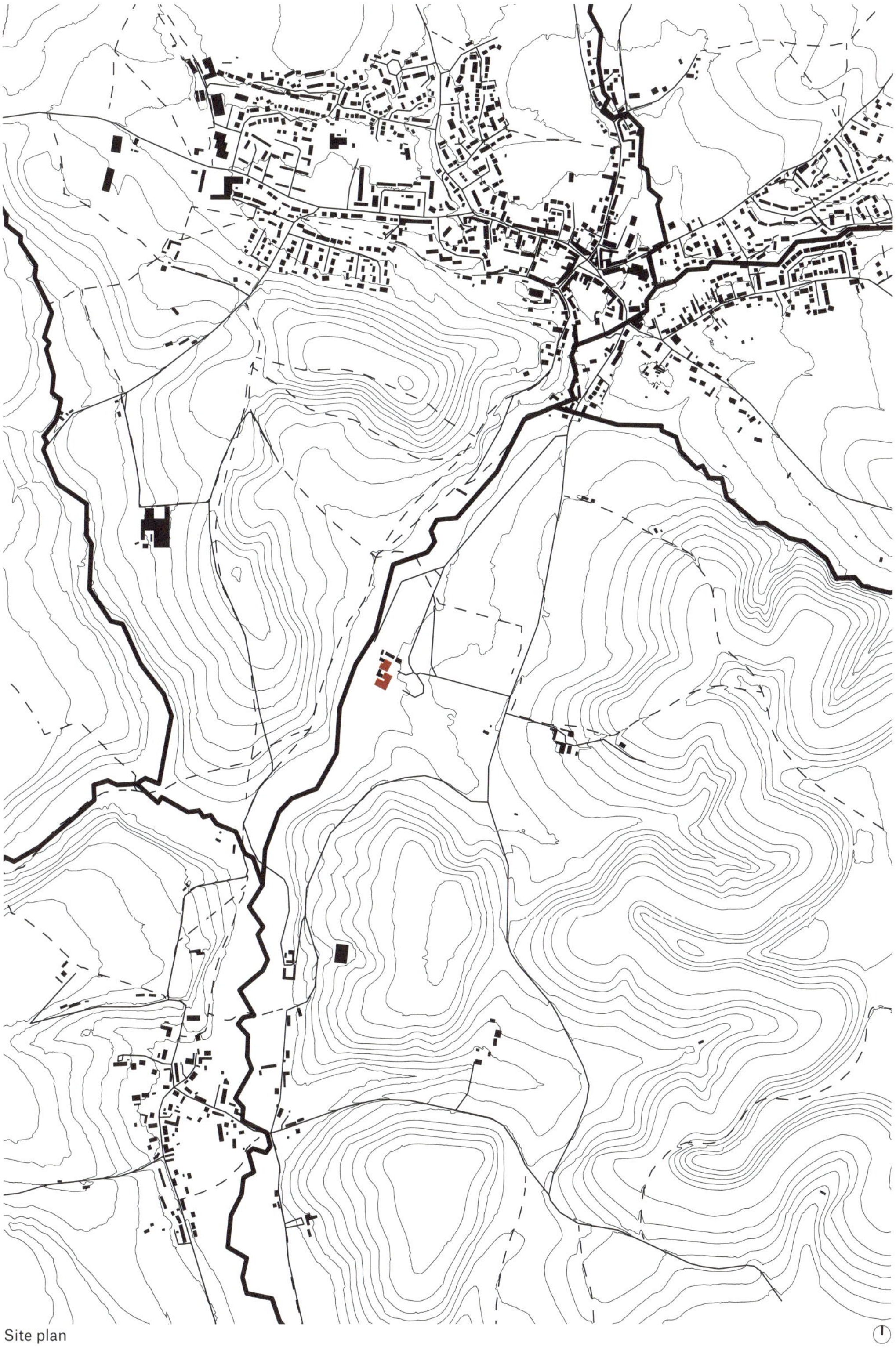

Site plan

Elevation

Architecture: Dorset Coast   149

The ruins the day after the fire in 2017 *iii*

Current state of the building

Woodworking School

Considering the lack of educational facilities in Dorset, the educational past of Parnham house, and the need for Hooke Park and the Architectural Association to extend their accumulated skills and knowledge, the project proposes for Parnham College to be turned into a vocational school specializing in woodworking. The school to be located inside the manor house would become the core of a system that goes much further than the house itself, creating links with Beaminster and Netherbury through its public library, restaurant, and student housing.

Ruins dissolve architecture to its essence, providing a unique opportunity to question what is considered as indoors or outdoors. The project for Parnham College and its accommodations explore exactly this theme. Material and spatial continuity between interior and exterior spaces are used to blur the spatial limits, with stone and wood becoming the only constants in this continuous environment.

In the manor house, walls are changing their status by transforming a previously exterior façade into a partition wall or a former interior space into a courtyard. Thresholds become porous as doors become arches. Materials contribute to blurring these limits as stone and wooden beams are to be found both within indoor and outdoor spaces. Courtyards highlight the fact that the manor has turned into a ruin, preserving all vegetation that has colonized the previously empty spaces.

The project proposes simplicity, sustainability, and environmental conscience by the use of local building resources. Sherborne stone, being the construction material of the old manor house, is used as load-bearing material and extracted from a quarry nearby. Compressed straw is used as the main insulation material, a resource found in abundance in Dorset. Finally, wood construction technology developed in Hooke Park is considered in the use of roundwood as beams in wood-concrete composite floors. In this way, traditional materials and local building techniques are revisited in a contemporary manner in a pursuit of an efficient, yet local architecture.

— *Juliette Armanet / Marina Garlatti*

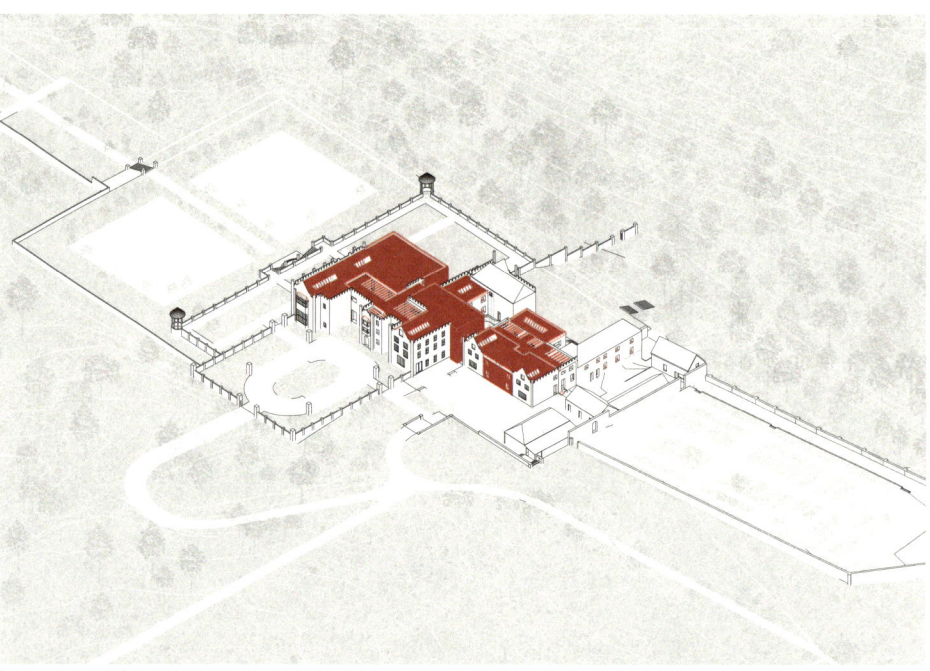
Axonometry of the project

Ground floor

Visualization: A new interior space

Visualization: Outside / inside

Architecture: Dorset Coast

Perspective section

Perspective section

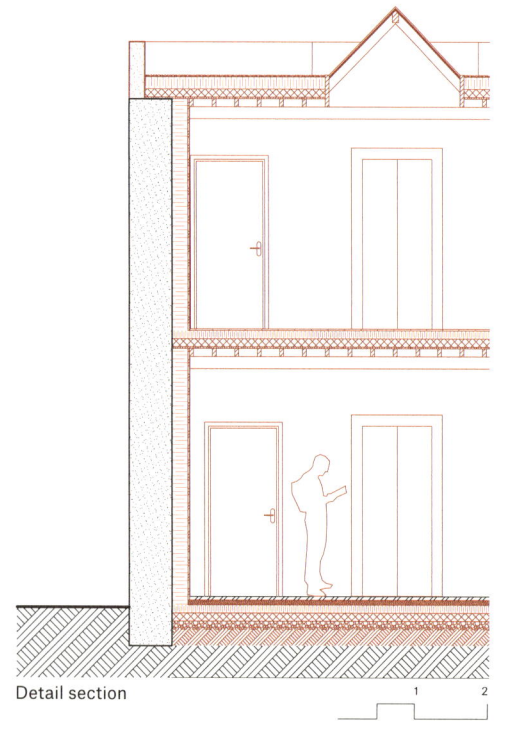
Detail section

Elevation

Visualization: View of the project from the park

5 Kingston Maurward Manor—Student Housing

Paul Trellu

Location: Dorchester, Dorset
Owner: Thomas Beeton
Architect: unknown
Date: 1591
Surface: unknown
Landscape architect: unknown

Kingston Maurward Manor

The original Elizabethan manor house was built in 1591. In the 18th century the Pitt family added the new Kingston Maurward House. At the same time a park and lake were laid out.

The formal gardens were designed from 1918 to 1920 by Sir Cecil and Lady Hanbury, who entertained leading politicians, and also Thomas Hardy. Lady Hanbury continued to live at Kingston Maurward, despite the requisition of the house and park during World War II, when it served as an important base in preparations for the D-Day landings. It was later sold to the Dorset County Council for use as the Dorset Farm Institute.

The farm institute, later to become the Agricultural and Horticultural College, opened at Kingston Maurward in 1949. The institute undertook an extensive program of repairs and consolidation, while from 1990 onwards the gardens and pleasure grounds have been restored along historic lines. The greater portion of the site remains in institutional use, while the 16th-century manor house is privately owned.

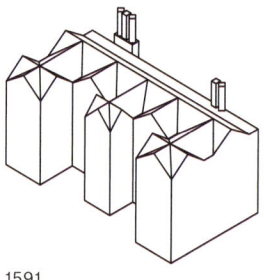
1591

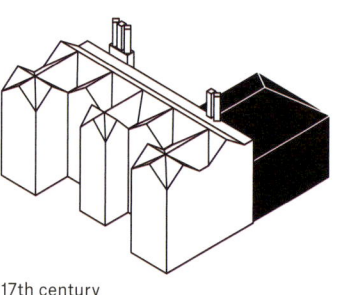
17th century

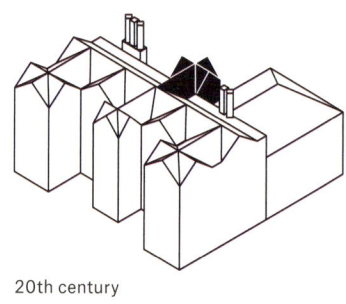
20th century

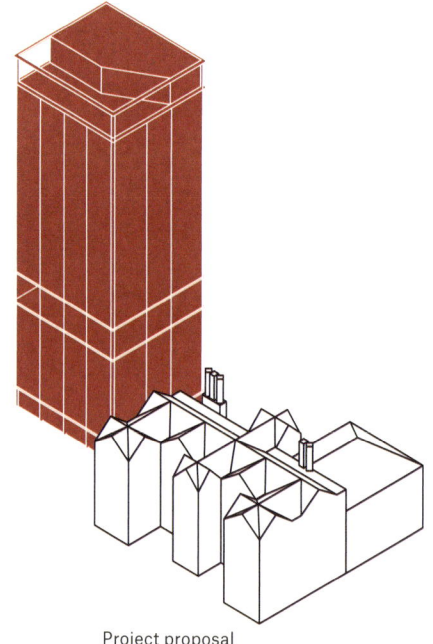
Project proposal

154

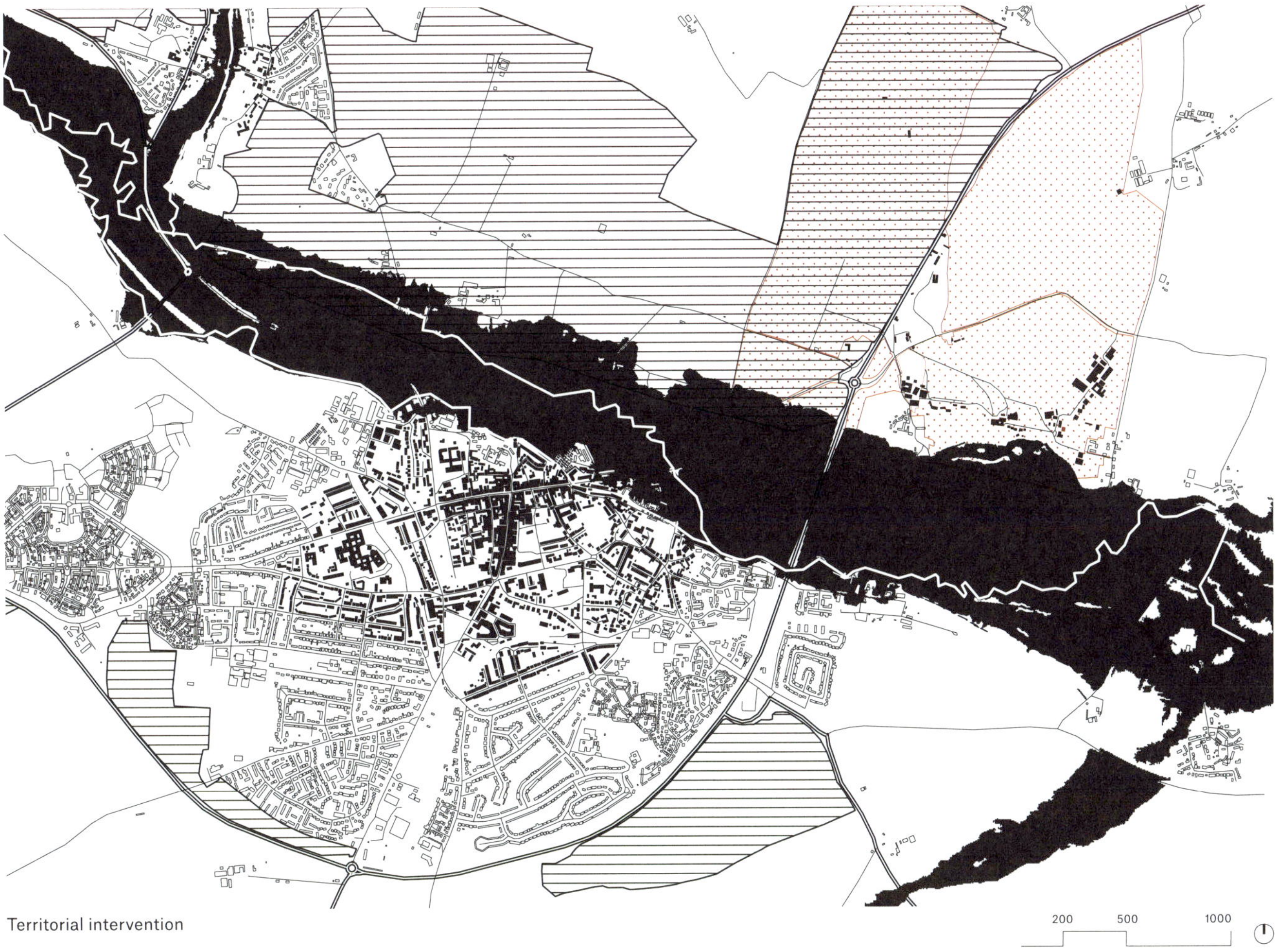

Territorial intervention

Elevation

Architecture: Dorset Coast

Site axonometry of the project

Student Housing

The project is located in the periphery of Dorchester, a town of 20,000 inhabitants. Kingston Maurward estate is currently used as a land-based college. Its land is directly affected by the Masterplan for Dorchester, a low-density urban development for 4,500 new homes in the next 15 years.

As the main provider of land-based education in the county of Dorset, Kingston Maurward College expects significant growth of its institution in the years to come. Today, of the 800 full-time students, only 50 are living on the campus. Hence, in the scope of contributing to the dwelling plans established by the masterplan, the college should consider building additional housing for its student population.

On site, a 16th-century manor house is currently used as a private dwelling. Situated halfway between the administrative center and the educational center of the campus, this manor house is an ideal site for the new student housing.

The project intends to minimize the building's footprint to the absolute minimum, establishing itself on the territory as a tower. The proportions of the new volume take into consideration the presence of the adjacent buildings and in particular that of the manor house. It is placed in a direct relationship to it, in order to profit from the same exterior spaces, but with a subtle recess so that each volume preserves its specificity. The manor house itself is converted to the Kingston Maurward College Faculty Club, becoming an integral part of campus life, benefitting students and visitors equally.

The dwelling typology organizes the tower's spaces into three levels of intimacy. This partition provides its residents a proper mix between the privacy one enjoys in everyday life while having generous and diverse shared spaces among the students. At first, the student's room represents the private nucleus. The second level of intimacy is the spacious common area preserved in each of the 10-room apartments spanning across two floors and containing a common cooking and dining area as well as a big living room. Finally, the tower provides a third level of common areas shared by all students such as a common game room, an outdoor rooftop kitchen, and a common study area on the sixth floor.

All of these spaces are organized vertically, linked by a central concrete core that stiffens the exterior wooden structure of the tower. The two different materials suit their respective program, with more functional spaces located at the concrete core, and more domestic areas positioned toward the façade built in wood. Being part of a hybrid structural system, wood is exposed on the façade. This accentuates the verticality of the building with a wooden grid that is interrupted to reveal common spaces. The rigid volume is nested close to the manor house. The composition of these two gravitating figures form a new centrality for the campus.

— *Paul Trellu*

Visualization: View of the new entrance

Ground floor

Architecture: Dorset Coast

Visualization: A student bedroom

Section

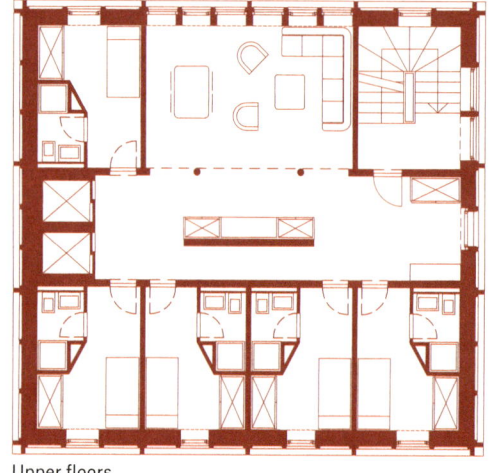

Upper floors

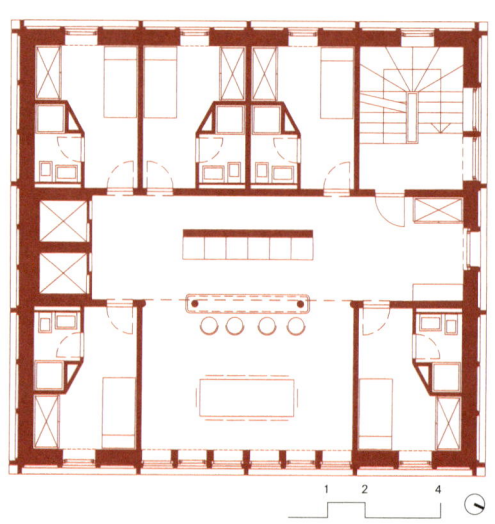

Visualization: The kitchen, a shared space

Axonometry of the project

Architecture: Dorset Coast 159

6 Creech Grange Manor—Institute of Architecture

Romain Barth / Sébastien Friess / Solène Hoffmann

Location: Steeple, Dorset
Owner: Norman Heyward
Architect: unknown
Date: 1540
Surface: 350 acres
Landscape architect: unknown

Creech Grange Manor

Creech Grange is a large estate of 350 acres located on the Isle of Purbeck in Dorset, with a manor house dating from the 16th century. It was built on land formerly owned by Bindon Abbey. The gardens and pleasure ground were laid out in the 17th century.

Only fragments remain of the original house, built by Sir Oliver Lawrence, an ancestor of George Washington, partly because it was damaged by a fire started by the Parliamentarians during the English Civil War, and also because the entire front was taken down and rebuilt in Tudor style in 1846.

The manor house we see today is the result of the long accumulation of heterogeneous fragments. As a whole, the building is a collage of strong and isolated interventions.

The site is made up of different geographical and architectural elements that highlight the manor house as well as the landscape. In 1746, a folly named Grange Arch was erected on the highest local point on the Purbeck Ridge, now owned by the National Trust.

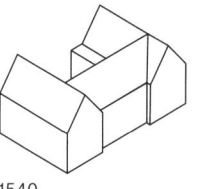
1540

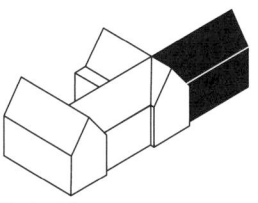
Early 17th century

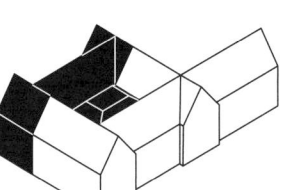
Later 17th century

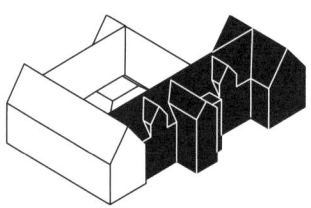
18th century

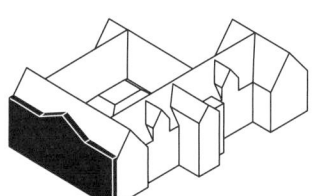
Mid-18th century

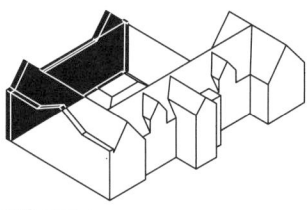
19th century

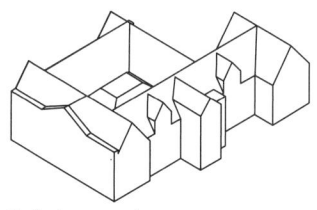
Project proposal

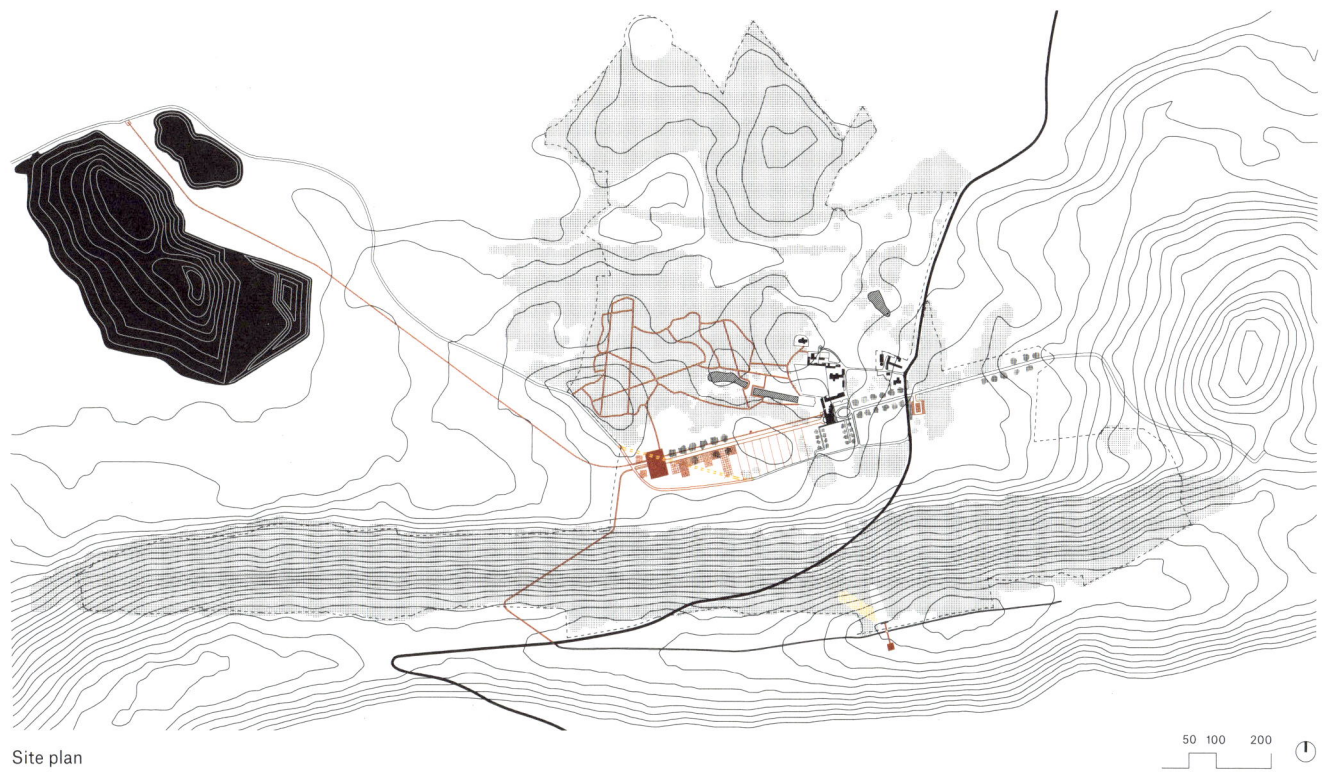

Site plan

View of the manor from the hill

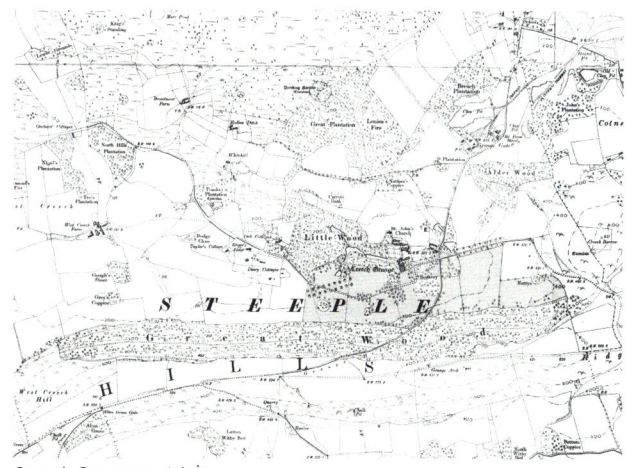

Creech Grange parish *iv*

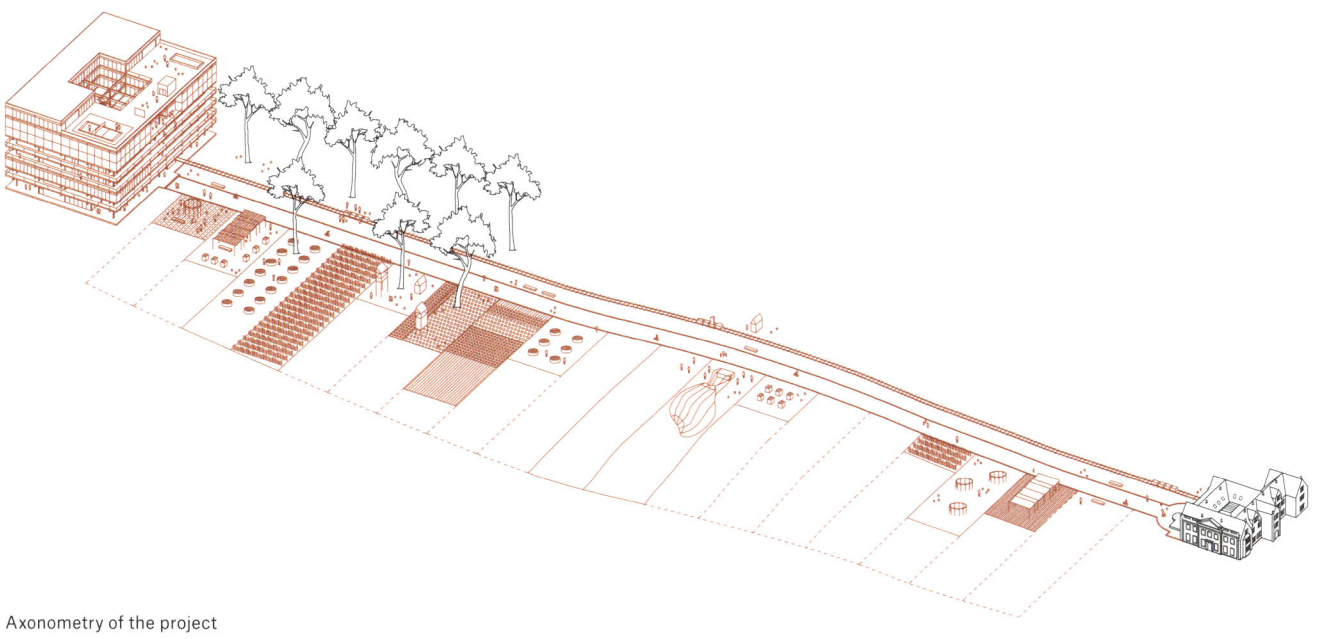

Axonometry of the project

Architecture: Dorset Coast 161

View from the park

The South façade

The West façade

Institute of Architecture

The proposed Institute of Architecture is planned for studies of the countryside, its architecture, and its ongoing transformations. The institute offers a postgraduate master's degree with a capacity of 250 students. The new building contains a complex program with housing, offices, studios, a library, and a parking lot, permitting living on-site. The school offers a direct application of the theories studied into its immediate context while enjoying the surrounding landscape.

In a context of global warming and the radicalization of capitalist productivism, the countryside is going through profound changes that are significant for the future. In order to understand these future transformations, it is necessary to be positioned in-situ, beyond the metropolitan framework. The island of Purbeck in Dorset offers an immersion in a territory where the existing tensions reflect the divergent expectations for the countryside.

The institute becomes a central place in the region from which to explore the countryside. Because of its location, its strong limits, and imposing dimensions, the new building challenges the codes of the existing manor house, which itself is rehabilitated into a leisure club that organizes cultural events open to the public, a place where the community of Purbeck and members of the school can meet. The new building sits on the main axis of the manor house connected to it by a pedestrian path along which outdoor activities are organized. A railway connects the manor to the quarry, crossing the ground floor of the new building where some outdoor and indoor workshops are located. From the school, different paths lead to a romantic promenade in Little Wood or to Grange Arch to enjoy the panorama of the territory. On the highest point of the scarp, a small pavilion turned toward the sea and hidden from the school offers a resting and meditation space.

Following the principles of compactness and congestion, the school's complex spatial program is gathered into a unique volume. The building has an expression of bare architecture organized in a strong grid to adapt to future programs. However, the relation with the manor and the surroundings defines the spatial organization of the school. The main vertical circulation sits at the end of the main axis of the manor house, allowing a strong visual connection to it. The horizontal circulation takes place at the perimeter of the plan, allowing many views of the territory. To free the ground from cars and open it to the surroundings, the parking lot is placed on the first floor and programs that do not require light are placed at the center of the building, such as the library. The housing units are located on the outside, with a direct connection to the library. On the upper floors studios are located in a double-height space with a mezzanine for more private meetings with the teachers and emphasizing the column-beam structure. On the top floor common and public activities take place, such as the exhibition space and the cafeteria with a generous roof terrace.

— *Romain Barth / Sébastien Friess / Solène Hoffmann*

Visualization: View from the aisle

Section

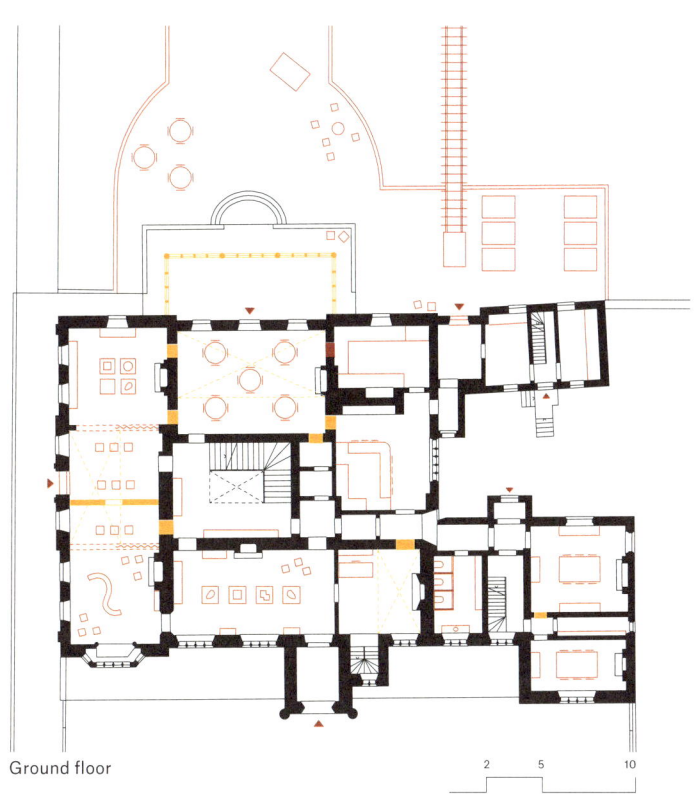
Ground floor

Architecture: Dorset Coast 163

Visualization: View from the balcony

Visualization: View from the workshop

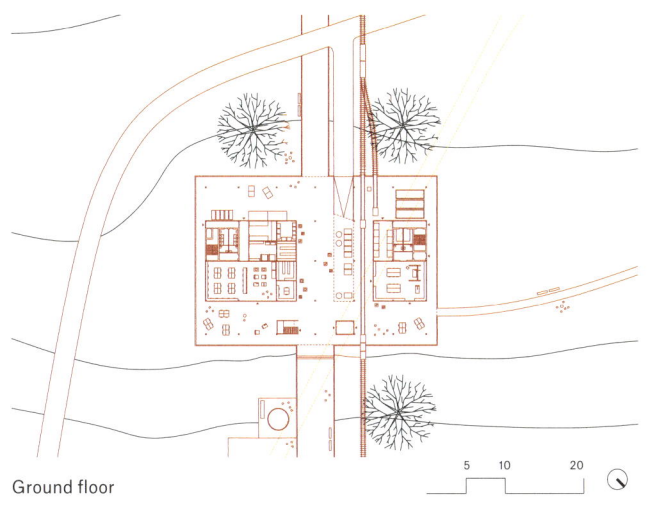
Ground floor

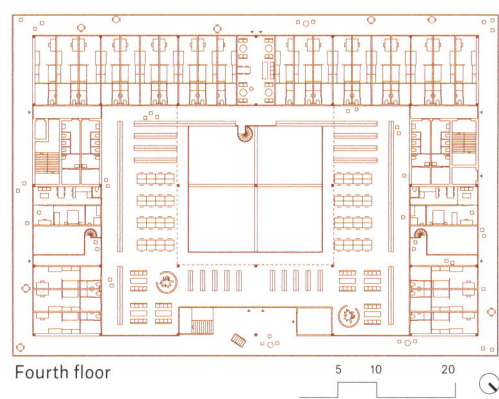
Fourth floor

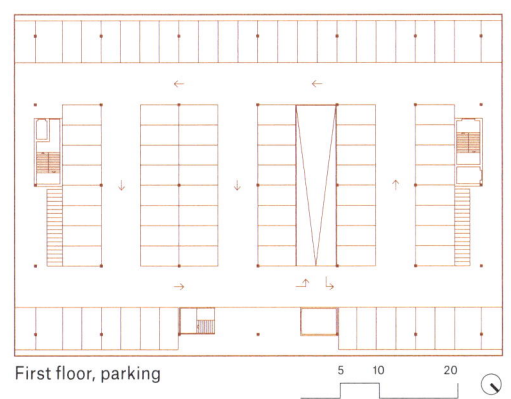
First floor, parking

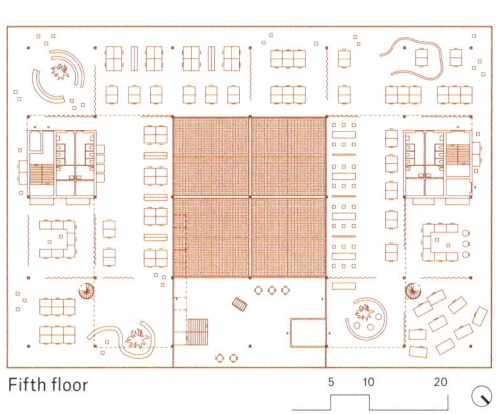
Fifth floor

Third floor

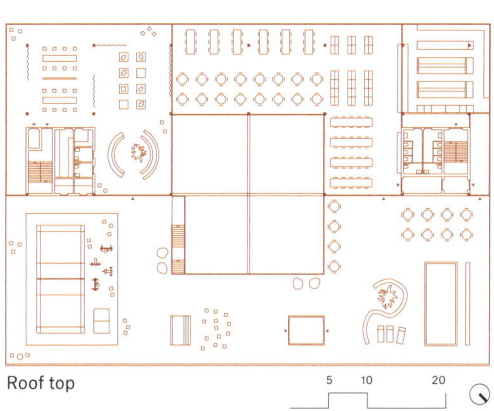
Roof top

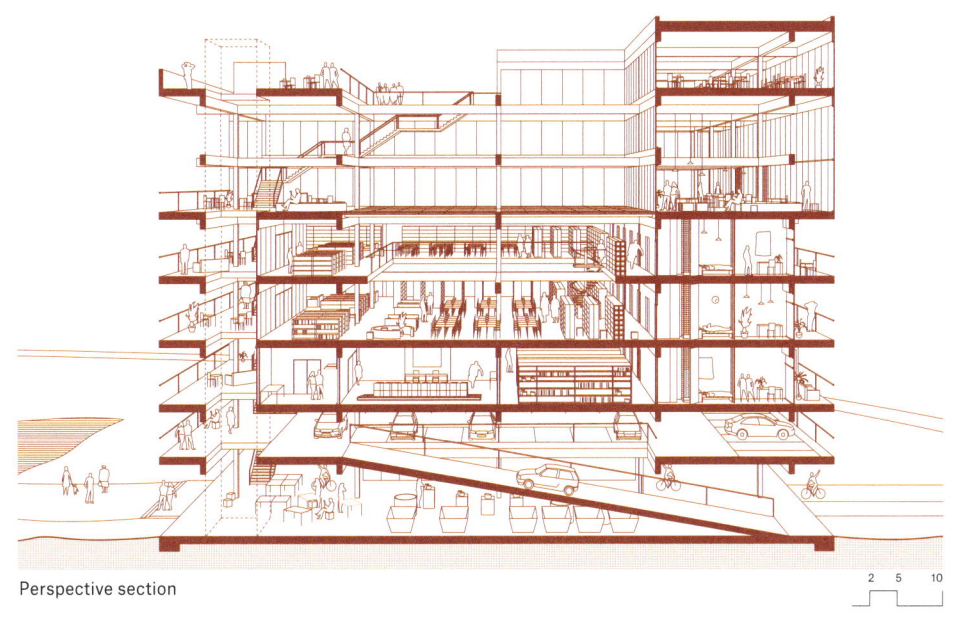
Perspective section

Architecture: Dorset Coast

7 Sharpham House—Eco-Communal Housing

Lucas Bastos Vieira / Elie Tournier

Location: Ashprington, South Devon
Owner: Sharpham Trust
Architect: Robert Taylor
Date: 16th century
Surface: 550 acres
Landscape architect: Capability Brown

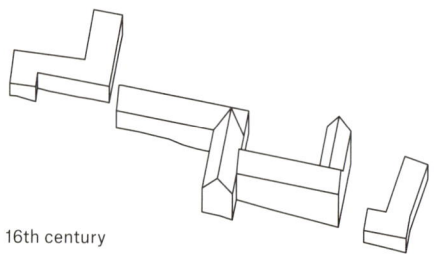
16th century

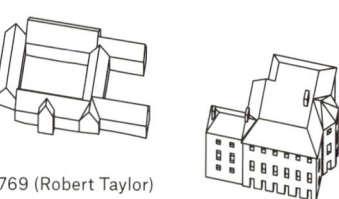
1769 (Robert Taylor)

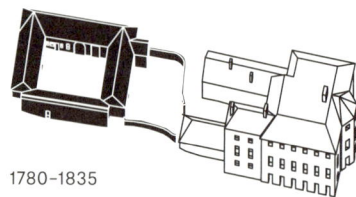
1780–1835

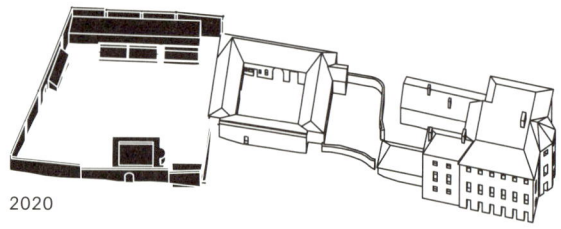
2020

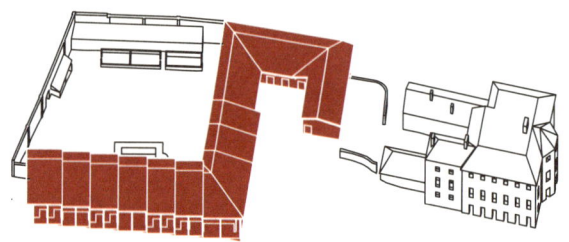
Project proposal

Sharpham House

Sharpham House is a Grade I listed building located in the parish of Ashprington, southeast of Totnes, high up on the west bank and within a tight bend of the River Dart.

The first traces of the manor date back to 1260. In 1765, Philemon Pownoll, a naval captain purchased the estate and commissioned the architect Sir Robert Taylor to convert the then existing Tudor mansion to a new villa in Palladian style. The construction of the house continued over an extended period, and it was probably only completed in its present form in 1820.

In addition, Taylor built a bathing house next to the river. The park and gardens are Grade II listed in the National Register of Historic Parks and Gardens and are thought to be designed by the famous landscape architect Capability Brown.

During the 1850s the Durant family contributed to the identity of Ashprington. They revamped the estate and the whole parish by widening the roads, refurbishing the church, building a schoolhouse, and creating new housing units called Holly Villas.

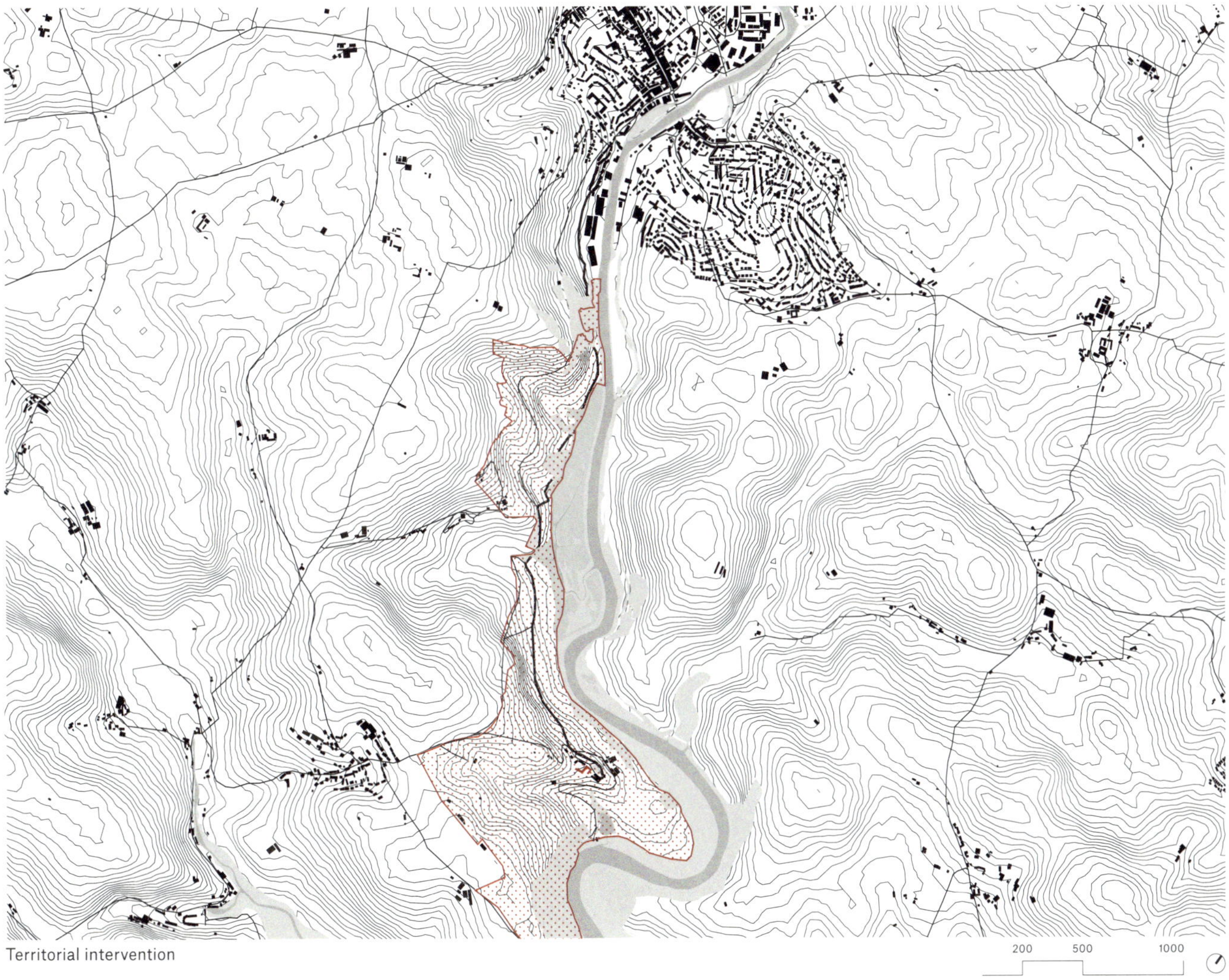

Territorial intervention

Elevation

Bird's-eye view of the manor

Architecture: South Hams 167

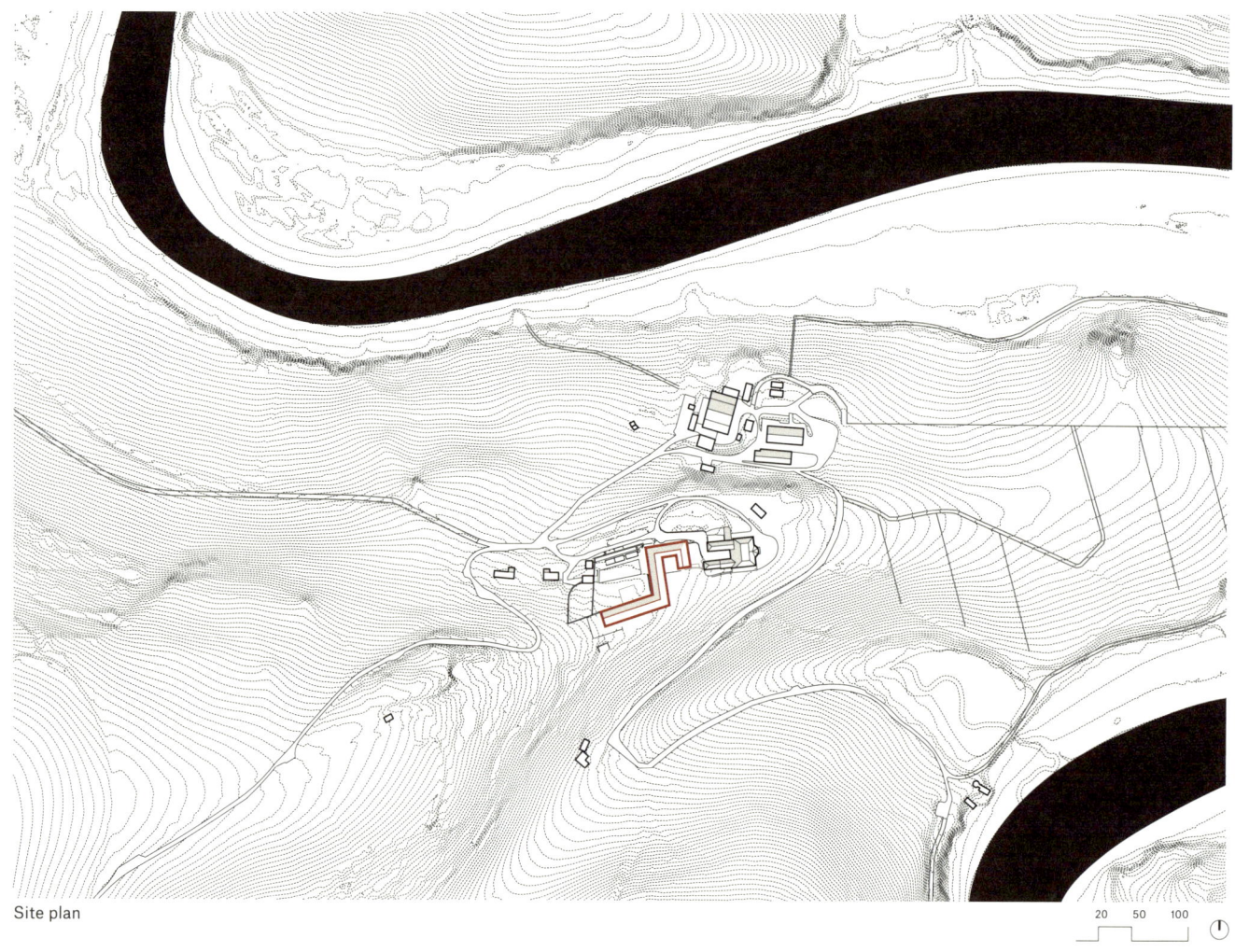

Site plan

Eco-Communal Housing

On the slopes running from the west toward the River Dart on the east, a mansion house with several walled gardens stands on a ridge of high ground overlooking the river. The Sharpham estate combines natural and manufactured beauty such as the 18th-century Palladian villa built by Robert Taylor and landscape interventions presumably planned by Capability Brown. It is not only an architectural heritage from the 18th century but also a 20th-century hub of radical but enduring ideas about land use, culture, the environment, and sustainability. Some of them are part of the Dartington Hall ethos, which had a major impact on Totnes's character and economy.

In order to pursue the ideological and historical character of the site, the project proposes the construction of an eco-hamlet: "a traditional or intentional community with the goal of becoming more socially, culturally, economically, and/or ecologically sustainable."[1]

To this aim, the proposal is to dwell in the garden and to promote community life and connection with the landscape. On a ridge, in line with the manor house and its extensions, the old coach house, and the walled garden, a light wooden structure is added onto the garden's south wall. This structure in fact uses the garden wall as its primary element, as the very backbone of the construction, and then extends to the coach house further north. The two-storied new construction falls in a cascade of levels adapting to the sites' topography.

In order to keep the essence of the preexisting wall, the north façade is an offset, leaving a space in between dedicated to circulation. This space occasionally expands giving place to the private unit entrances as well as the common areas. This in-between space works as an inhabited winter garden, which links not only the wall to the project but also the existing walled garden and the new garden to the south. On the second floor, over the wall, a glazed façade highlights this displacement and opens up the view on the communal gardens.

The common and public programs are located on the ground floor of the coach house and in the manor house. The manor becomes the very symbol of this community and hosts all the collective activities such as cooking, eating, meeting, celebrating, learning, and working. The project is in line with a return to the back-to-the-land movement by promoting the benefits of cohabitation and the search for self-sufficiency and resilience at individual and collective levels.

— *Lucas Bastos Vieira / Elie Tournier*

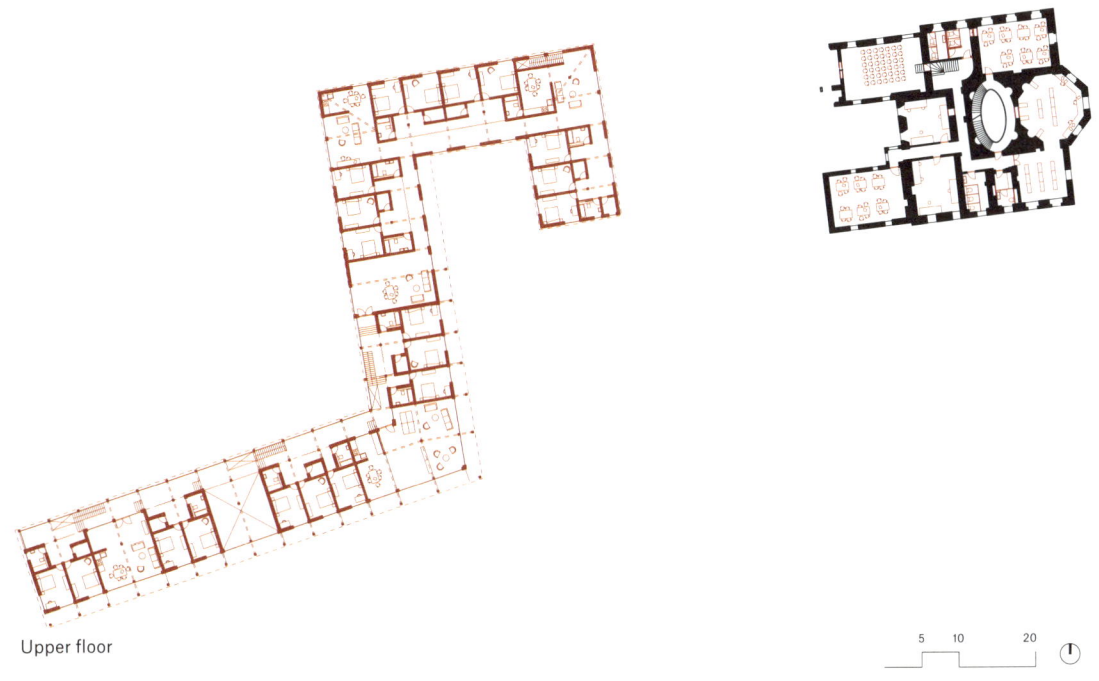
Upper floor

Ground floor

Architecture: South Hams

Aquarelle of the Southill House *vi*

The east façade *vii*

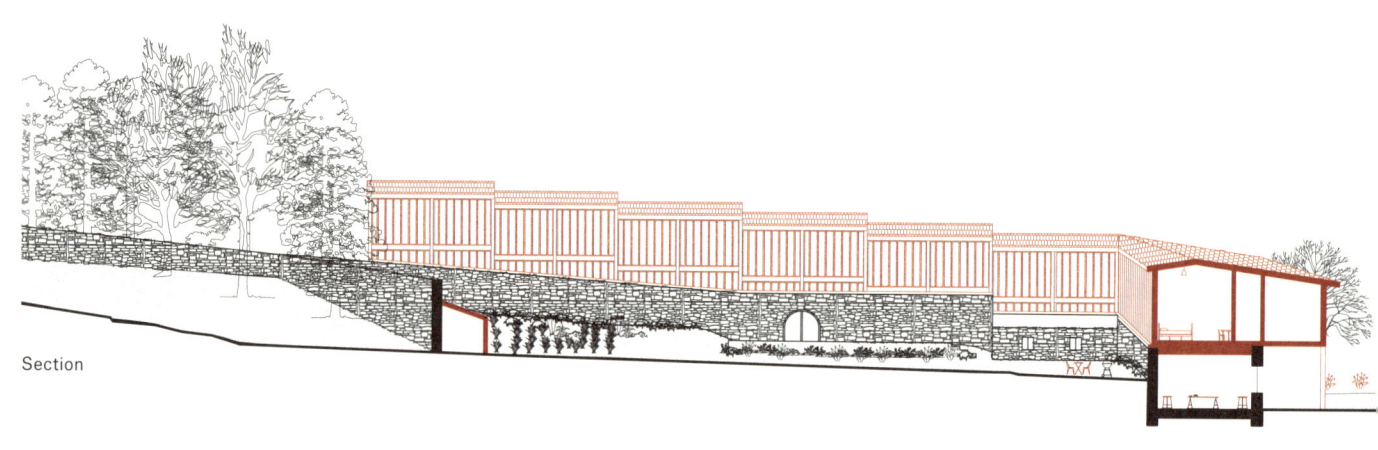
Section

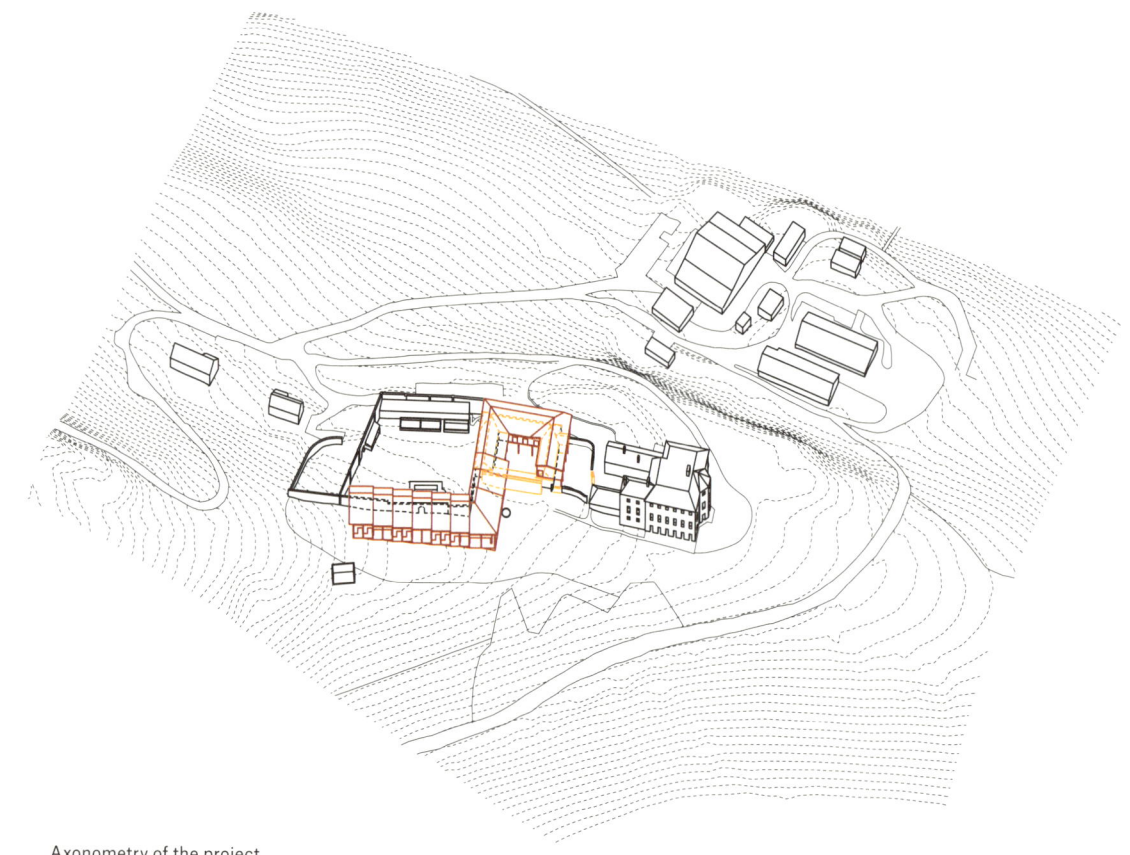
Axonometry of the project

Visualization: View into the shared spaces

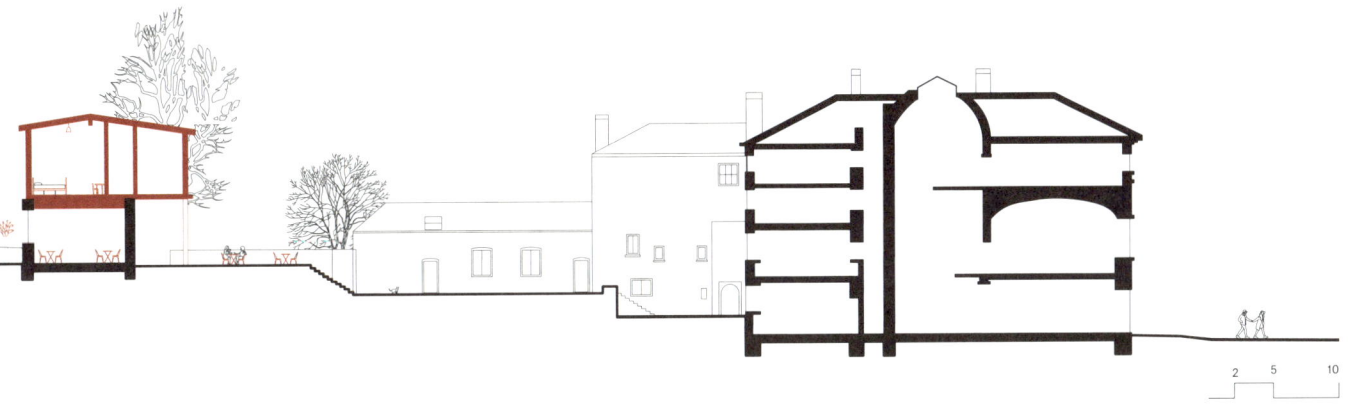

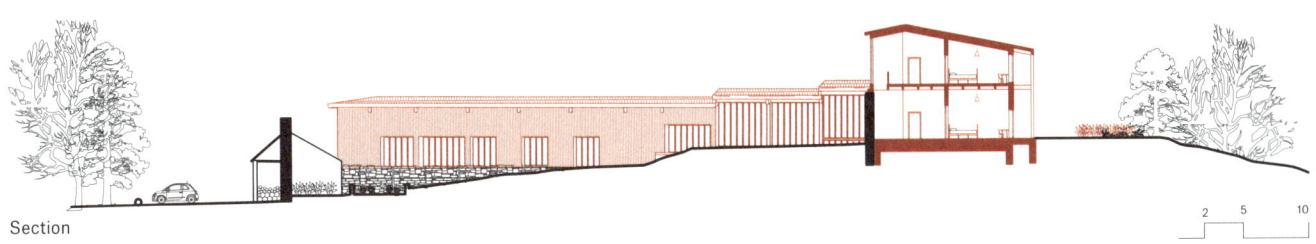
Section

Architecture: South Hams

8 Sharpham Marsh—Inhabited Path

Vincent Bianchi / Raphael Delmuè

viii

Location: Ashprington, South Devon
Owner: Sharpham Trust
Architect: Robert Taylor
Date: 16th century
Surface: 550 acres
Landscape architect: Capability Brown

Sharpham Marsh

Sharpham Marsh is located southeast of Totnes where the River Dart, originating in Dartmoor National Park, flows through its estuary into the English Channel. It is an ecosystem that has been greatly modified by humans over the last two centuries. Originally, there was a wide meander of the river. The territory was ameliorated around 1840 to create a proper navigation channel and an area of summer pastures.

However, a century later, due to neglect, subsidence, and slow sea-level rise, the retaining walls delineating these pastures were overwhelmed by the highest tides of the year, causing the dyke to break at a point known as the "hole in the wall." A new marshland has developed over the last 60 years to the present situation. Today, the dyke is mostly absent, turning the site's perimeter into an intertidal zone, which causes many erosion problems. If tides persist, the navigation channel will eventually disappear.

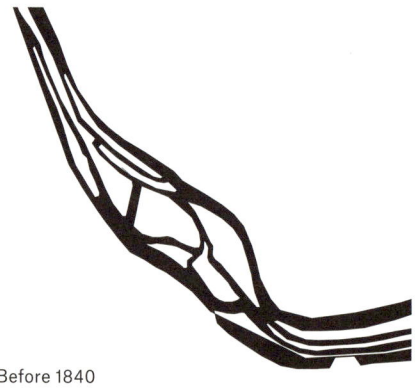

Before 1840

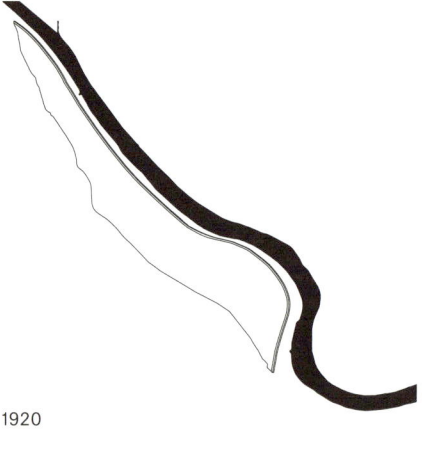

1920

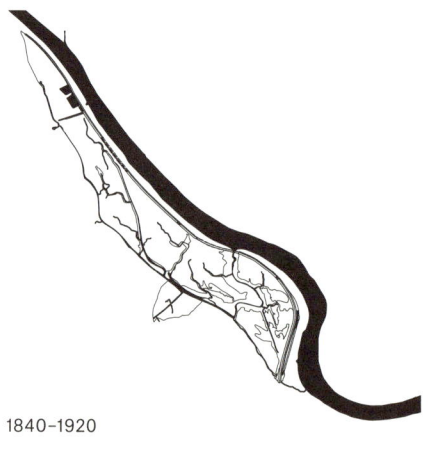

1840–1920

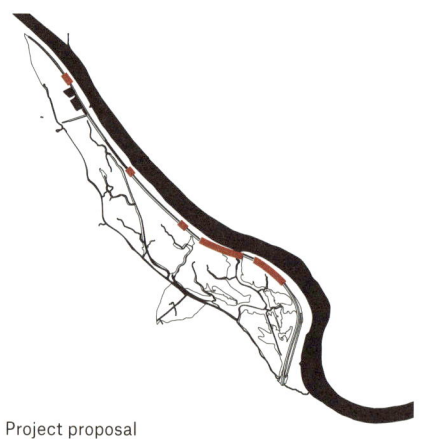

Project proposal

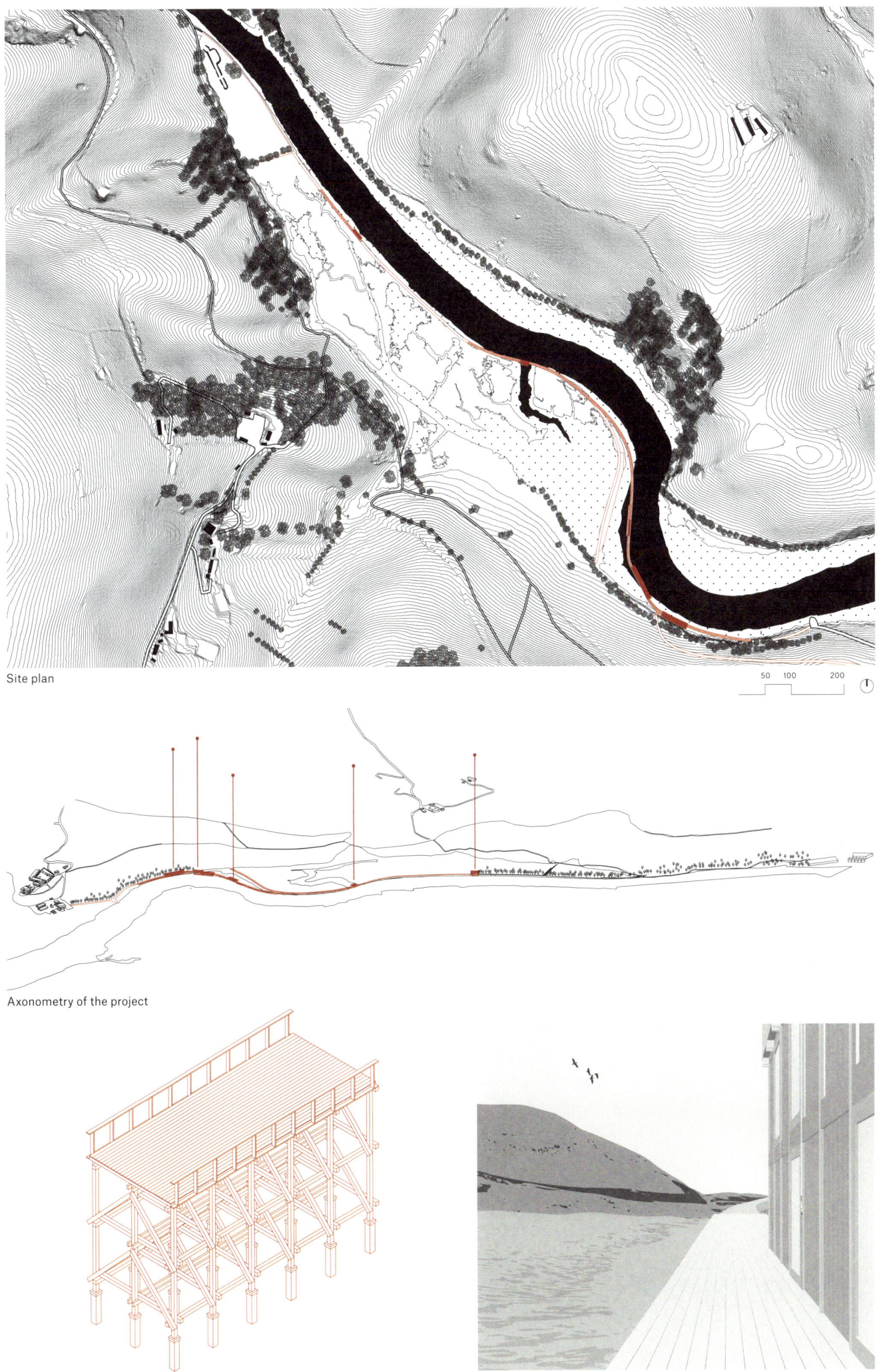

Site plan

Axonometry of the project

Axonometry of the deck

View from the deck

Architecture: South Hams

1809 First Ordnance Survey map

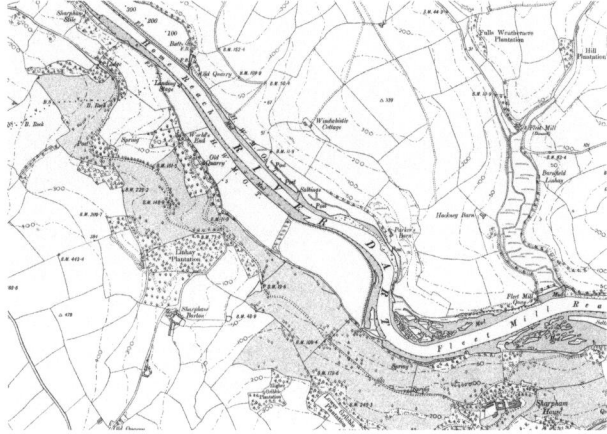
1905 Ordnance Survey map *ix*

Territorial link

Inhabited Path

In accordance to the site constitution developed for South Devon, with the aim of transforming this territory into an even more resilient system and to respond to urgent global challenges, a network of manor houses is proposed to activate the four dimensions of sustainability: social, cultural, economic, and ecological. This network is formed by production lines that corresponded to the axial system of rivers flowing from Dartmoor National Park to the sea. At the same time, these lines were connected to settlements that served as poles of attraction.

The project integrates this principle by being one of the links associating the town of Totnes to Sharpham Manor through walking. Indeed, this practice, well anchored in the English imagination and aesthetic reveals forgotten corners, hidden beauties, and the poetry of abandoned places as well as reconnecting the people with their environment, allowing them to physically experience the passage from the city to the countryside.

The proposed path along the Sharpham salt marsh forms the heart of the project. This territory is a partly manufactured neo-ecosystem. It was therefore decided to insert several interventions along this path that cultivate the idea of a co-evolution between human settlement and the surrounding environment.

The estuary of the River Dart is subject to tides that erode the banks of the marsh and thus risk making the river impassable. Improving the existing dyke would not only help to contain this problem and protect the ecosystem of the marsh, but it also allows for the production of hydroelectric power by the tides.

The new path is made of wood, being in line with the collective imaginary of the marshland landscape. The structure of our intervention follows a grid, determined by the width of the existing embankment, which is 4.5 meters. This structure is an obsessive repetition of wooden beams and columns of 18 × 18 centimeter sections. The use of simple technology—adjacent joints bolted together, without wedges between the parts—has allowed its quick and clean assembly and flexibility in its maintenance.

The height of the pathway is guided by the embankment while the vertical position of the different interventions depends on their necessity to be close to the water or not. This compositional rigor results in an architectural homogeneity between the different programs. However, the layout of the roofs allows each of the entities to keep an identity of its own.

The flaneur coming from the manor house will first be confronted with a part of the project located on the water. It contains a restaurant, which is placed at the beginning of the pathway to connect to the wine and cheese farm located at the Sharpham estate. It will be complemented by a landing stage, linking Sharpham to the rest of the estuary. A recreation area, in the form of public baths, connects the people of Ashprington and the new community of Sharpham to the river. An outpost of the nature conservation center of Ambios completes the project toward Totnes.

— *Vincent Bianchi / Raphael Delmuè*

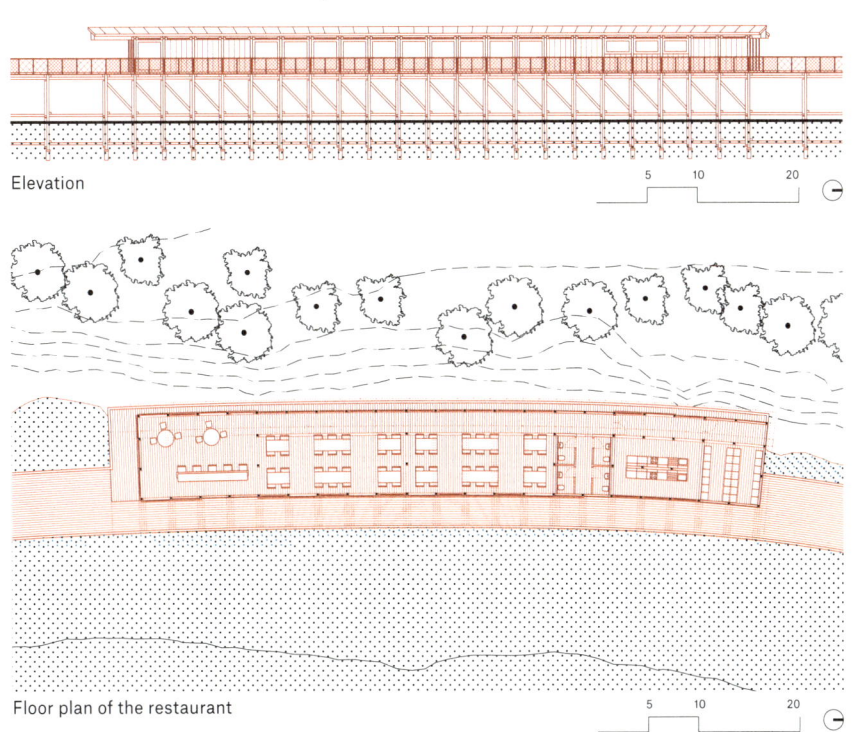

Elevation

Floor plan of the restaurant

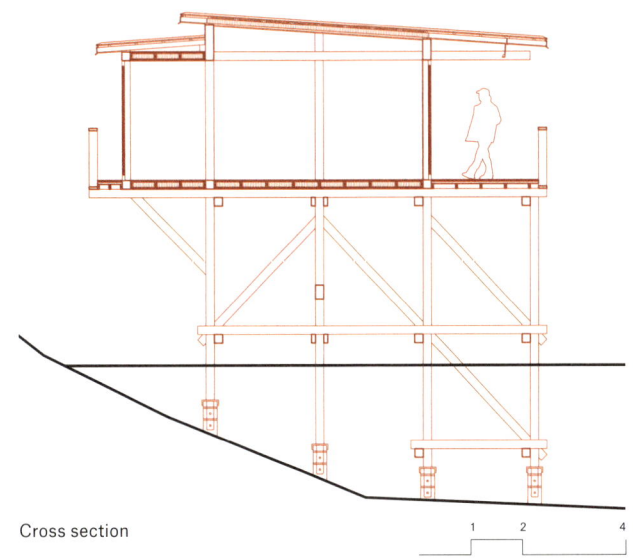

Cross section

Visualization: View from the restaurant

Architecture: South Hams 175

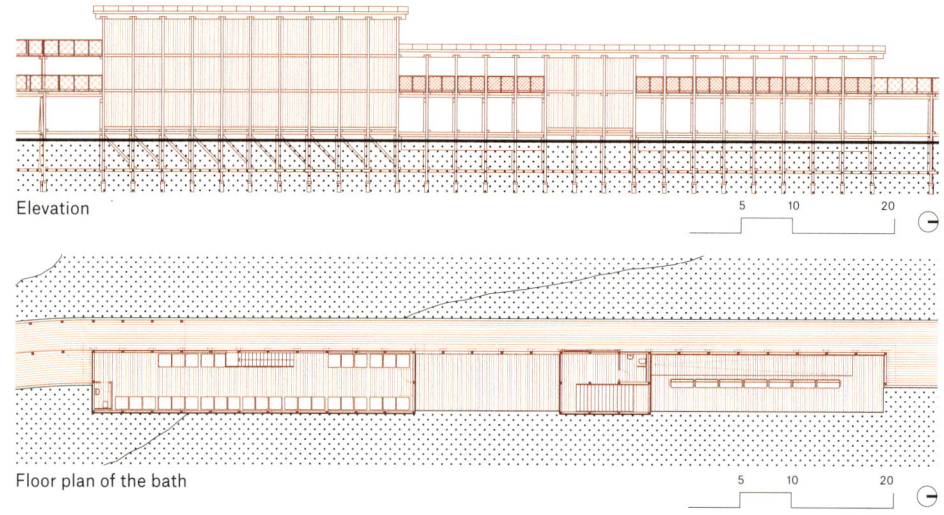

Elevation

Floor plan of the bath

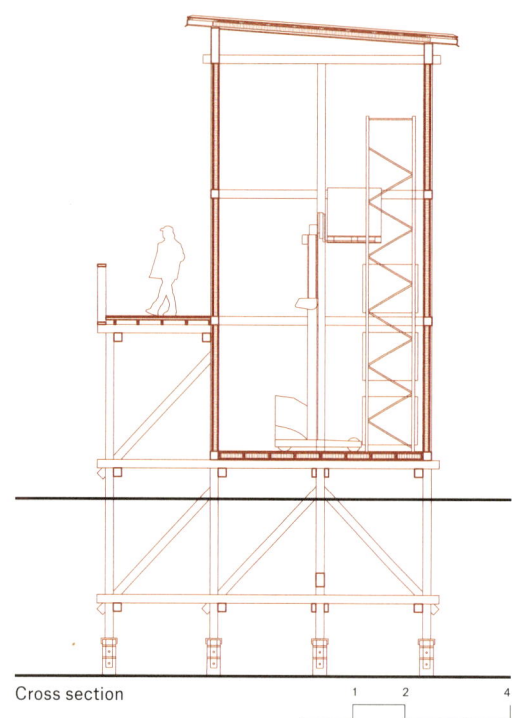

Cross section

Visualization: View from the changing room

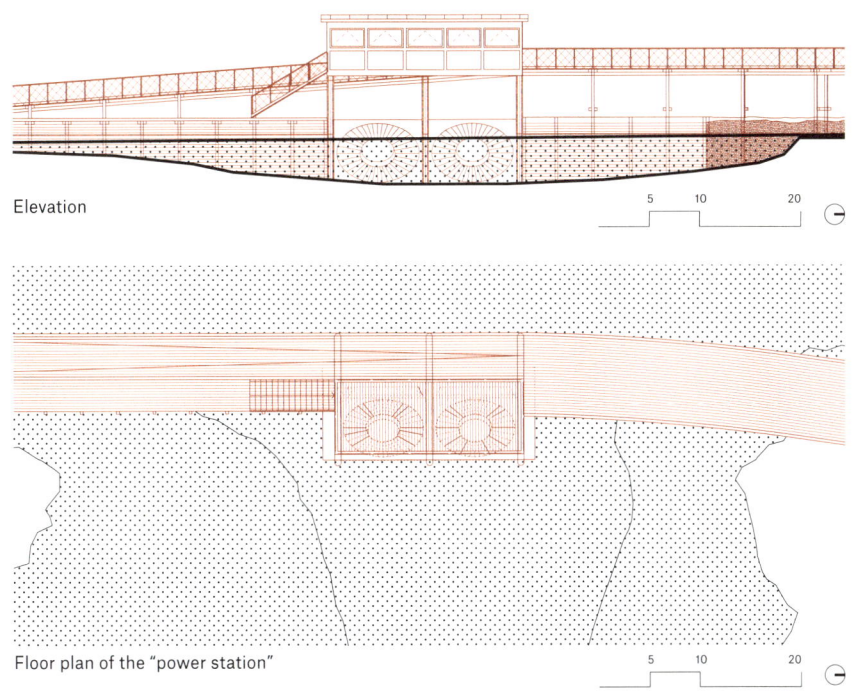

Elevation

Floor plan of the "power station"

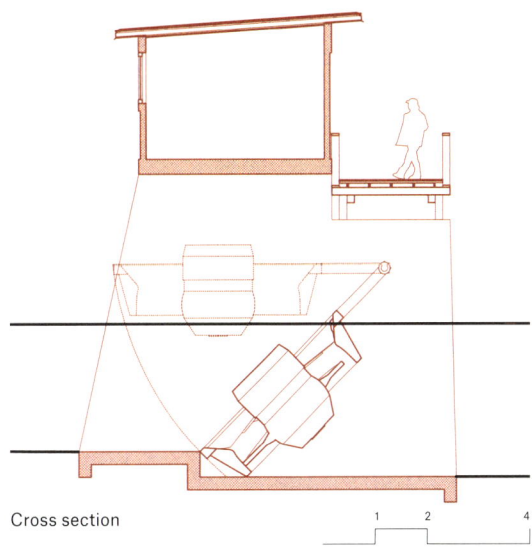

Cross section

Visualization: View toward the "power station"

Architecture: South Hams   177

9 Nettlecombe Court—Refuges for Hikers

Marion Aubert / Océane Perrone

Location: Willington, Exmoor National Park
Owner: John Wolseley
Architect: unknown
Date: 1599
Surface: 290 acres
Landscape architect: unknown

Nettlecombe Court

Nettlecombe Court and Park is an estate, situated on the northern fringes of the Brendon Hills, within the Exmoor National Park in Somerset. Before the Norman conquest in the 11th century, it was held by the son of King Harold. William the Conqueror assumed possession of Nettlecombe after defeating King Harold at the Battle of Hastings.

The 16th-century Elizabethan, Tudor, and Medieval architecture with Georgian refinements includes a mansion, a medieval hall, a church, a monumental oak grove, and a farm.

The house is surrounded by Nettlecombe Park, a 90-hectares Site of Special Scientific Interest (SSI). The park blends into woodlands. Today the house serves as the Leonard Wills Field Centre run by the Field Studies Council, which offers residential and non-residential fieldwork for schools, colleges, and universities as well as holiday accommodation and professional and leisure courses in natural history and the arts.

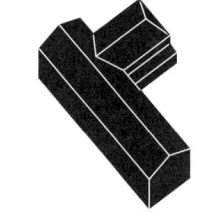
Late medieval

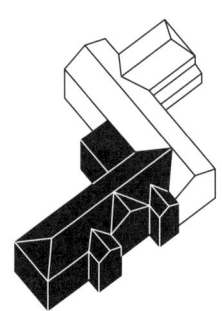
15th century

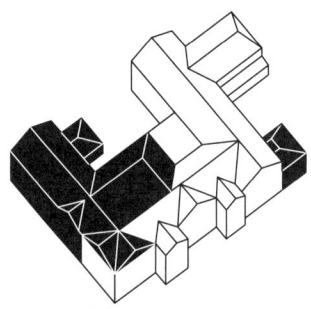
17th century

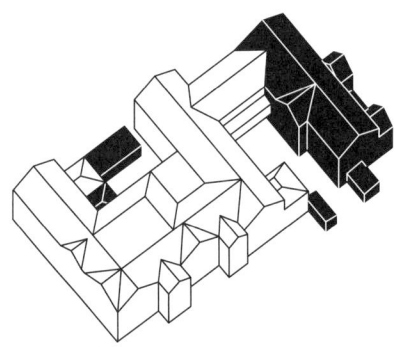
19th century

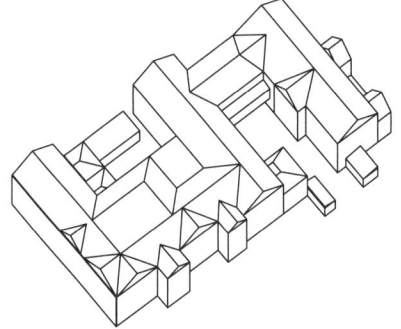
Project proposal

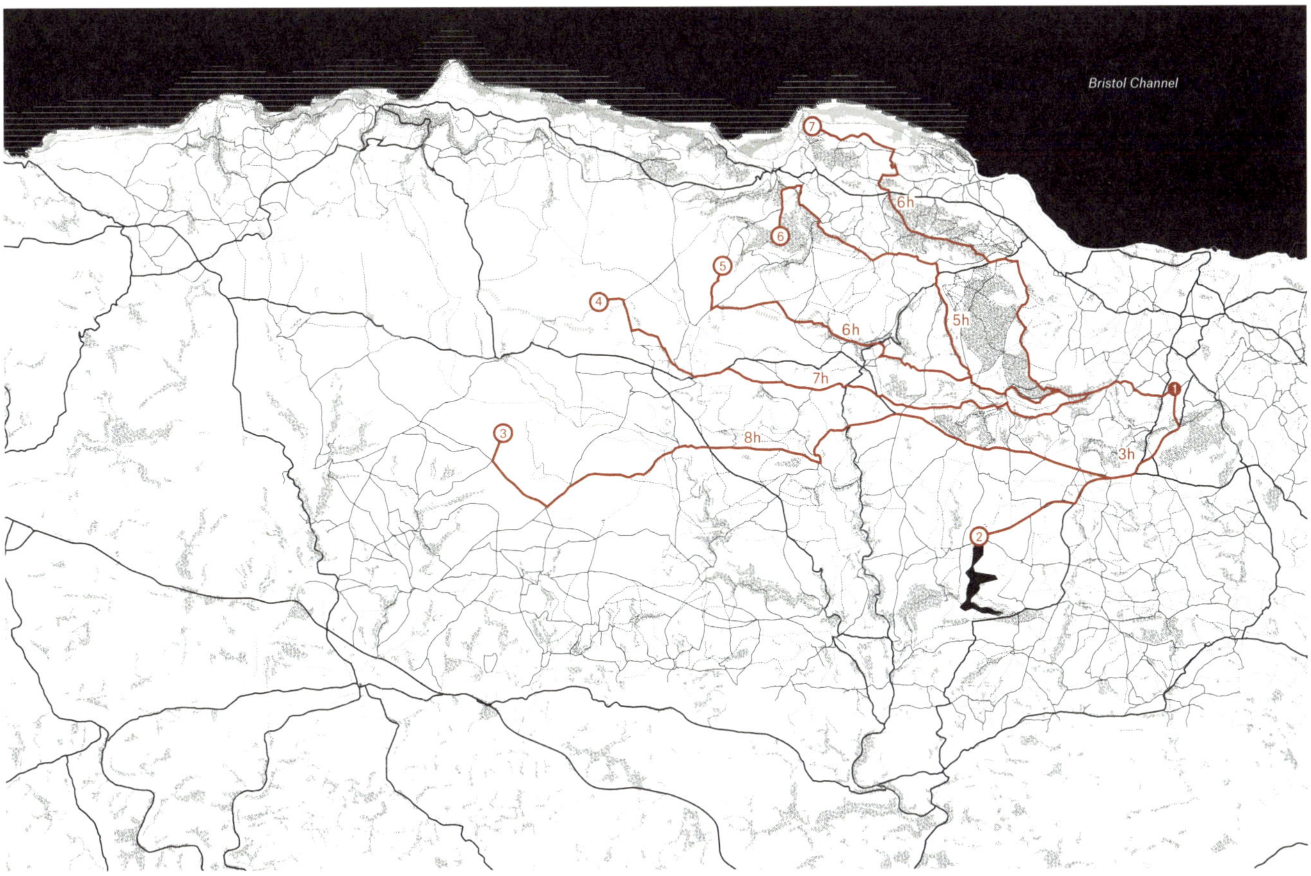

Site plan

Nettlecombe Court, engraved by W. Angus in 1793 ˣ

Site plan

Refuges for Hikers

The seven proposed refuges for Exmoor National Park respond to the request of the park authority and its visitors for more public access to the various natural landscapes. Six of the refuges are placed across the park in different habitats, with a program allowing hikers to stay in the various landscapes the park provides. They are located on the highpoints of the territory in order to be visible in the distance and act as landmarks.

The hiking trails leading to the refuges start at Nettlecombe Court Manor located in the northeast of Exmoor Park. Nowadays, the manor houses an environmental school, which plays an important role promoting natural heritage. The seventh refuge, the only one in a valley, is located near the manor and serves as a meeting place for residents of the manor and the hikers.

The architectural language for all of the refuges is one and the same so that they keep a recognizable identity throughout the park. Wood is used as a main construction material, for structural, aesthetic, and sustainability issues. The façades of the project are wooden claddings, which are only pierced to allow the gaze of the inhabitants toward the landscapes. Access to the shelters is provided with board walks allowing pedestrians to penetrate the surrounding vegetation without harming it before arriving at the refuges.

The main module of the construction is a façade module of 100 × 240 centimeters in which the openings are integrated. The spaces are grouped into three modules that make up the program: a day module, a night module, and a module dedicated to observation. Being in landscapes with very varied characteristics, the refuges react to their specific milieu. In each refuge the space modules position themselves in response to the various environments and influence the overall volume of construction.

The views are a key element of the project. They organize the interior spaces and the openings in order to guide the gaze into the landscape. The interior of the project is designed with minimal spaces, integrated into the grid dictated by the façade module. A little generosity is given to the common spaces in order to allow a relaxed exchange between the inhabitants. In order to utilize the space economically, the furniture is integrated into the wall and façade modules. Also, different spaces have different climatic conditions, providing isolated and heated spaces, intermediate temperate spaces, and the observatory, which is not conditioned at all. Materiality follows the logic of the climatic condition of each space. The wood is therefore tinted white in the heated spaces, while in the observatory the wood is uncovered.

The project aims to be self-sufficient in both water and energy resources. This is why the building services are adapted to rainwater collection. Solar panels on the roof cover the electricity needs, and the façades are designed to provide sufficient passive solar gain to heat the spaces.

— *Marion Aubert / Océane Perrone*

Ground floor

Top floor

Elevation

Architecture: Taw & Exe Valley

10 Colleton Manor—Public House

Alexis Corre / Tanguy Mulard

Location: Chulmleigh, North Devon
Owner: Simon and Grania Philipps
Architect: unknown / renovated in 1988 by Knapp Hicks & Partners
Date: 11th century
Surface: 620 acres
Landscape architect: unknown

Colleton Manor

Colleton is a hamlet and former manor in the parish of Chulmleigh, in the North Devon district. It is situated on the east side of the valley formed by the river Taw. The river Taw is followed by the A377 and the railway which constitute a dynamic axis connecting Barnstable in the north and Exeter in the south. Colleton lies between this axis and the village of Chulmleigh, which lies about 2 kilometers further east.

The manor dates from the 11th century. It was substantially extended and rebuilt during the 17th century. Most of what we see today is the result of this intervention. Colleton is actually the former barton, referring to the demesne farm of Chulmleigh's manor; it only obtained the status of a "manor" during the 20th century. Colleton is made of several buildings, among them a gatehouse, a chapel, and a few barns. Acting almost like a village itself, the buildings create many outside conditions, similar to an urban setting. It also benefits from its elevation by offering splendid views into the valley.

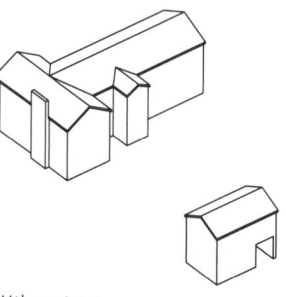

11th century

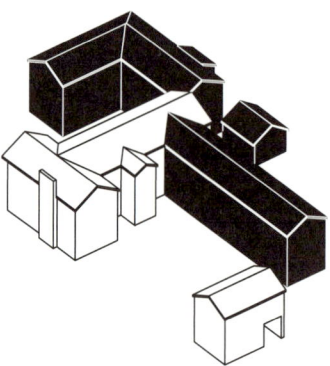

17th century

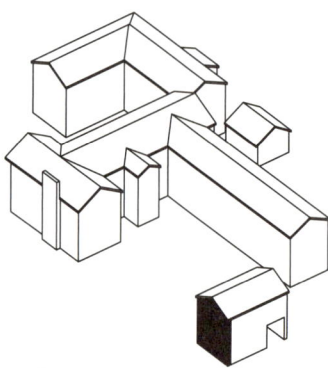

20th century

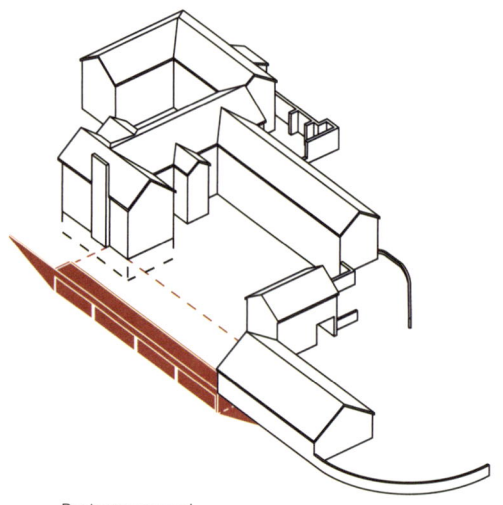

Project proposal

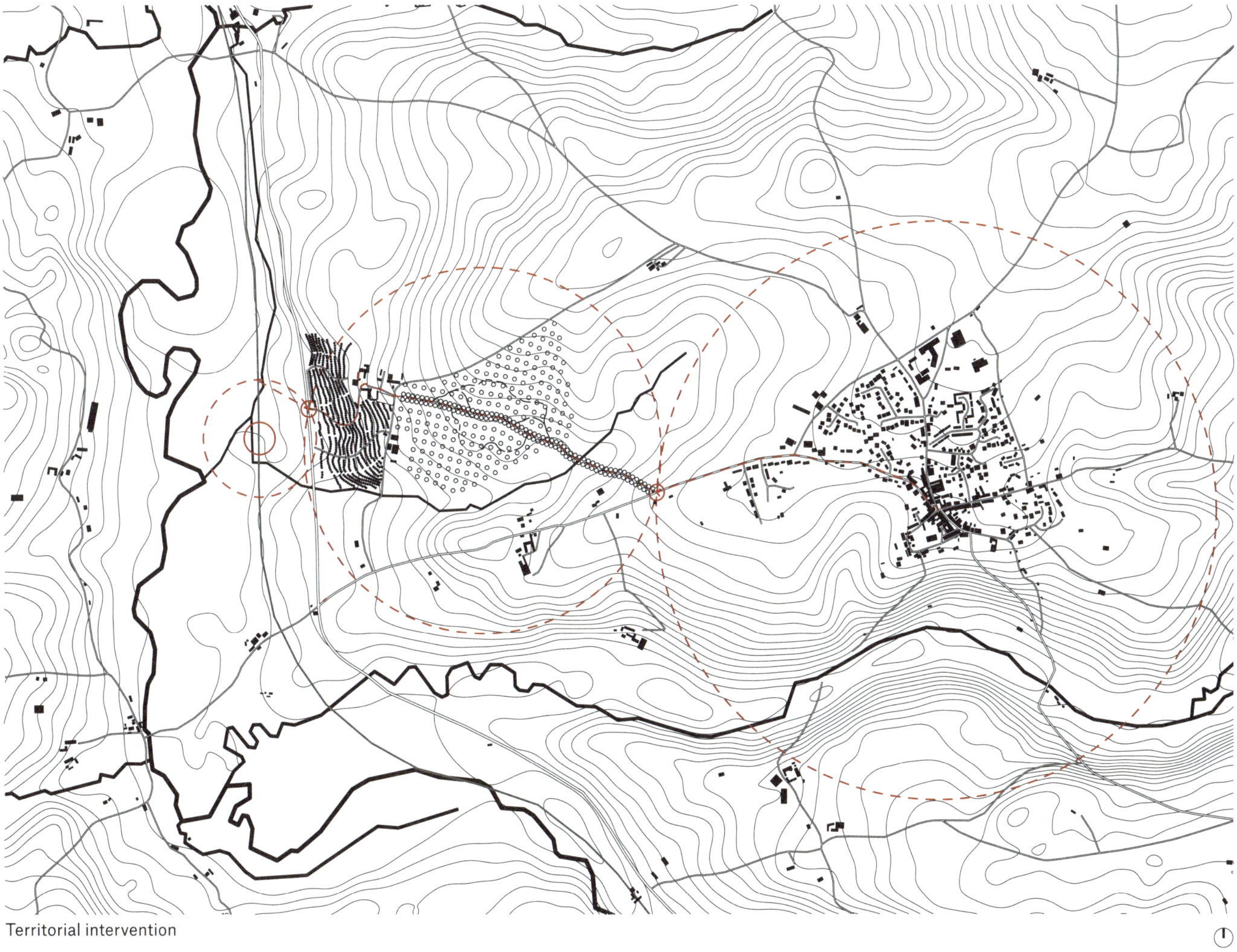

Territorial intervention

Elevation

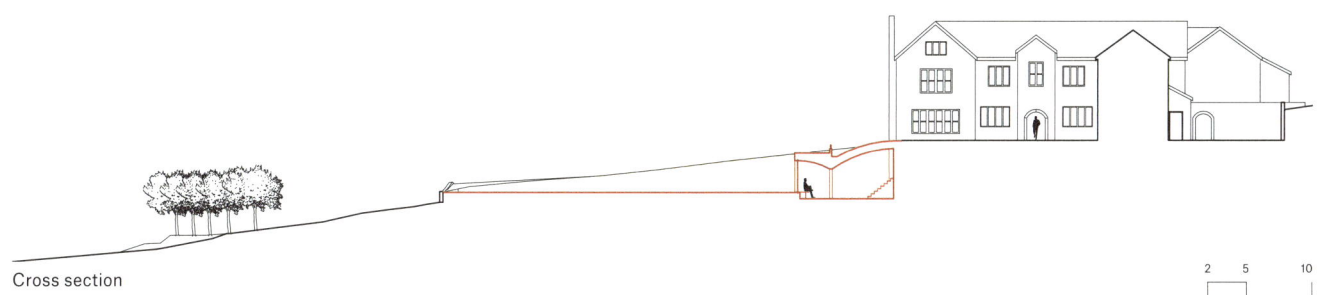

Cross section

Architecture: Taw & Exe Valley 183

Colleton Barton viewed from south west, showing the River Taw at the bottom of the valley [xi]

Drawing of the manor by Edward Ashworth, 1892 [xii]

Entrance of the manor

Partial view of the park from the manor

Public House

North Devon, a rural area sparsely settled, is left out of the economic development of the region, which is concentrated in two poles: the cities of Exeter and Barnstaple. This remote region is crossed by the valleys of the rivers of Taw and Exe, holding the infrastructure spine formed by the railway and the A377, which links Barnstaple and Exeter. Chulmleigh village is a local center for a large area due to the sparse settlement and the lack of other facilities in the surrounding area. Its regional importance offers the possibility of renewal of sociability in the general scope of improving the social dynamism in the area.

Located on the axis linking Chulmleigh to the Taw-Exe spine, Colleton Manor can constitute a new gate for Chulmleigh, becoming a landmark for the social identity and dynamism of the whole area. The project is viewed as part of a territorial strategy aiming to link Chulmleigh to the dynamic spine with a new axis crossing Colleton Manor. This new axis is established by infrastructures such as a new train station, a road reaching Chulmleigh, and landscape elements, such as a new orchard.

The project intends to form the threshold between the new orchard and the manor. It is articulated by using the existing cellar as a transition space to an underground extension. The threshold is constituted by a space in the garden with an elongated glass façade allowing the visual relationship with the orchard. The terrain above the extension is slightly undulated in order to preserve the direct view from the manor. The unhindered view reaches the existing ha-ha that separates the manor's garden and the first trees of the orchard where the new path crosses to the main entrance. The entire intervention remains imperceivable from the manor in order not to put in question the manor's immediate relationship to the landscape, nor its precious view.

The extension is accessed from the manor by the quite exiguous stairs leading to the cellar. Since the extension is underground, the whole structure is made in concrete. To adapt to the material of the manor, existing stones are used as an aggregate for the concrete. In this way the new walls will gradually resemble the existing buildings. The ceiling adapts itself to the terrain above. Two curves underline the two different ambiences. On the darker side, the space creates more intimate conditions including the typical British pub booth. The sill of the windows is expanded inwards, forming a long continuous bench. Sitting on this bench one rests at level with the ha-ha and has a direct experience of the landscape, within a more contemplative ambience.

— *Alexis Corre / Tanguy Mulard*

Ground floor

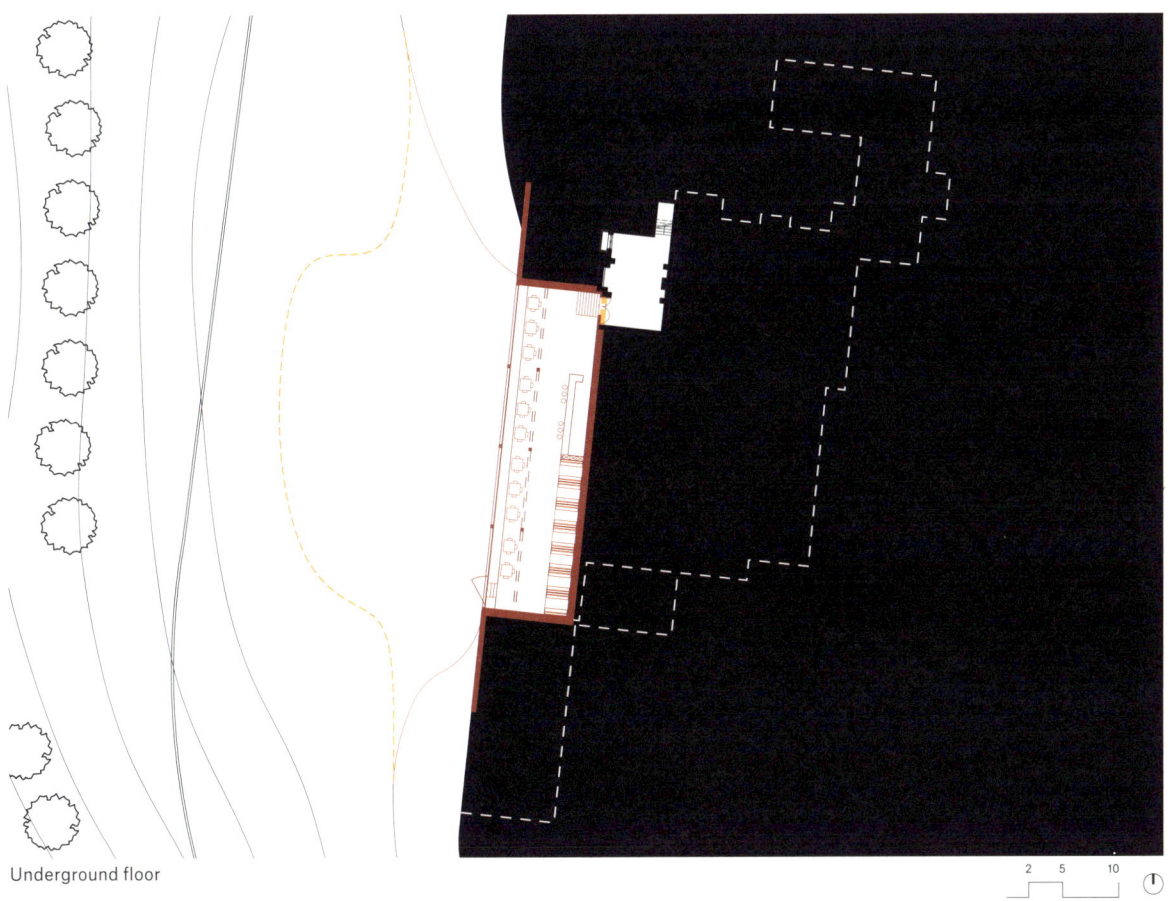

Underground floor

Architecture: Taw & Exe Valley 185

Visualization: View of the park from the window

Visualization: View of the bar

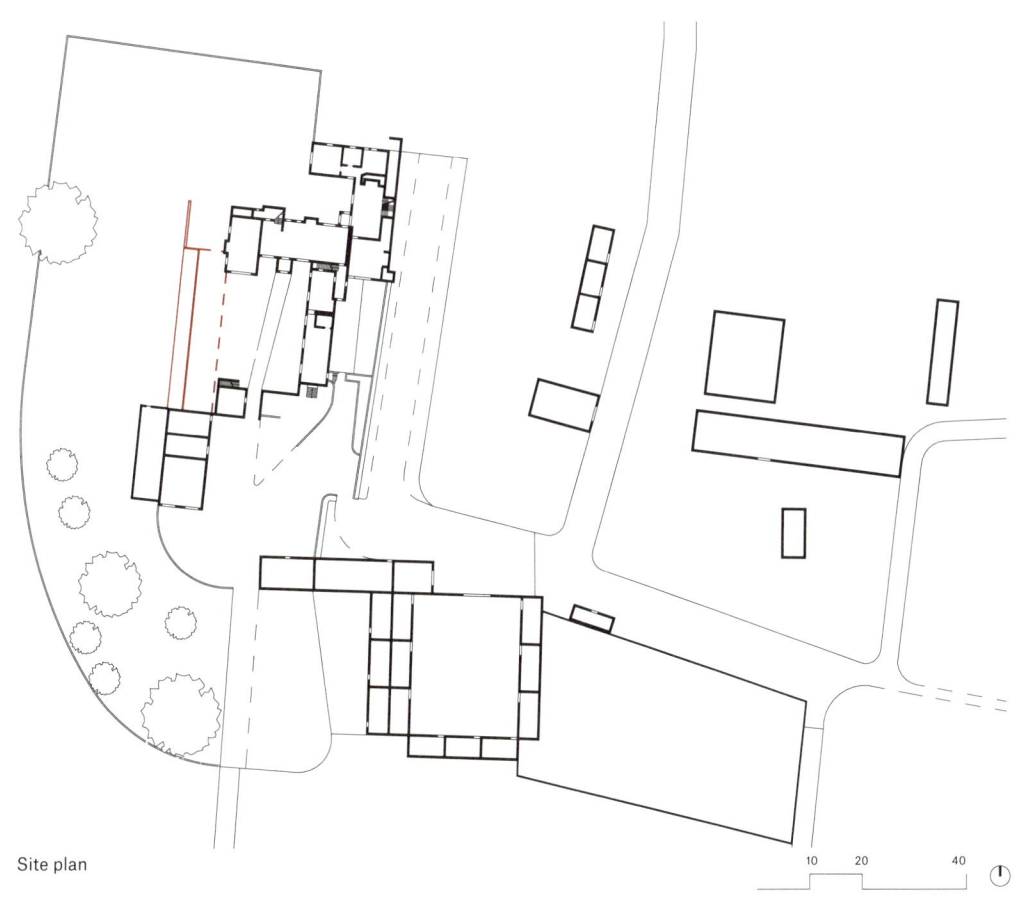

Site plan

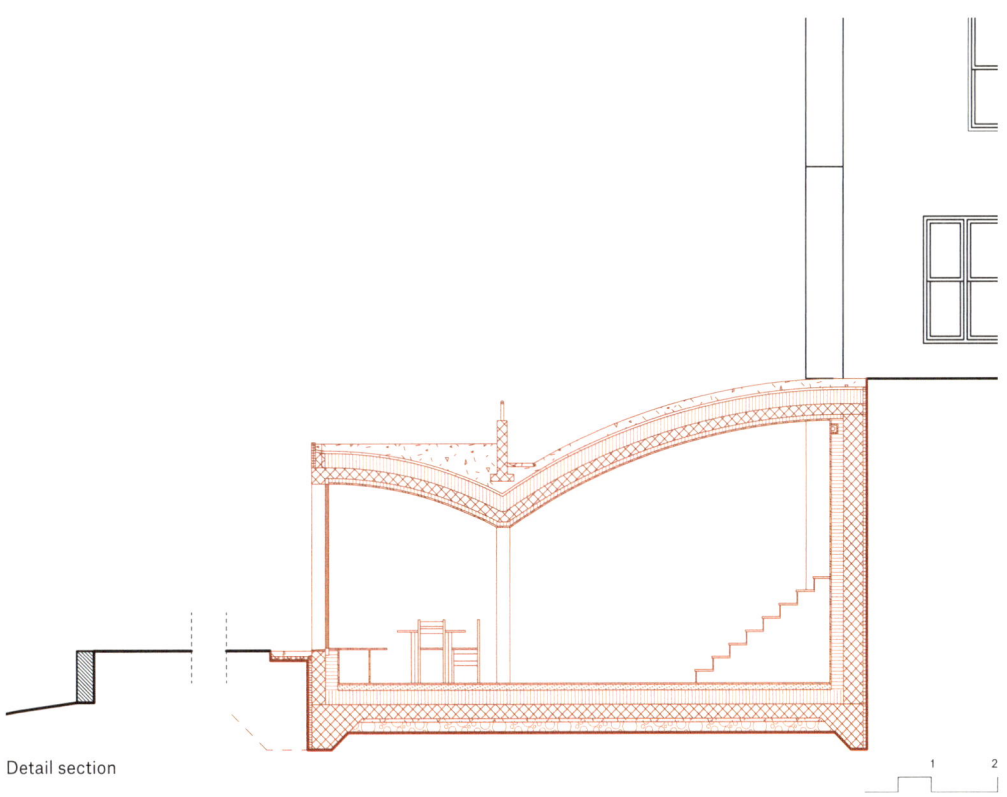

Detail section

Architecture: Taw & Exe Valley 187

11 Eggesford House — Student Housing

Camille Ehrensperger / Tania Versteegh

Location: Chulmleigh, North Devon
Owner: Edward and Jo Howell
Architect: Thomas Lee
Date: 1830s
Surface: unknown
Landscape architect: Nathaniel Richmond

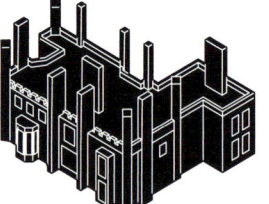

1826–1832
Construction

Eggesford House

Eggesford House was constructed in the 1820s on the Eggesford estate at the Heywood Barton, located up a hill and overlooking the parkland in the valley below. The Tudor-Gothic-style building was crowned by an astonishing number of chimneys, turrets, battlements, and buttresses. In 1873, Eggesford was tied to an estate of nearly 16,500 acres, the seventh largest in the county.

After the Eggesford station was built in 1854, the manor house was extended, and a small tower was added next to the manor. This is when the house was at its most developed stage.

In 1923, after the abandonment of the house and its decay, a demolition sale was organized and resulted in the distribution of the house's architectural elements across the whole county. The house remained a ruin until the London architect Ed Howell and his wife Jo bought it in 1992. They decided to restore it and inserted a new construction within the surviving walls of the main body of the building.

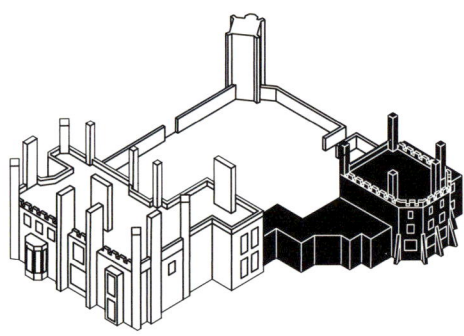

1853–1889
Lymington wing and tower

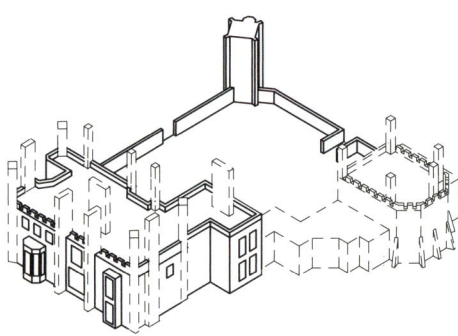

1927–1992
Demolition sales and decay

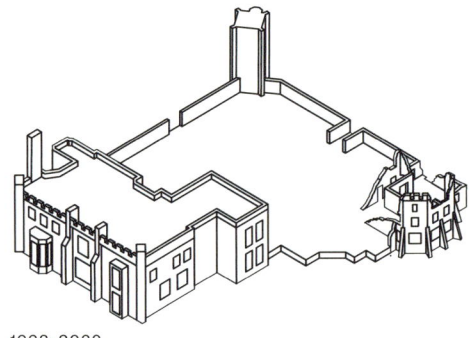

1992–2020
Renovation

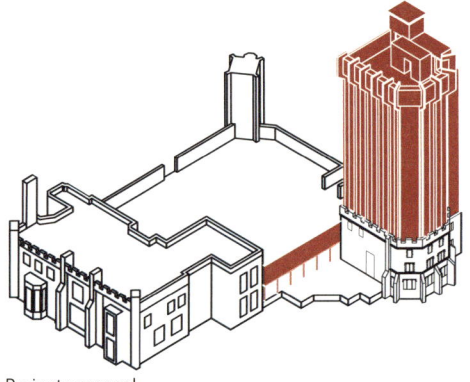

Project proposal

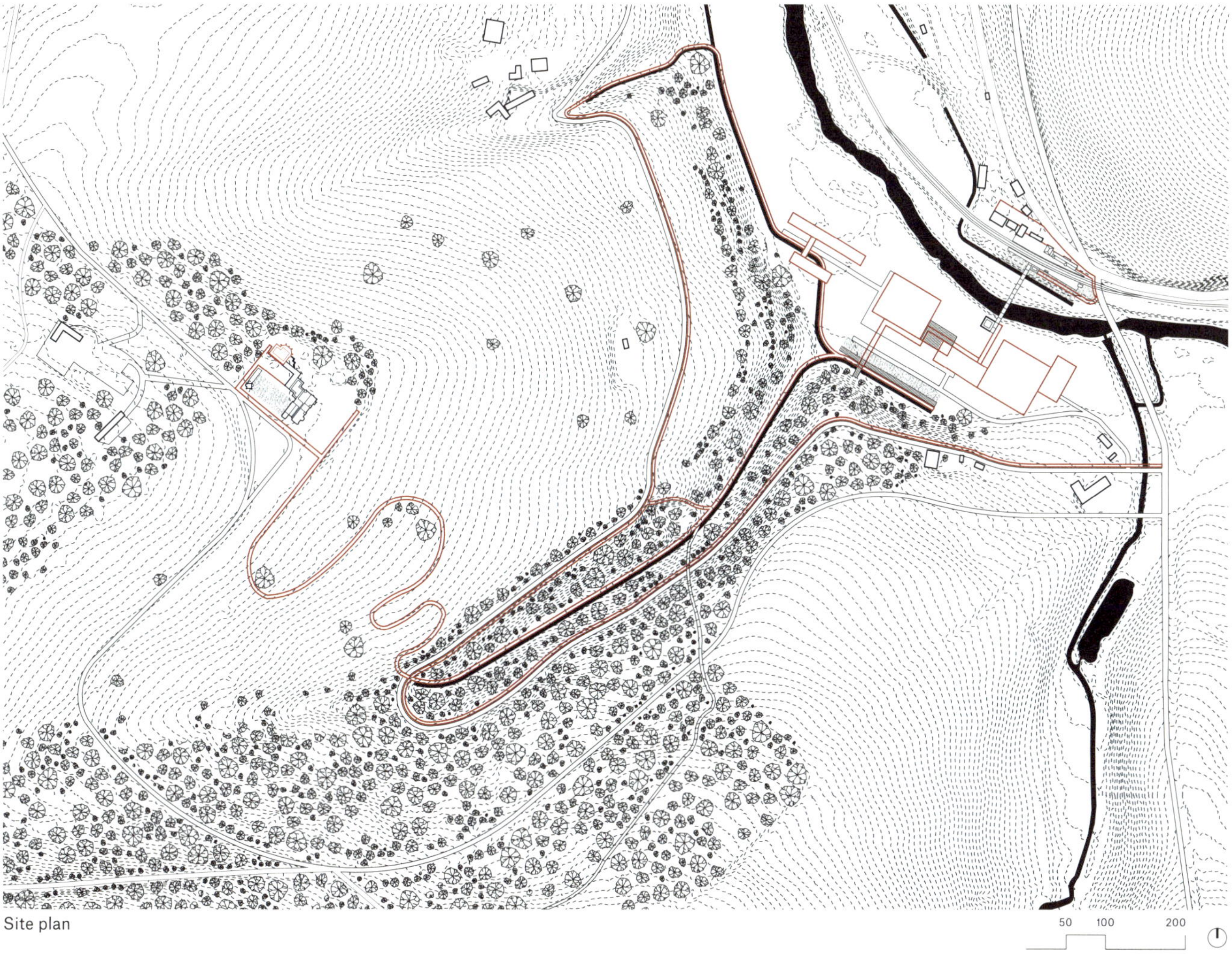

Site plan

Old picture of the manor in its original state

View of the ruin

Elevation

Architecture: Taw & Exe Valley

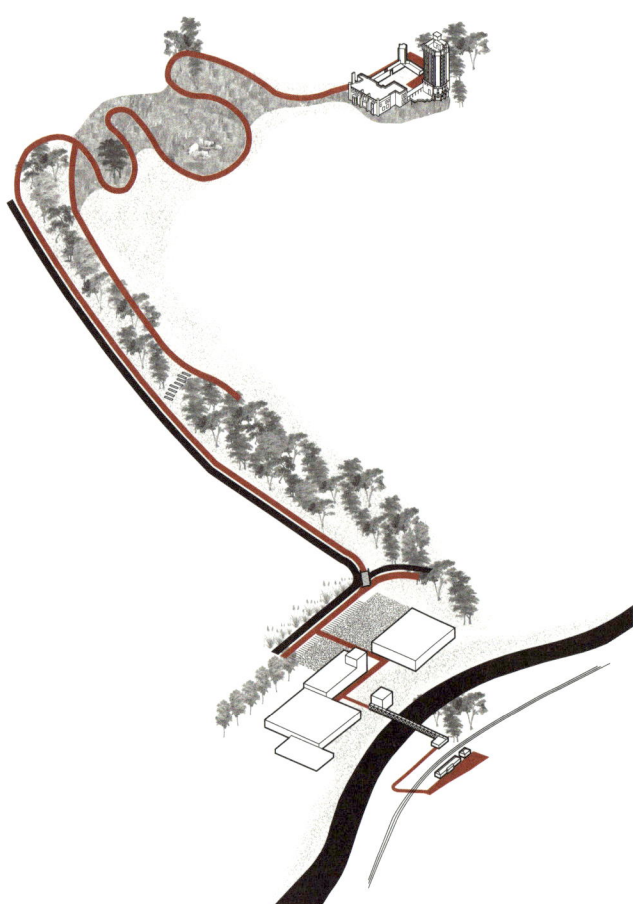

The path from the train to the manor

Part of the ruin *xiv*

The manor before renovation *xv*

Student Housing

Eggesford is part of a territorial system characterized by an infrastructural spine running through the Taw Valley. This spine is constituted by the River Taw, a main road, and a railway line. By connecting the two coasts of the South West and the cities of Barnstaple and Exeter, this figure forms the main communication axis within the territory. Despite their strategic position along this spine, Eggesford and the region are facing some major challenges, such as a massive exodus of young people due to limited employment opportunities.

At the same time the region strongly conveys the imaginary of the idyllic English countryside. Sited within the hilly and dense woodlands, Eggesford House is part of this imaginary. Standing up on a hill and surrounded by the woods of the Taw Valley, the house has been a source of inspiration for artists and poets since its construction in the 1820s. The landscape around the house and its idyllic views were depicted and described by the topographer and artist John Swete and the English novelist and poet Thomas Hardy. After his stay in Eggesford House, Hardy described the enchanting walk from the train station to the manor house.

Using Eggesford train station for access and Eggesford forest as a resource, the project proposes a new carpentry school at the station in order to counteract the exodus of young people and create new job opportunities. To offer the students a residence, Eggesford house would be partly turned into student housing.

The project proposes new sequenced promenades within the landscape to access the manor house easily from the train station. The paths, adapting to the topography, refer to John Swete's paintings and the English garden imaginary. Up on the hill, the student housing, a 40-meters high structure, acts as landmark. It articulates itself next to the existing courtyard of Eggesford House and uses the ruin of the former Lymington wing tower as foundation. The courtyard is divided into two distinctive parts, one accessible by the current owner, the other by the students. This allows the exterior spaces to be shared while offering privacy for the users.

The common space of the garden extends to the first two floors of the student housing, where a double height lobby welcomes students and visitors. From the third floor on, the tower contains the bedrooms and the common living spaces for the students. The tower is conceived as stacked houses, with four bedrooms on each floor. A double-height kitchen allows the dining area to be visually connected to the living room located above.

To achieve a robust structure in line with the architectural language of the ruin, mineral materials are used. The use of bricks and glass allows the tower to blend in with the existing building. The structural elements, made out of concrete, underline the verticality of the ruin. Strengthening the walls, they reinterpret the imaginary of the Gothic buttresses and refer to the vertical elements that once crowned the manor.

— *Camille Ehrensperger / Tania Versteegh*

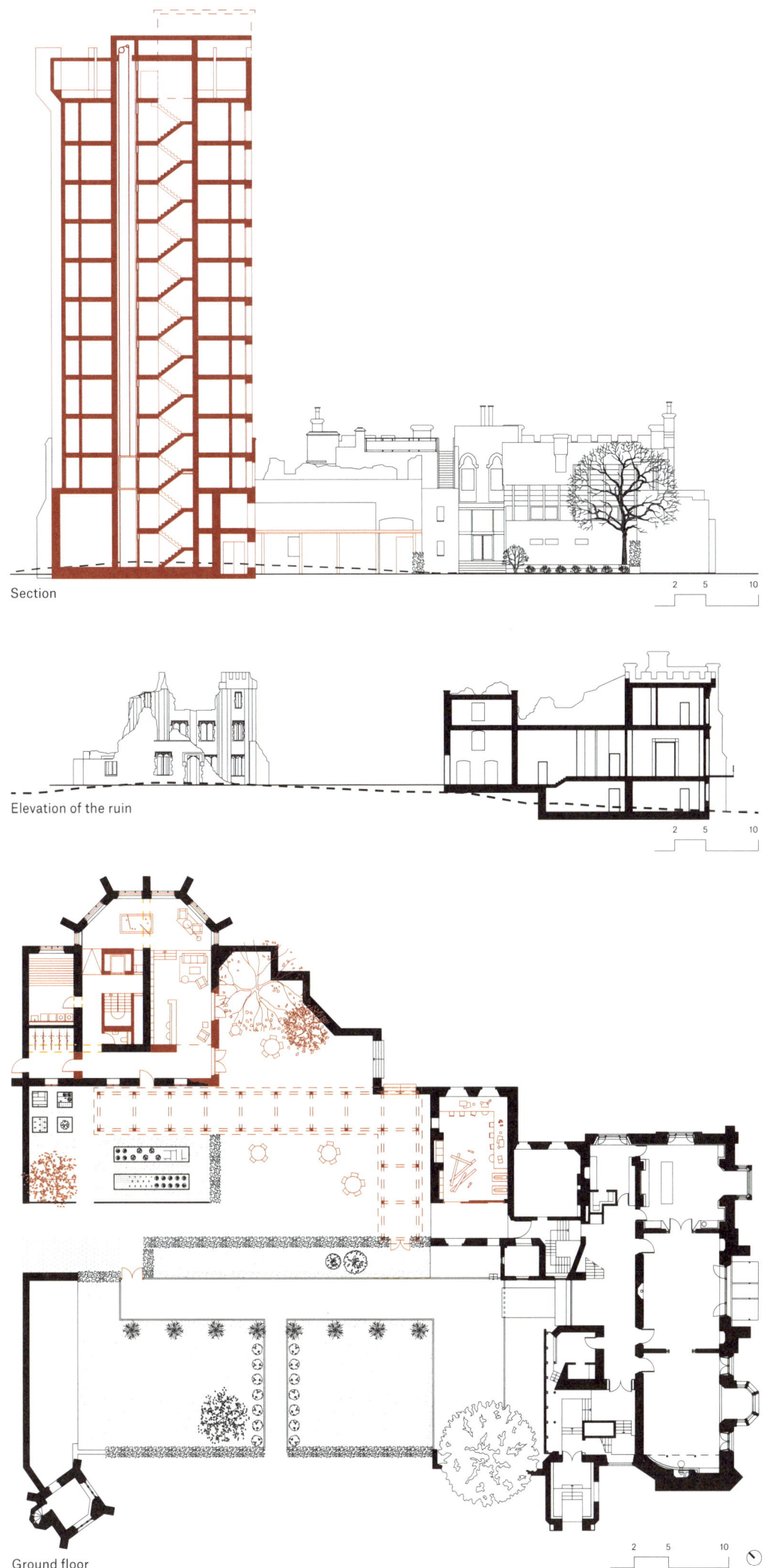

Section

Elevation of the ruin

Ground floor

Architecture: Taw & Exe Valley 191

Visualization: View of the living room

Visualization: View of the roof terrace

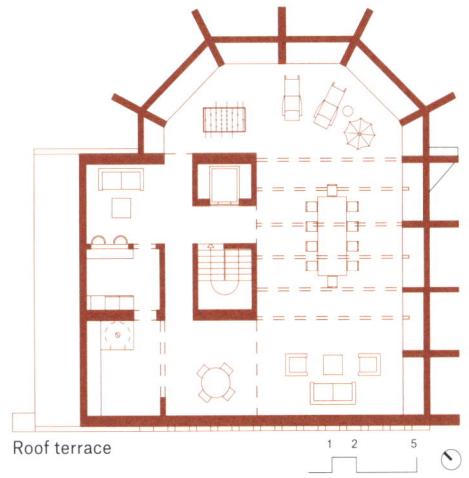
Roof terrace

Bedroom floor

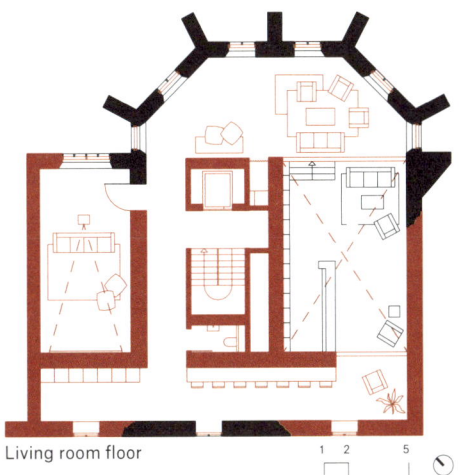
Living room floor

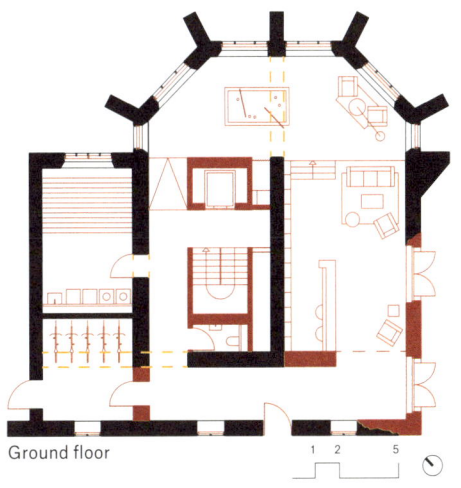
Ground floor

Visualization: View of the project at arrival

Architecture: Taw & Exe Valley 193

Notes and References

Teaching and Research in Architecture

1. E.-E. Viollet-le-Duc, "XIV Entretien," *Entretiens sur l'architecture*, vol. 2 (Paris: A. Morel et Cie Editeurs, 1872), p. 173.
2. William Morris, *Hopes and Fears for Art* (1882; Worcestershire: Read Books, 2012).

The Commons Revisited

1. Bruno Wollheim, *A Bigger Picture* (London: Coluga Pictures Ltd., 2010), https://www.a-bigger-picture.com.
2. Wollheim, *Bigger Picture*.
3. Ernest Pollard, Max D. Hooper, and Norman Winfrid Moore, *Hedges* (London: Collins, 1974).
4. Harry Mount, *How England Made the English* (London: Penguin, 2012), pp. 120–144.
5. Peter Linebaugh, "Enclosures from the Bottom Up," *Radical History Review* 108 (Fall 2010), p. 14.
6. Garrett Hardin, "The Tragedy of the Commons," *Science*, New Series, vol. 162, no. 3859 (Dec. 13, 1968), pp. 1243–1248
7. See: Elinor Ostrom, *Governing the Commons: The Evolution of Institutions for Collective Action* (Cambridge: Cambridge University Press, 1995), Linebaugh, "Enclosures from the Bottom Up," pp. 11–27, John E. Martin, *Feudalism to Capitalism: Peasant and Landlord in English Agrarian Development* (New Jersey: Humanities Press, 1983), Silvia Federici, *Caliban and the Witch: Women, the Body, and Primitive Accumulation*, (Brooklyn : Autonomedia, 2014), David Harvey, "The Future of the Commons," *Radical History Review* 109 (Winter 2011), pp. 101–107, Allan Greer, "Commons and Enclosure in the Colonization of North America," *American Historical Review*, 117, no. 2, (April 2012), pp. 365–386.
8. Linebaugh, "Enclosures from the Bottom Up."
9. Peter Linebaugh and Marcus Rediker, *The Many Headed Hydra: Sailors, Slaves, Commoners, and the Hidden History of the Revolutionary Atlantic* (London: Verso, 2000), p. 44.
10. Raymond Williams, *The Country and the City* (New York: Oxford University Press, 1973), p. 37.
11. Anthony D. Smith, "Memory and Modernity," *Nations and Nationalism* 2 (1996), 371–388, p. 385.
12. Robert Frost, "Mending Wall", *Gleeditions*, 17, Apr. 2011, www.gleeditions.com/mendingwall/students/pages.asp?lid=305&pg=5. Originally published in *Tendencies in Modern American Poetry*, edited by Amy Lowell (Macmillan, 1917), pp. 92–93.
13. Paul Readman, *Storied Ground* (Cambridge: Cambridge University Press, 2018).
14. Ibid., p. 9.
15. Williams, *Country and the City*, p. 42.
16. Ibid., pp. 35–36.
17. Readman, *Storied Ground*, p. 19.
18. Estimated by Paul Readman in *Storied Ground*, p. 126, derived from the list of acquisitions given in National Trust, Annual Reports, Swindon, National Trust Archives.
19. The Domesday Book is a detailed survey and valuation of landed property in England at the end of the 11th century. The survey was ordered by William the Conqueror at Christmas 1085 and undertaken the following year. It records who held the land and how it was used, and also includes information on how this had changed since the Norman Conquest in 1066.
20. Keith Feiling, *A History of England: From the Coming of the English to 1918* (London: Macmillan & Co., 1950), p. 98.
21. Equivalent to one Acre, that being the most efficient division of land when ploughing the soil with an ox. One Acre is made up of four Furlongs which is the length a single ploughman with an ox can plough without rest, four of these Furlongs is the area which can be ploughed in one day.
22. Fredric Seebohm, *The English Village Community, Examined in Its Relations to the Manorial and Tribal Systems and to the Common or Open-Field System of Husbandry; an Essay in Economic History* (London: Longmans Green and Co., 1883) pp. 1–12.
23. Martin, *Feudalism to Capitalism*, pp. 27–45.
24. Linebaugh, "Enclosures from the Bottom Up."
25. Williams, *Country and the City*, p. 39.
26. E. P. Thompson, *The Making of the English Working Class* (New York: Vintage Books, 1966), p. 197.
27. Williams, *Country and the City*, p. 39.
28. Williams, *Country and the City*, p. 39.
29. David Littlejohn, *The Fate of the English Country House* (New York: Oxford University Press, 1997), p. 19.

[*Fig. 1*] © David Hockney. Photo credit: Prudence Cuming Associates, Collection of Fine Arts, Boston.
[*Fig. 2*] Creative Commons License (CC BY-SA 3.0).
[*Fig. 3*] 1895. 8.6 x 15.8 cm, framed, in Hardy's 1891 novel *Tess of the D'Urbervilles: A Pure Woman*, vol. 1 of the McIlvaine Osgood, Complete Uniform Edition of the Wessex Novels, in 17 vols. (1895–1897)
[*Fig. 4*] Derek Harper / Reave below White Tor / CC BY-SA 2.0. Creative Commons Attribution Share-alike license 2.0.
[*Fig. 5*] Andrew Fleming, *The Dartmoor Reaves*, (Oxford: Oxbow Books, 1988).
[*Fig. 6*] William R. Shepherd, *Historical Atlas* (New York: Henry Holt and Company, 1923).
[*Fig. 7*] William Cobbett, *Rural Rides* (1830; repr., Harmondsworth: Penguin Books, 1979), p. 313.

Territory: General Facts

1. www.metoffice.gov.uk/binaries/content/assets/metofficegovuk/pdf/weather/learn-about/uk-past-events/regional-climates/south-west-england_-climate---met-office.pdf.
2. G. Metcalf, F. Chambers, A. Charlesworth, V. Forrest, J. Hunt, K. McEwen, K. Russell, and S. Schofield, eds., Warming to the Idea, Technical Report, South West Region Climate Change Impacts Scoping Study, Cheltenham, UK, 2003.
3. Eddie Smith, "Portrait of the South West," *Reg Trends* 42 (2010), 43–59. https://doi.org/10.1057/rt.2010.4.
4. Office for National Statistics. Contains public sector information licensed under the Open Government Licence v3.0.
5. Smith, "Portrait of the South West."

[*Fig. 1*] laba.
[*Fig. 2*] David Thomas, *An Advanced Geography of the Bristish Isles* (Hulton Educational Publications Ltd., 1974), p. 169.
[*Fig. 3*] BGS Geology in British Geological Survey, accessed October 16, 2020, https://www.bgs.ac.uk/products/digitalmaps/DiGMapGB_625.html.
[*Fig. 4*] Met Office, accessed October 16, 2020, https://www.metoffice.gov.uk/research/climate/maps-and-data/uk-actual-and-anomaly-maps.
[*Fig. 5*] Met Office.
[*Fig. 6*] Met Office.
[*Fig. 7*] Thomas, *An Advanced Geography of the British Isles*.
[*Fig. 8*] Provisional Agricultural Land Classification (ALC) in Data Gov., accessed October 16, 2020, https://data.gov.uk/dataset/952421ecda63-4569-817d-4d6399df40a1/provisional-agricultural-land-classification-alc.
[*Fig. 9*] Office for National Statistics, accessed October 16, 2020, https://www.ons.gov.uk/peoplepopulationandcommunity/populationandmigration/populationestimates/articles/overviewoftheukpopulation/july2017.
[*Fig. 10*] laba students.
[*Fig. 11*] Ordnance Survey Open Roads, accessed October 16, 2020, https://www.ordnancesurvey.co.uk/business-government/products/open-map-roads.
[*Fig. 12a*] Leigh Shaw-Taylor and Xuesheng You, *The Development of the Railway Network in Britain 1825-1911* (Semantic Scholar, 2018), p. 16.
[*Fig. 12b*] Ibid., p. 19.
[*Fig. 12c*] Ibid., p. 22.
[*Fig. 12d*] laba, Open Street Map.

i. Office for National Statistics, National Records of Scotland, and Northern Ireland Statistics and Research Agency, 2011 Census Aggregate Data. UK Data Service, June 2016, accessed September 14, 2020, DOI: http://dx.doi.org/10.5257/census/aggregate-2011-1.
ii. laba student.
iii. laba student.
iv. laba student.
v. laba student.
vi. laba student.

Territory: Avon Green Belt

1. David Northrup, ed., *The Atlantic Slave Trade* (Lexington, MA: D. C. Heath and Company, 1994), 134.
2. Madge Dresser, *Slavery Obscured–The Social History of the Slave Trade in an English Provincial Port* (London: Continuum, 2001).
3. Office for National Statistics. Contains public sector information licensed under the Open Government Licence v3.0.
4. UK Tech on the Global Stage, Tech Nation Report 2018, https://technation.io/insights/report-2018/bristol/.
5. Bristol Economic Briefing, September 2019, https://www.bristol.gov.uk/business-support-advice/economic-information-and-analysis www.bristol.gov.uk/documents/20182/33191/Bristol+Economic+Briefing+Web+Final+SGU+Sep19.pdf/8647105e-0b5d-f38c-5168-05c38f0b91ef.
6. Ebenezer Howard, *Garden Cities of Tomorrow* (London: Swan Sinnenschein & Co., 1902), p. 24.
7. Frederic James Osborn, *Green-belt Cities* (New York: Schocken, 1969), p. 15.
8. Rowan Moore, "Is it time to rethink Britain's green belt," *The Observer*, October 19, 2014, www.theguardian.com/politics/2014/oct/19/is-it-time-to-rethink-the-green-belt.
9. West of England Joint Spatial Plan Green Belt Assessment, November 2015.
10. UK House Price Index search tool available under the Open Government License v3.0, https://landregistry.data.gov.uk/.

11 Department for Farming and Rural Affairs, Agriculture in the United Kingdom 2018, © Crown, 2019, https://www.gov.uk/government/statistics/agriculture-in-the-united-kingdom-2018.
12 Food Chain Analysis Group, DEFRA, Food Security and the UK: An Evidence and Analysis Paper, December 2006.
13 Bristol City Council, Bristol Development Framework—Core Strategy, adopted June 2011.
14 Bath and North East Somerset Council, Bath and North East Somerset Core Strategy—part 1 of the Local Plan, adopted July 2014.
15 Kevin Lynch, *Good City Form* (Cambridge, MA: MIT Press, 1981), 294.
[Fig. 1] Northrup, *The Atlantic Slave Trade,* p. 22.
[Fig. 2] R.W. Gallois, *The Geology of the Hot Springs at Bath Spa, Somerset*, Geoscience in South-West England, vol. 11, p. 169.
[Fig. 3] Accessed October 16, 2020, https://www.plumplot.co.uk/.
[Fig. 4] Quartet Communitiy Foundation, Bristol: Area Profile, July 2014, accessed October 30, 2020, https://quartetcf.org.uk/wp-content/uploads/2015/05/bristol-area-profile-final.pdf.
[Fig. 5] Strategic Planning, Bristol City Council, Office for National Statistics, Ordnance Survey 100023406, 2013.
[Fig. 6] Ibid.
[Fig. 7] World Population Review, accessed October 30, 2020, https://worldpopulationreview.com/world-cities/bath-population.
[Fig. 8] Office for National Statistics, www.ons.gov.uk.
[Fig. 9] laba.
[Fig. 10] laba.
[Fig. 11] laba.
[Fig. 12] Green Belt in Natural England, accessed October 16, 2020, https://www.cpre.org.uk/what-we-do/housing-and-planning/green-belts.
[Fig. 13] West of England, Strategic Green Infrastructure Framework, p. 1, accessed October 16, 2020, http://www.westofengland.org/media/216918/gi%20framework%20020611.pdf.
[Fig. 14] Campaign to Protect Rural England, Avon Green Belt, accessed October 30, 2020, www.cpre.org.uk/wp-content/uploads/2019/11/Avon_factsheet_2018.pdf.
[Fig. 15] West of England, Strategic Green Infrastructure Framework, p. 18, accessed October 16, 2020, http://www.westofengland.org/media/216918/gi%20framework%20020611.pdf.
[Fig. 16] Ibid., p. 21.
[Fig. 17] Hometrack, accessed October 30, 2020, https://www.hometrack.com/uk/insight/uk-house-price-index/.
[Fig. 18] laba.
[Fig. 19] laba.
[Fig. 20] laba.
[Fig. 21] laba.
[Fig. 22] laba.
i   commons.wikimedia.org.
ii laba student.
iii © Robert Cutts, Edward Colston, and Borad Quay, Bristol / Flickr / CC BY-SA 2.0.
iv Photo credit: Nicholas Ostrowski, Twitter@nicklalor, https://twitter.com/nicklalor/status/1273928378345758720.
v   Ben Birchall/PA Wire/PA Images.
vi laba student.
vii laba student.
viii laba student.
ix Photo credit: getabanksy.com.
x   © Ebenezer Howard, *To-morrow: A Peaceful Path to Real Reform* (London: Swan Sonnenschein & Co., Ltd., 1898).
xi Ibid.
xii laba student.
xiii Google maps, 2020, www.google.com/maps
xiv Mirroxpix/Reach Licensing.
xv Source unknown.
xvi laba student.

Territory: Dorset Coast

1   Guidance: Areas of Outstanding Natural Beauty (AONBs): Designation and Management. All content is available under the Open Government Licence v3.0, except where otherwise stated, © Crown.
2   City status in the UK does not automatically apply based on any particular criteria but was historically granted to towns with diocesan cathedrals. City status is given by royal designation by the reigning monarch. The holding of city status confers no special rights and as of 2020 there are 69 cities in the United Kingdom.
3   Thomas Hardy, *Return of the Native* (New York: Random House, 2001), p. 5.
4   Ibid., p. 1.
5   David Glover, Landscapes Review—Final Report, 2019, https://assets.publishing.service.gov.uk/government/uploads/system/uploads/attachment_data/file/833726/landscapes-review-final-report.pdf.
6   Ibid.
7   Ibid.
8   Ibid.
9   Martin Boddy and Hannah Hickman, "The Demise of Strategic Planning? The Impact of the Abolition of Regional Spatial Strategy in a Growth Region," *The Town Planning Review* 84, January 2013.
10 CPRE, What's the Plan? May 2020, https://www.cpre.org.uk/wp-content/uploads/2020/05/Whats-the-plan-_Full-report_2020.pdf.
11 West Dorset, Weymouth & Portland Local Plan, 2015, https://www.dorsetcouncil.gov.uk/planning-buildings-land/planning-policy/west-dorset-and-weymouth-portland/adopted-local-plan/pdfs/alp/west-dorset-weymouth-portland-local-plan-2015.pdf.
12 Ministry of Housing, Communities and Local Government, National Planning Policy Framework, February 2019, p. 21, https://assets.publishing.service.gov.uk/government/uploads/system/uploads/attachment_data/file/810197/NPPF_Feb_2019_revised.pdf.
13 The Right to Buy Scheme, legislated under the Thatcher government in 1979, gave all tenants of government-owned housing the opportunity to purchase their home at a discounted rate. Local Authorities were obliged to offer mortgages on these properties with no deposit. By 1987 more than 1 million council houses had been sold to their tenants. Central government required that Local Councils use the revenue generated from the sales to clear all council debts, before it could be used for building new housing stock, effectively drastically reducing the number of council houses in Britain.
14 Lewis Mumford, *The City In Its History: Its Origins, Its Transformations, and Its Prospects*, (New York: Harcourt, Brace & World, 1961), 421.
15 Mumford, *The City In Its History*, 500.

[Fig. 1] Natural England Open Data, accessed October 16, 2020, https://naturalengland-defra.opendata.arcgis.com/datasets/6f2ad07d-91304ad79cdecd52489d5046_0.
[Fig. 2] Ibid.
[Fig. 3] Ibid.
[Fig. 4] Accessed October 16, 2020, https://www.plumplot.co.uk/.
[Fig. 5] Department for Environment, Food & Rural Affairs DEFR; Landscapes Review, Final Report 2019.
[Fig. 6] National Statistics, accessed October 30, 2020, https://www.gov.uk/government/statistics/english-housing-survey-2018-to-2019-second-homes-fact-sheet.
[Fig. 7] The countryside charity, What's the Plan? May, 2020, accessed October 16, 2020, https://www.cpre.org.uk/resources/whats-the-plan-full-report/.
[Fig. 8] Ibid.
[Fig. 9] laba.
[Fig. 10] Dorset Council, West Dorset Mapping, accessed October 16, 2020, https://westdorsetdc.maps.arcgis.com/apps/webappviewer/index.html?id=209d87c-9c6624c3386cda6eaee755a4e.
[Fig. 11] Dorset Council, accessed October 16, 2020 https://www.dorsetcouncil.gov.uk/planning-buildings-land/planning-policy/adopted-local-plans/west-dorset-weymouth-and-portland-adopted-local-plan.aspx.
[Fig. 12] Lewes Community Land Trust, accessed October 30, 2020, https://www.lewesclt.com/about-land-trust.
[Fig. 13] laba.
[Fig. 14] Natural England, accessed October 16, 2020 https://www.gov.uk/government/publications/national-character-area-profiles-data-for-local-decision-making/national-character-area-profiles#ncas-in-south-west-england.
[Fig. 15] laba.
[Fig. 16] laba.
i   laba student.
ii laba student.
iii © Ingrid Pollard
iv laba student.
v   laba student.
vi laba student.
vii laba student.
viii laba student.
ix James Thormod.
x   Students from London Metropolitan University, Unit 15.
xi laba student.
xii laba student.
xiii laba student.

Territory: South Hams

1   British Geological Survey, Regional Geological Summaries, South-west England v2, www.bgs.ac.uk/research/ukgeology/regionalGeology/home.html.
2   John Leland, *The Itinerary of John Leland in or about the years 1535–1543*, ed. Lucy Toulmin Smith (London: George Bell and Sons, 1906).
3   Hardy, *Return of the Native*, p. 5.
4   Rod Edward, Visitor Attraction Trends in England 2018—Full Report, August 2019, www.visitbritain.org/sites/default/files/vb-corporate/Documents-Library/documents/England-documents/annual_attractions_survey_2018_trends_report.pdf.
5   Ina Horlings and Yoko Kanemasu, Towards an Eco-Economy? Rural Development and Farm

Tourism in Devon (UK), Cardiff University, September 2010, https://edepot.wur.nl/175640.
6 https://ec.europa.eu/info/food-farming-fisheries/key-policies/common-agricultural-policy/cap-glance_en#documents.
7 Harry Mount, *How England Made the English* (London: Penguin, 2013), 195.
8 Andrew Wasley and Madlen Davies, "The Rise of the 'Megafarm': How British Meat is Made," published online in July 17, 2017 by the Bureau of Investigation,. www.thebureauinvestigates.com/stories/2017-07-17/megafarms-uk-intensive-farming-meat.
9 DEFRA, Agriculture in the United Kingdom, © Crown, 2019.
[*Fig. 1*] British Geological Survey, Natural Environment Research Council, accessed October 16, 2020, https://mapapps.bgs.ac.uk/geologyofbritain/home.html.
[*Fig. 2*] Met Office, accessed October 16, 2020, https://www.metoffice.gov.uk/research/climate/maps-and-data/uk-actual-and-anomaly-maps.
[*Fig. 3*] laba.
[*Fig. 4*] Accessed October 16, 2020, https://www.plumplot.co.uk/.
[*Fig. 5*] laba.
[*Fig. 6*] Visit England, accessed October 30, 2020, https://trade.visitbritain.com/wp-content/uploads/2017/07/discover_england_initial_summary_report_v7_140817.pdf.
[*Fig. 7*] Devon Farms, accessed October 16, 2020, https://www.devonfarms.co.uk/.
[*Fig. 8*] European Comission, The Common Agricultural Policy, accessed October 30, 2020, https://ec.europa.eu/info/sites/info/files/food-farming-fisheries/key_policies/documents/cap-separating-facts-from-fiction_en.pdf.
[*Fig. 9*] Accessed October 16, 2020, https://www.devonlive.com/news/devon-news/rise-megafarms-how-style-563315.
[*Fig. 10*] Duchy College, The South West Diary Industry–A Vital Cog in the Economy, October 2016, accessed October 30, 2020, https://www.nfuonline.com/assets/67942.
[*Fig. 11*] Office of National Statistics, 2011.
[*Fig. 12*] Office for National Statistics, accessed October 16, 2020, https://www.ons.gov.uk/peoplepopulationandcommunity/populationandmigration/populationestimates/articles/overviewoftheukpopulation/july2017.
[*Fig. 13*] Office of National Statistics, 2011.
[*Fig. 14*] Accessed October 16, 2020, https://www.southhams.gov.uk/article/3538/South-Hams-Overview-Report.
[*Fig. 15*] The Guardian, accessed October 16, 2020, https://www.theguardian.com/news/datablog/2012/oct/22/second-homes-england-wales-detailed.
[*Fig. 16*] Regeneration economic development communities (REDC) for Devon County Council, Low carbon workspace to meet the needs of micro and small businesses in Devon, accessed October 16, 2020, https://mk0partnersdevooxv4n.kinstacdn.com/wp-content/uploads/sites/3/2020/02/RedC-Final-Report.pdf.
[*Fig. 17*] Ibid.
[*Fig. 18*] Teignbridge District Councils, accessed October 30, 2020, https://www.teignbridge.gov.uk/media/8060/2019-factsheet-2-employment.pdf.
[*Fig. 19*] laba.
[*Fig. 20*] laba.
[*Fig. 21*] laba.
[*Fig. 22*] laba.
i   laba student.
ii   laba student.
iii laba student.
iv   laba student.
v   laba student.
vi   laba student.
vii laba student.
viii laba student.
ix   laba student.

Territory: Taw & Exe Valley

1 Alisdair Rogers, Noel Castree and Rob Kitchin, *A Dictionary of Human Geography* (Oxford: Oxford University Press, 2013).
2 Local Economic Assessment, 2018 and Strategy for Growth Discussion Paper, Report to Devon County Council, April 2018.
3 Ibid.
4 Revenue Expenditure and Financing, 2019–20 Final Outturn, Statistical Release, © Crown, 2019, https://assets.publishing.service.gov.uk/government/uploads/system/uploads/attachment_data/file/812505/Local_Authority_Revenue_Expenditure_and_Financing_2019-20_Budget__England.pdf.
5 "Education, education, education," BBC News, May 14, 2007, http://news.bbc.co.uk/2/hi/uk_news/education/6564933.stm.
6 Nomis official labour market statistics. Source: ONS population survey, www.nomisweb.co.uk/reports/lmp/gor/2092957698/report.aspx?#tabquals.
7 Patrick J. Carr and Maria J. Kefalas, *Hollowing Out the Middle—The Rural Brain Drain and What it Means for America* (Boston: Beacon Press, 2009), p. 5.
8 Sébastien Marot, *Taking the Country's Side* (Lisbon: Polígrafa, 2019), p. 15.
9 Ibid., p. 111.
[*Fig. 1*] Accessed October 16, 2020, https://en-gb.topographic-map.com/maps/b9/England/.
[*Fig. 2*] laba.
[*Fig. 3*] laba.
[*Fig. 4*] laba.
[*Fig. 5*] Accessed October 16, 2020, Office for National Statistics, https://www.ons.gov.uk/economy/grossvalueaddedgva.
[*Fig. 6*] Ibid.
[*Fig. 7*] Ibid.
[*Fig. 8*] Accessed October 30, 2020, Revenue Expenditure and Financing, 2019-20 Final Outturn, Statistical Release, © Crown, 2019, https://assets.publishing.service.gov.uk/government/uploads/system/uploads/attachment_data/file/812505/Local_Authority_Revenue_Expenditure_and_Financing_2019-20_Budget__England.pdf.
[*Fig. 9*] Ibid.
[*Fig. 10*] Carr and Kefalas, *Hollowing Out the Middle*, p. 5.
[*Fig. 11*] laba.
[*Fig. 12*] Google Maps, 2020. www.google.com/maps.
[*Fig. 13*] laba.
[*Fig. 14*] Westcountry Rivers Trust, The Taw River Improvement Project, 2015, p. 5, accessed October 16, 2020, https://wrt.org.uk/documents/WRT_CRF_TRIP_Report.pdf.
[*Fig. 15*] laba.
[*Fig. 16*] laba.
i   James Clancy / Alamy Stock Photo.
ii   laba student.
iii laba student.
iv   laba student.
v   laba student.
vi   laba student.
vii laba student.
viii laba student.

Architecture

1 Wikipedia, https://en.wikipedia.org/wiki/Ecovillage#:~:text=An%20ecovillage%20is%20a%20traditional,%2C%20and%-2For%20ecologically%20sustainable.&-text=It%20is%20consciously%20designed%20through,its%20social%20and%20natural%20environments.
i   Author unknown.
ii   © Knight Frank / SWNS.
iii   © GrahamHunt / BNPS.
iv   © Crown copyright and database right 2020, Contains public sector information licensed under the Open Government Licence v3.0.
v   © Sharpham Trust.
vi   © Sharpham Trust.
vii   © Sharpham Trust.
viii © Sharpham Trust.
ix   © Crown copyright and database right 2020, Contains public sector information licensed under the Open Government Licence v3.0.
x   Image source: https://commons.wikimedia.org/.
xi   Image source: https://en.wikipedia.org/wiki/Colleton,_Chulmleigh, Public Domain.
xii   Image source: https://en.wikipedia.org/wiki/Colleton,_Chulmleigh, Public Domain.
xiii Photo: Ed Howell.
xiv   Photo: James Ravilious.
xv   Photo: Ed Howell.

Participants

Studio Director
Harry Gugger

laba Team
Sarah Barth
Augustin Clément
Bárbara Maçães Costa
Helen Ebert
Juliette Fong
Alexandros Fotakis
Amy Perkins
Tiago Trigo

laba Students
Juliette Armanet
Marion Aubert
Romain Barth
Lucas Bastos Vieira
Vincent Bianchi
Clara Brun
Alexis Corre
Raphael Delmuè
Camille Ehrensperger
Sébastien Friess
Marina Garlatti
Ombline Heili
Solène Hoffmann
Alix Houlon
Vianney Huart
Tanguy Mulard
Océane Perrone
Aurora Pizziolo
Lucia Quintela
Lucia Santosbuceta
Elie Tournier
Paul Trellu
Tania Versteegh
Raphaël Vouilloz

Acknowledgments

Thanks to the lecturers mentioned below as well as the invited reviewers: Martina Barcelloni Corte, Eik Frenzel, Catherine Gay, Christophe Girot, Henriette Gugger, Metaxia Markaki, Charles Tashima, Günther Vogt, and Martina Voser.

Lectures at the laba Symposium "Commons Revisited," September 30, 2019, EPFL
— Jörg Stollmann, TU Berlin
— Florian Hertweck, University of Luxembourg

Lectures at the laba Symposium "Commons Revisited," November 12, 2019, EPFL
— Irina Davidovici, ETHZ
— Tim Crabtree, Wessex Community Assets
— James Grasby, National Trust

Lectures at the Symposium "Commons Revisited," February 10, 2020, University of Bath
— Peter Clegg, Feilden Clegg Bradley Studios
— Tim Osborne, to-studio landscape architecture
— Marion Harney, University of Bath

The symposium "Commons Revisited" in Bath was organized in collaboration with Alexander Wright and Toby Lewis from University of Bath, to whom we are grateful.
Thanks to Jayne Barlow and Rowan Morris for the wonderful tour and kind hospitality at the Whitehall Farm, and to Tim Crabtree for his invaluable help with the student workshops at the EPFL, for sharing his brilliant tips and the relevant contacts to plan our study trip, and for providing an extensive tour of Hooke Park. Thanks also to Zachary Mollica for the introduction at Hooke Park.
Thank you, Alex Lewis, Andrew Owens, and Paule Glade at Fowlescombe, an organic farm in the South Hams, for the presentation and tour.
Thanks to Niall Hobhouse at Drawing Matters for the group tour and letting us explore the archives.
Thanks to Brian Boylan for hosting the laba team at his wonderful home at Dart Cottage.
Thanks to Martin Cross from Centurion Travel for providing great background information and for getting us across the West Country safely, and to Miranda Litchfield from Centurion Travel for meticulous travel arrangements.
The School of Architecture and Environmental Engineering ENAC EPFL has provided funding for this publication. Thank you.

Student Assistants
Paul Trellu
Raphaël Vouilloz

Imprint

Editors
Harry Gugger
Amy Perkins
Sarah Barth
Augustin Clément
Alexandros Fotakis

Introduction
Amy Perkins
Harry Gugger

Copy Editor
Margaret Puskar-Pasewicz
www.margaretedits.com

Editorial Concept and Graphic Design
© Helen Ebert, Zurich
www.helen-ebert.eu

Typefaces
Atlas Grotesk, Berthold Baskerville

Field Photography
© laba staff and students

Lithography, Printing and Binding
DZA Druckerei zu Altenburg GmbH, Germany

Every reasonable attempt has been made by the authors, editors, and publishers to identify owners of copyrights. Errors or omissions will be corrected in subsequent editions.

This work is subject to copyright. All rights are reserved, whether the whole or part of the material is concerned, specifically the rights of translation, reprinting, re-use of illustrations, recitation, broadcasting, reproduction on microfilms or in any other ways, and storage in databases. For any kind of use, permission of the copyright owner must be obtained.

© 2021 Laboratoire Bâle (laba)
Institut d'Architecture Faculté ENAC
École Polytechnique Fédérale de Lausanne
and Park Books, Zurich

EPFL ENAC IA laba
Ackermannshof
St. Johanns-Vorstadt 19–21
4056 Basel
http://laba.epfl.ch

Park Books
Niederdorfstrasse 54
8001 Zurich
Switzerland
www.park-books.com

Park Books is being supported by the Swiss Federal Office of Culture with a general subsidy for the years 2021–2024.

ISBN 978-3-03860-196-8

PARK BOOKS